# SAINTS
# AND
# SINNERS

# SAINTS
# AND
# SINNERS

The career of
Kapitänleutnant Erich Gerth
1886-1943

CHRIS HEAL

Published by Chattaway and Spottiswood
Four Marks, Hampshire

candspublishing.org.uk
chrisheal@candspublishing.org.uk

This is a historical work of non-fiction. It is a much abridged version of *Sound of
Hunger*, published in hardback by Uniform in 2018, ISBN: 978-1-911604-41-9, 754
pages, RRP: £30. The names, characters and quotes of the principal characters,
events and incidents are taken from contemporary archives, except where stated
otherwise.
Opinions about characters, events and incidents are the views of the author.

A catalogue record for this book is available from
the British Library.

ISBN 978-1-9161944-8-9

Design and typeset: Mary Woolley, www.battlefield-design.co.uk
Cover design, maps and advertisements: Paul Hewitt, www.battlefield-design.co.uk
Print liaison and website: Andy Severn, www.oxford-ebooks.com

Printed on demand: www.ingramspark.com

# CONTENTS

Author's note                                          7
Introduction: Preparing for war                        9
List of maps                                          11

1    Canaris: Master spy                              17
2    Gerth: To the Baltic                             26
3    Gerth: U-Boats in the Adriatic                   39
4    Gerth: Into the Mediterranean                    47
5    Gerth: Balance sheet                             62
6    Gerth: Welcome home                              64
7    Trotha: Illegal U-Boats                          71
8    Marx: The Jewish Countess                        80
9    Marx: Freikorps and easy murder                  95
10   Marx: Power behind the throne                   117
11   Canaris: Rearmament                             124
12   Marx: Films for propaganda                      127
13   Marx: Murder, murder, everywhere               132
14   Gerth: The Foreign Office                       151
15   Gerth: Rupture in Christian unity               163
16   Gerth: The beginning of the end                 171
17   Marx: The humiliation                           176
18   Gerth: On the run                               180
19   Gerth: Life after death                         189
20   Gerth: The long arm of the war                  195

Abbreviations & common German words                  199
Bibliography                                          201

# Author's note

In 2016, I was asked by the Maritime Archaeology Trust, based in Southampton, to assist in a small way with a five-year Heritage Lottery-funded project as part of the Centenary of the First World War. The project was called *Forgotten Wrecks, intended* to chart and record some 700 South Coast sites that resulted from the conflict. My short-term assignment became a multi-year investigation that led to the u-boat war, famine as a weapon by both sides in the conflict and a close view of many of the characters involved in either plotting against or supporting the rise of Adolf Hitler.

At the heart of the story were two brothers, Berliners, both u-boat captains, Erich and Georg Gerth. The two men had very different wars. Erich began as a naval spy in South America and managed only one operational u-boat patrol in 1918 in the Mediterranean which was responsible eventually for many deaths. Georg fought through much of 1917 in the North Sea and the English Channel and became a prisoner of war.

The brothers' inter-war years could not have contrasted more: Erich caught up in society, the *Freikorps* and their murderous escapades and religious conflict between Lutherans, Jews and Catholics; Georg seeking the life of a hermit philosopher until his home city was fire-bombed by the British in a raid more devastating than Dresden.

At each new shocking and unexpected revelation, my co-researcher, Jacqui Squire, used to say, 'This is the story that keeps on giving.'

I wrote a book, *Sound of Hunger*, published in 2018, over 750 pages, a true doorstop, which told of all that we had found. Erich and Georg's careers allowed the inclusion of many of the awful things that that occurred before, during and after the war and as much context as I found useful. I wanted to explore events that were integral to the Gerth brothers, to see how they were altered by what they were taught and experienced. The part of *Sound of Hunger* that concerned *UC 61* was later translated into French (with additional material) by Lt Col Henri Lesoin in a book titled *La dernière patrouille de l'UC 61*.

This year, I was asked to extract the lives of Erich and Georg into two conventional paperbacks starting from the time when they finished their naval training and ending with their deaths: this book, *Saints & Sinners*, is about Erich; its companion, *The War of The Raven*, is about Georg.

They are fascinating and independent stories of how war, beliefs and the search for power changes everything within a family.

# Introduction
# PREPARING FOR WAR

One of the things that has served to convince us that the Prussian autocracy was not and could never be our friend is that from the very outset of the present war it has filled our unsuspecting communities and even our offices of government with spies and set criminal intrigues everywhere afoot against our national unity of counsel, our peace within and without our industries and our commerce.

Indeed it is now evident that its spies were here even before the war began; and it is unhappily not a matter of conjecture but a fact proved in our courts of justice that the intrigues which have more than once come perilously near to disturbing the peace and dislocating the industries of the country have been carried on at the instigation, with the support, and even under the personal direction of official agents of the Imperial Government accredited to the Government of the United States.

Even in checking these things and trying to extirpate them we have sought to put the most generous interpretation possible upon them because we knew that their source lay, not in any hostile feeling or purpose of the German people towards us (who were, no doubt, as ignorant of them as we ourselves were), but only in the selfish designs of a Government that did what it pleased and told its people nothing.

But they have played their part in serving to convince us at last that their Government entertains no real friendship for us and means to act against our peace and security at its convenience. It means to stir up enemies against us at our very doors.

President Woodrow Wilson,
US Congress, 22 April 1917[1]

---

1    *War Messages*, 65th Congress, 1st Session, Senate Document No. 5, Serial No. 7264, Washington, DC, pp. 3-8.

# List of maps

Page

Wilhem Canaris and Erich Gerth in South America, 1907-1916    13

Erich and Georg Gerth in the Baltic to 1917    14

Erich Gerth and the Mediterranean War    15

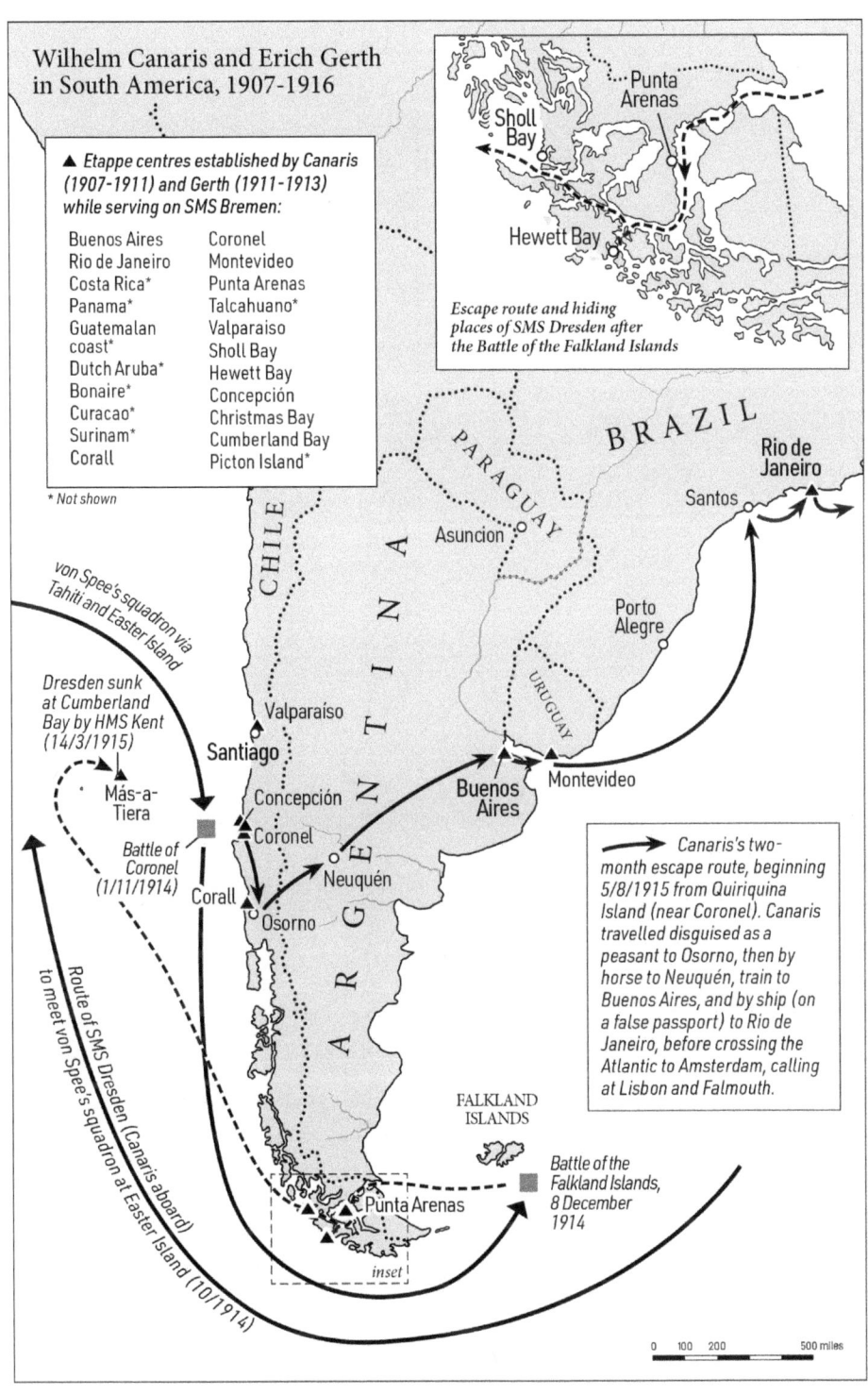

# Wilhelm Canaris and Erich Gerth in South America, 1907-1916

▲ *Etappe centres established by Canaris (1907-1911) and Gerth (1911-1913) while serving on SMS Bremen:*

| | |
|---|---|
| Buenos Aires | Coronel |
| Rio de Janeiro | Montevideo |
| Costa Rica* | Punta Arenas |
| Panama* | Talcahuano* |
| Guatemalan | Valparaiso |
| coast* | Sholl Bay |
| Dutch Aruba* | Hewett Bay |
| Bonaire* | Concepción |
| Curacao* | Christmas Bay |
| Surinam* | Cumberland Bay |
| Corall | Picton Island* |

*\* Not shown*

*Escape route and hiding places of SMS Dresden after the Battle of the Falkland Islands*

Punta Arenas

Sholl Bay

Hewett Bay

BRAZIL

Rio de Janeiro

Santos

PARAGUAY

Asuncion

Porto Alegre

URUGUAY

CHILE

ARGENTINA

von Spee's squadron via Tahiti and Easter Island

Dresden sunk at Cumberland Bay by HMS Kent (14/3/1915)

Valparaiso

Santiago

Más-a-Tiera

Concepción

Battle of Coronel (1/11/1914)

Coronel

Corall

Neuquén

Osorno

Buenos Aires

Montevideo

Route of SMS Dresden (Canaris aboard) to meet von Spee's squadron at Easter Island (10/1914)

FALKLAND ISLANDS

Punta Arenas

*inset*

Battle of the Falkland Islands, 8 December 1914

→ Canaris's two-month escape route, beginning 5/8/1915 from Quiriquina Island (near Coronel). Canaris travelled disguised as a peasant to Osorno, then by horse to Neuquén, train to Buenos Aires, and by ship (on a false passport) to Rio de Janeiro, before crossing the Atlantic to Amsterdam, calling at Lisbon and Falmouth.

0   100   200        500 miles

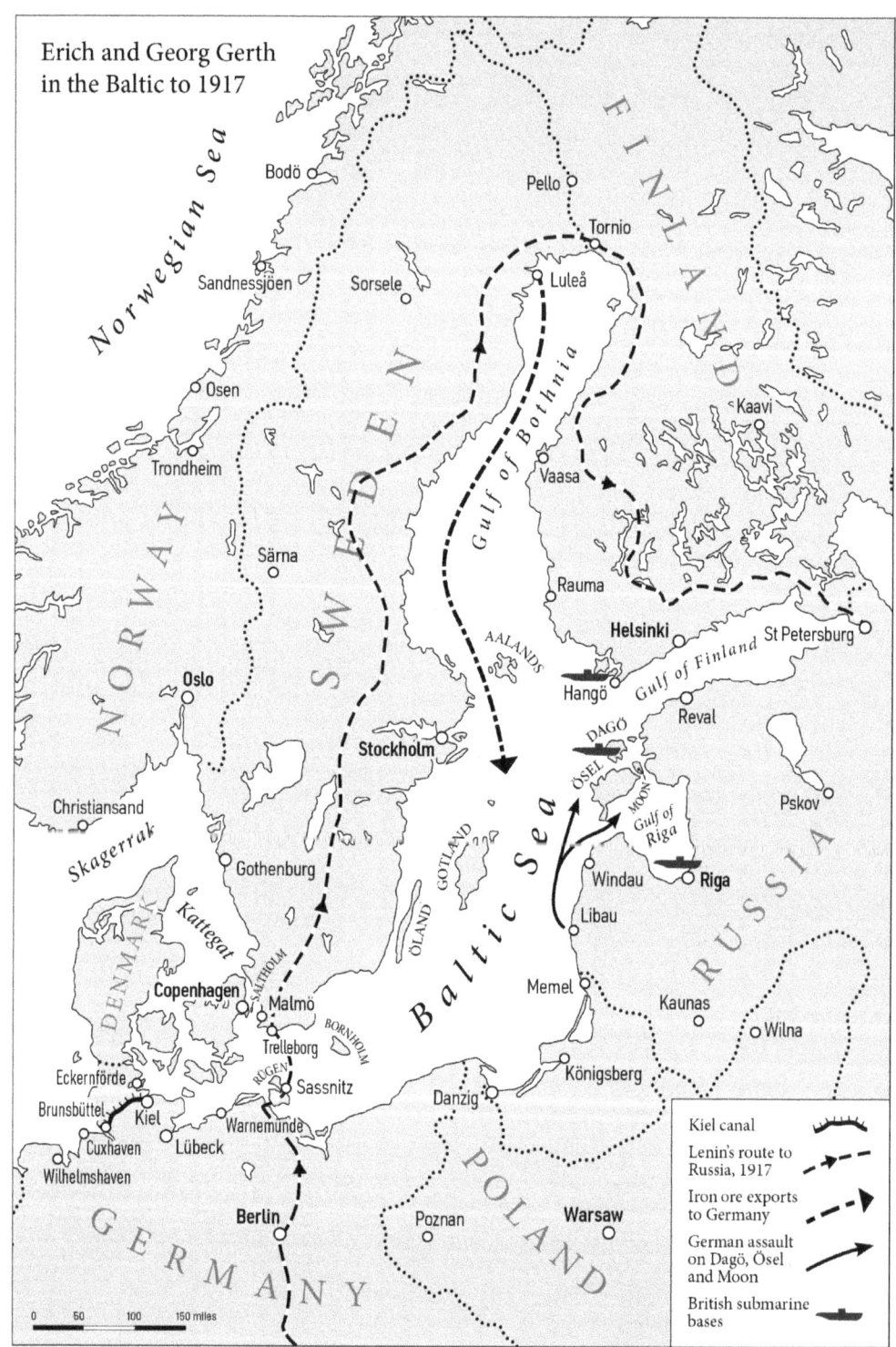

Erich and Georg Gerth
in the Baltic to 1917

*Norwegian Sea*

Bodö

Pello

Tornio

FINLAND

Sandnessjöen

Sorsele

Luleå

*Gulf of Bothnia*

Kaavi

Osen

Vaasa

Trondheim

N O R W A Y

S W E D E N

Särna

Rauma

Helsinki

St Petersburg

Oslo

AALANDS

Hangö

*Gulf of Finland*

Reval

Stockholm

DAGÖ

ÖSEL

MOON

Pskov

Christiansand

*Skagerrak*

Gothenburg

*Kattegat*

ÖLAND

GOTLAND

*B a l t i c   S e a*

*Gulf of Riga*

Windau

Riga

R U S S I A

Libau

DENMARK

SALTHOLM

Copenhagen

Malmö

BORNHOLM

Memel

Kaunas

Wilna

Trelleborg

RÜGEN

Sassnitz

Königsberg

Eckernförde

Brunsbüttel

Kiel

Warnemünde

Danzig

Cuxhaven

Lübeck

Wilhelmshaven

G E R M A N Y

Berlin

Poznan

Warsaw

P O L A N D

0    50    100    150 miles

| | |
|---|---|
| Kiel canal | |
| Lenin's route to Russia, 1917 | |
| Iron ore exports to Germany | |
| German assault on Dagö, Ösel and Moon | |
| British submarine bases | |

14

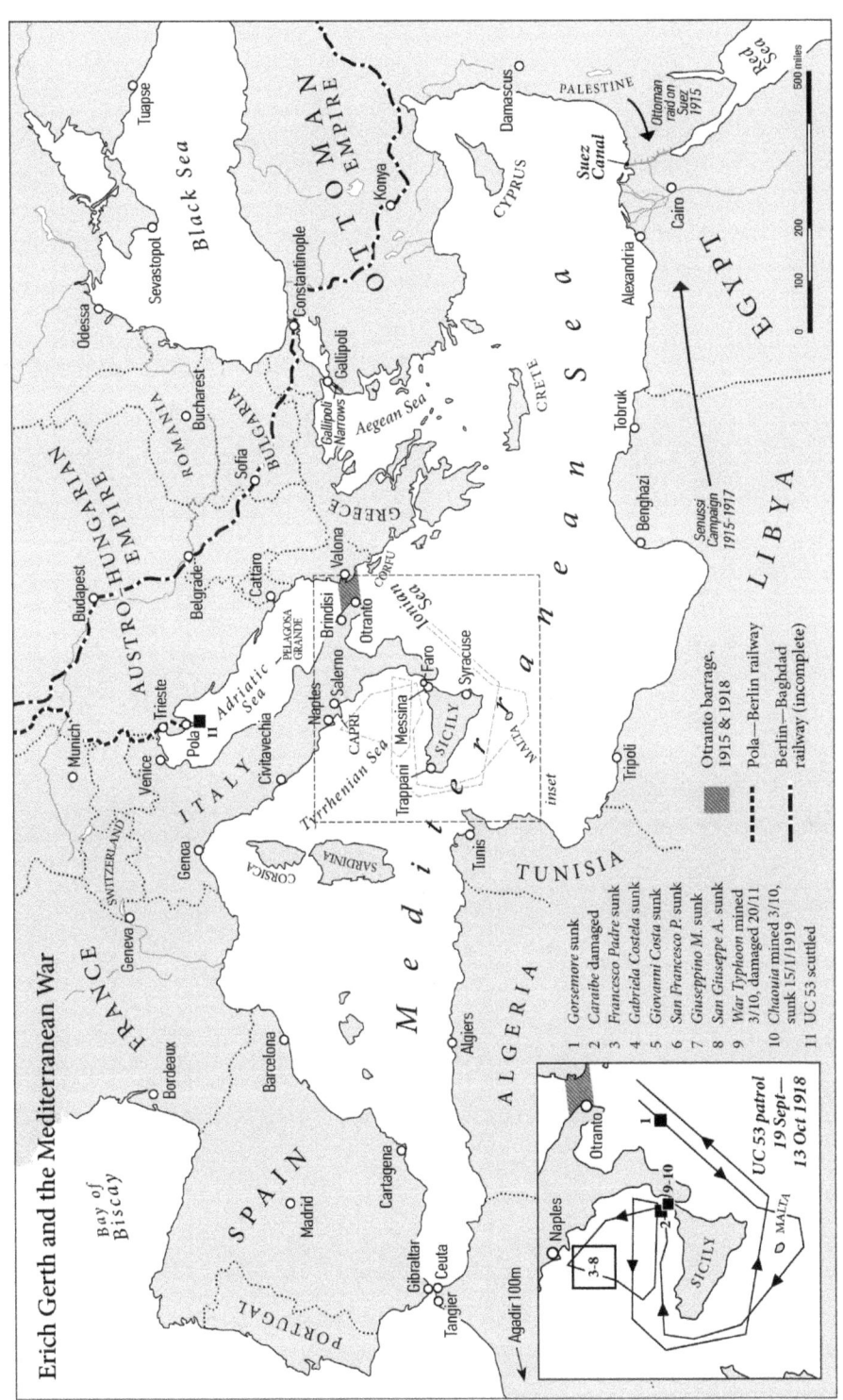

# Erich Gerth and the Mediterranean War

500 miles

**Ottoman raid on Suez 1915**

PALESTINE

Suez Canal

Damascus

Konya

CYPRUS

Alexandria

Cairo

EGYPT

Tuapse

Black Sea

Sevastopol

Odessa

OTTOMAN EMPIRE

CRETE

Mediterranean Sea

Tobruk

Benghazi

Senussi Campaign 1915-1917

LIBYA

Tripoli

Bucharest

ROMANIA

Constantinople

Gallipoli

Aegean Sea

Sofia

BULGARIA

Gallipoli Narrows

GREECE

Budapest

AUSTRO-HUNGARIAN EMPIRE

Belgrade

Cattaro

Valona

CORFU

Ionian Sea

Trieste

Pola

II

Adriatic Sea

PELAGOSA GRANDE

Brindisi

Otranto

Munich

Venice

Civitavecchia

Naples

Salerno

CAPRI

Faro

Messina

Syracuse

SICILY

Trappani

Tyrrhenian Sea

MALTA

inset

SWITZERLAND

Geneva

Genoa

CORSICA

SARDINIA

ITALY

FRANCE

Bordeaux

Bay of Biscay

Barcelona

Tunis

TUNISIA

Algiers

ALGERIA

Madrid

SPAIN

Cartagena

PORTUGAL

Gibraltar

Ceuta

Tangier

Agadir 100m

Otranto barrage, 1915 & 1918

Pola—Berlin railway

Berlin—Baghdad railway (incomplete)

1  Gorsemore sunk
2  Caraibe damaged
3  Francesco Padre sunk
4  Gabriela Costela sunk
5  Giovanni Costa sunk
6  San Francesco P. sunk
7  Giuseppino M. sunk
8  San Giuseppe A. sunk
9  War Typhoon mined 3/10, damaged 20/11
10 Chaouia mined 3/10, sunk 15/11/1919
11 UC 53 scuttled

Otranto

Naples

SICILY

MALTA

UC 53 patrol 19 Sept— 13 Oct 1918

1

9-10

2

3-8

# 1

# CANARIS: MASTER SPY

Erich Gerth's war began long before the shooting started. In the spring of 1911 he took the port railway from Bremen to Bremerhaven to claim one of the fifty cabins on the Norddeutscher Lloyd steamer *Chemnitz*.[1] Gerth was a member of small party of new officers travelling to join the light cruiser *Bremen* on its East American Station. *Chemnitz* arrived at Galveston in Texas on 25 May; *Bremen* was waiting in port to collect her replacements who reported the next day.

Gerth's own posting was unusual: he was to become an agent for German naval intelligence.

*Bremen* was seven years into a ten-year posting charged with promoting and protecting German commercial endeavours in Central and South America and with flying the flag in visits to the United States.[2] The ship was built in 1902 at the AG Weser yard in Bremen, which provided her name, and also built both of the u-boats commanded during the coming war by Erich's brother, Georg. At almost 4,000 tons, *Bremen* carried a main battery of ten 4.1-inch guns and two eighteen-inch torpedo tubes. She was accounted a good sea boat although, when reaching her top speed of around twenty-three knots, she took a lot of water while rolling up to twenty per cent.[3]

---

1    *Deutsches U-Boot Museum*, Cuxhaven, Löhr, 'Obituary and naval record: Erich Gerth'. norwayheritage.com.

2    Mueller, *Canaris*, p. 6.

3    Gröner, *German Warships*, Vol. 1, pp. 102-4.

Erich Gerth's career before joining the *Bremen* had been conventional for a new officer. After concluding his sea cadet training and receiving his commission as Leutnant zur See in 1908, he joined the High Seas Fleet for a year and a half aboard the light cruiser *Königsberg*. Then followed a year with the Naval Artillery Department during which time he gained his automatic promotion to Oberleutnant.

Something had marked Gerth out as suitable for his new role. Apart from the intellect evident during training, and his natural urbane and sociable manner, it may have been his association with the man who preceded him as a spy in South America, Wilhelm Canaris.

Towards the end of their time together as sea cadets, in November 1907, both Gerth and Canaris were awarded the *Kronenorrden*, the Prussian Order of the Crown, in the gift of the Kaiser, which came in six levels of importance. Their junior medal was given to commissioned officers for services to the crown of a general nature, more of a thank you or a pat on the back than a reward of great honour. The Kaiser doled out at least three to British worthies in 1899 for making the arrangements for his official visit to Great Britain which, of course, included time to see his grandmother, Queen Victoria. A further two British officials received awards for similar duties when the Prince of Wales visited the Kaiser in Berlin in 1902 for birthday celebrations. At least forty-two sea cadets who went on to become u-boat commanders received the *Kronenorrden* before the war began. As these officers' dates of entry are spread over time, it is possible that the top cadets in each year were recognised in this way.

Officers were promoted in the German naval officer corps because of time served, not because of competence. By an imperial decree in 1899, all officers were listed in order of length of service and promotion from one rank to the other followed strictly according to whoever headed these lists. The final decision always rested with the Kaiser.

The system concentrated on the 'expulsion of the undesirable rather than on the promotion of the most highly desirable'.[4] 'Only in the case of submarine commanders in World War One were exceptions made, as the road from Leutnant to Kapitänleutnant was [later] somewhat shortened by the exigencies of war.' Normally it took three years from leutnant to Oberleutnant and a further four years to Kapitänleutnant. Canaris and Gerth received their

---

early promotions within days of each other: Fähnrich (midshipman), April 1906; Leutnant, September 1908; but then it seems Gerth slipped a little behind: Oberleutnant, August 1910 (Canaris), January 1911 (Gerth); and Kapitänleutnant, November 1915 (Canaris), December 1915 (Gerth), although some records suggest Gerth's last promotion was delayed until August 1916.

Kapitänleutnant is the rank at which Gerth's career rested, while Canaris went on in 1938 to become a Vizeamiral and the head of the *Abwehr*, the Nazi military intelligence. Canaris led a complex life with many secrets; there is much evidence that he traded information with the British whom he certainly met during the second world war. He was tortured and garrotted in 1945 at the Flossenbürg concentration camp after he finally admitted playing a leading part in the plot to assassinate Adolf Hitler on 20 July the year before.

Canaris preceded Gerth by just over a year in the *Bremen*; his tour of South American duty lasted two years from November 1907 to November 1909, including a visit to Haiti during the revolution of 1908. Canaris became the adjutant of *Bremen*'s commander, Kapitän Albert Hopman, and accompanied him on visits to friends in the South American interior.[5]

*Bremen* travelled widely: her duties took her round Cape Horn to Chilean ports like Punta Arenas, but most of her time was spent near the principal German interests on the east coast. In 1908, *Bremen* began a five-month tour of South America with stops at Buenos Aires, Rio de Janeiro, Costa Rica, Panama, Guatemala and the Dutch Antilles. In the autumn of 1909, she joined other cruisers including the *Dresden* in celebrations in the United States and, early in 1912, was there again, this time with the battlecruiser *Moltke*, on a goodwill cruise recognising US President William Taft.

Wherever she went, great parties were thrown for the *Bremen*'s crew as she received the 'typical fanatical welcome accorded to German warships by the patriotic and nationalistic expatriate community' of those times.[6] There were 10,000 Germans in Buenos Aires and 30,000 across Argentina; the bread winners were mostly business people, engineers, technicians and farmers, but the number also included many military instructors who trained the Argentine Army.

---

5    *BA-MA*, Freiburg, N 326/5, Albert Hopman: 'Diary'.
6    Mueller, *Canaris*, p. 6.

All in all, there was plenty of time and opportunity for Canaris and Gerth to be about their covert tasks. These duties involved the setting up and development of what the Germans called Etappe Centres; an etappe was historically a staging post or a place where troops on the march stayed overnight. From 1898, naval officers overseas began establishing secret intelligence posts.[7] These *Etappendienst* could be run by several men, or a single person, depending on the ports and countries in which they operated. The centres gathered and transmitted by radio intelligence on the shipping movements of Germany's future enemies. They also negotiated berthing contracts within neutral states; sought information on secluded anchorages on the mainland and on coastal islands; and investigated options for coal and wood for refuelling in emergency. The British had a parallel and equally concealed world-wide network that used brokerage firms, ships' captains and consulates.

Canaris was given contact addresses in Brazil, Chile and Argentina to set up networks of informers. He expanded the circle of agents and set up an offshore message re-transmission system using ships fitted with wireless telegraphy owned by Norddeutsche Lloyd, HAPAG, and the Kosmos Line. Their task was to make night-time calls at Corall, Coronel, Talcahuano and Valparaiso to collect telegrams from ashore and to signal their contents to German warships at sea. It was at these meetings with land agents that Canaris began to acquire the Spanish language as he became familiar with the countries of Central and South America. The system worked and 'later the entire cruiser squadron operating in South American waters relied on the network of Canaris's spies and report ships'.

When Gerth arrived in South America, he took over Canaris's work. This is recognised by Gerth's obituary written many years later by Matthias Löhr, an official at the German Foreign Office in Berlin with access to ministry files.[8] Löhr's information about Gerth's intelligence career is based in part on Gerth's hand-written, sanitised application to join the German Foreign Office in 1922. Gerth wrote:

---

7    Mueller, *Canaris*, pp. 7-12.

8    Herr Löhr's interest in u-boats stems from his twice great uncle Alfred Gerke who died when *U 102* was sunk by a mine on the Northern Barrage while homeward bound in September 1918. All forty-two crew were lost. Löhr was instrumental in the identification of *U 102* when it was found by sonar in 2006 and investigated by divers in 2007.

*I spent many years abroad, in particular, Spain, Italy and the remaining Mediterranean countries, in North and South America and in Africa. During a permanent stay abroad which lasted several years as a member of the admiralty staff I was involved in a special military political mission and had the opportunity to study political and economic conditions, write military-political reports, extend my knowledge in foreign languages, adapt to foreign ways of thinking and gain confidence in official communication with foreign personalities and offices.* [9]

The document contains subtle gilding, immediately recognisable today to anyone whose duties include reading job applications. There is, also, the first hint of a little more, the beginnings of untestable exaggerations, the borrowing of the overheard experiences of others.

As Gerth's story unfolds, especially after the war, it is evident that Gerth had a much-welcomed personality, instantly popular with many, a party-goer, and a good teller of stories. The international extravaganzas with their swirling dances and enthusiastic ladies that Gerth enjoyed aboard the *Bremen* were a long way from his fatherless teenage years in Berlin. As a young adult, life initially came easily. Perhaps inventing some small and harmless excitements in his past so as to move nearer to the centre of the 'in-crowd' was a natural thing to do.

*We were inundated with invitations, ate at tables covered with the most glorious mantles, adorned with the rarest orchids, the finest porcelain, silver plate and golden dessert spoons, were seated next to stylish ladies who wore expensive perfume and metre-long necklaces of pearls: we made trips in automobiles and dog-carts, danced the two-step and generally 'had a good time'.* [10]

Ten years later in 1932, Gerth was pleading special circumstances because of his past military service while employed in the Foreign Office. He wrote that he was used on 'various different' missions at home and abroad. 'For example', he explained, 'I was entrusted for three years with the organisation of the intelligence service in North and South America and the cruiser war in the

---

9    *Auswärtige Amt*, Das Politische Archiv, Berlin, 004389, Vol. 2.

10   Hopman, 'Assessments', Canaris-IfZ, quoted in Mueller, *Canaris*, p. 7.

Atlantic Ocean in case of war, a task that I fulfilled to the full satisfaction of the admiralty staff.'[11]

Note the multiplicity of 'missions' of which he was the 'organiser'. Twenty-eight months away was increased to thirty-six. Now, we have included 'North America', something his predecessor, Canaris, never discussed. North America did not offer the opportunities for refuelling or hiding armed cruisers than were provided in the south. As a neutral country, ship movements were readily discussed in the American newspapers and needed no cloak and dagger discovery. Work in North America would entail something darker, perhaps the establishment of sleeper cells for later, possible, terrorist attacks.

The Germans were particularly upset that the United States, despite being neutral, sent munitions to the Allies from 1914. Indeed, before the British blockade, many Americans, driven by profit, defended their neutral right to supply whomever they wished. One arch culprit from Germany's perspective was the giant Bethlehem Steel Company. The Germans, somewhat naively, did nothing to hide their intentions in circulars from their military representative, Dr E Fischer, which were reprinted in the Swiss press in 1914. These called for volunteers to look for employment in munitions companies like Bethlehem Steel and, when settled, to undertake sabotage – unless, of course, the notice was engineered by the British or the French as an elaborate defamatory ruse to arouse American indignation.

*In all branch establishments of German banking houses in Sweden, Norway, Switzerland, China and the United States, special military accounts have been opened for special war necessities. Main headquarters authorizes you to use these credits to an unlimited extent for the purpose of destroying factories, workshops, camps, and the most important centres of military and civil supply belonging to the enemy. In addition to the incitement of labour troubles, measures must be taken for the damaging of engines and machinery plants, the destruction of vessels carrying war material to enemy countries, the burning of stocks of raw materials and finished goods, and the depriving of large industrial centres of electric power, fuel and food. Special agents, who will be placed at your disposal, will supply you with the necessary means for*

---

*effecting explosions and fires, as well as with a list of people in the country under your*
*supervision who are willing to undertake the task of destruction.*[12]

Widespread sabotage certainly occurred before and after the United States entered the war in 1917. Fifty acts of terrorism are on record and thirty of these took place around New York City and the New Jersey area. These acts were managed through the German embassies in New York and Washington, headed by the diplomat Count Johann von Bernstorff, and all vigorously denied at the time. They included $10 million in damages to thirty-six cargo ships as they crossed the Atlantic and caused by the placement in cargo holds of pencil bombs with delayed timers. This team was led by master spy Franz von Rintelen.

Elsewhere, munitions factories were hit by explosion. A large ammunition store near the Statue of Liberty, its contents destined for the Allies in Europe, was blown up in 1916. It is possible, of course, that Gerth was involved in some of the advanced planning for this mayhem, but it does seem unusual that, after the conclusion of his tour on the *Bremen*, he was shipped back to a deck position in the Baltic with all his North American contacts and skills left behind.

When President Wilson urged Congress on 22 April 1917 to confirm a declaration of war on Germany, he gave the German spy system in America as the fourth of his reasons alongside the use of unrestricted submarine warfare, the sinking of neutral merchant ships and embarrassment of the discovery of the 'Zimmermann telegram' which encouraged Mexico to attack the United States.[13]

In his Foreign Office application of 1922, Gerth claimed that during his naval years he took language examinations in English, French and Spanish and that he achieved fluency in all three. He also claimed to be able to communicate in Italian. However, when asked if he was prepared to take a preliminary language examination in English and French, he requested a delay. This seems a little odd for an applicant for a scarce and prestigious position in the tough times just a few years after the end of the Great War. But, there may have been good reasons.

---

12    *Freie Zeitung*, Berne, 2/11/1914, placed by German General Headquarters.
13    'Introduction' to this book.

In fairness, Gerth's secondary school in Berlin, the Konigliches Kaiser Wilhelm's Realgymnasium, provided its pupils in their last two years with thirty-one compulsory lessons a week, including four in Latin and three each in English and French.[14] His mother was reported to speak French well and his brother, Georg, was competent in English and French. As well as the Spanish, which would have greatly benefitted from South American travels, there was an extensive Italian community in Montevideo which may well have been on Gerth's itinerary and provided important fodder for his intelligence network.[15]

Gerth, foreign adventure over, travelled home in September 1913 on the *Hans Woermann*, a 4,000-ton passenger, freight and mail ship of the Woermann Line of Hamburg. For the next two years until the end of 1915, Gerth served as watch officer on fleet duties in the Baltic on SMS *Hessen*, sister ship to the SMS *Preussen* on which brother Georg spent eighteen months around 1909.

No doubt both Canaris and Gerth wrote detailed notes of their intelligence network; presumably Gerth's work in South America was an updating and an improvement of that already done by Canaris. Contact details and emergency bases and their facilities would then be issued to warships sent to fight in the South Atlantic and to the auxiliaries ordered to supply them. Ironically, it was Canaris who came to make use of their combined knowledge and, therefore, in a way, be grateful to Gerth for his efforts.

In 1914, Canaris was again appointed an adjutant, this time on the cruiser SMS *Dresden* which was sent to replace *Bremen* on the East American Station. *Dresden* arrived off the Mexican naval base of Veracruz in January to be greeted by two Mexican gunboats. Civil war had broken out. The newly-installed President Victoriano Huerta faced a revolt led by the 'bandit' Pancho Villa. American oil workers and their families came under threat and US troops were landed. Because of his language skills, Canaris was in the thick of negotiations and often conducted dangerous trips ashore.

With the European war declared in 1914, *Dresden* was ordered to stay on station and to carry out a 'trade war', common code for sinking enemy merchant shipping. After much naval activity, the expansion of Canaris's spy network, and the regular use of the etappe facilities on the mainland, *Dresden* joined at Easter Island with Admiral Count Maximilian von Spee's squadron

---

14    'School records' (digital.ub.uni-dusseldorf.de), accessed 3/2017.
15    Trevelyan, *Garibaldi's Defence of the Roman Republic*, Vol. 1, pp. 26-41.

of heavy cruisers crossing the Pacific from China.[16] The fleet ran into three British cruisers at Coronel off the coast of Chile on 1 November 1914, two of which were sunk with all hands.[17] This was the first British naval defeat since 1812.

A month later and seeking rapid revenge, 'two hastily despatched British battle cruisers' with workmen still on board - *Invincible* and *Inflexible* - caught up with Spee near the Falkland Islands as he attempted to raid the British supply base at Port Stanley. Spee believed rumours, against the advice of his senior commanders, that the islands were undefended because their ships had left to put down a new Boer uprising in South Africa.

The British fleet, commanded by Vice Admiral Doveton Sturdee, caught Spee at his most vulnerable. Sturdee rapidly sank six of Spee's ships, including the sister heavy cruisers *Scharnhorst* and *Gneisenau*, killing 2,200 men, including Spee and his two sons.[18] The one German escapee was the *Dresden* whose cat and mouse flight from the British involved use of several scouted havens and etappes including Sholl and Hewett Bays, near Punta Arenas; Christmas Island; and eventually Cumberland Bay on Robinson Crusoe's island of Más-a-Tierra. Here she was eventually found and sunk illegally in neutral waters by the British cruiser *Kent*.

Canaris conducted negotiations with the British under the roar of *Kent*'s guns. He escaped from Chilean internment in August 1915 and after a 'boy's own' two-month trip home involving horseback, train and ships on a false passport, and which included a stopover in Falmouth, England, reached Germany.[19] Canaris received a hero's welcome. However, another of his and Erich Gerth's classmates, Oberleutnant Kurt Hartwig, was also on the *Dresden* as torpedo officer. He also escaped internment and got back to Germany in July before Canaris made his attempt to little applause.[20]

16    Mueller, *Canaris*, Chapter 2, 'The Last Epic Voyage of the Dresden'.
17    Asprey, *German High Command*, p. 133. Marder, *Dreadnought*, Vol. II, pp. 104-18.
18    Marder, *Dreadnought*, Vol. II, pp. 118-29. Mueller, *Canaris*, pp. 14-15.
19    Mueller, *Canaris*, pp. 19-20.
20    wikipedia.

# 2

# GERTH: TO THE BALTIC

At the beginning of 1914, Gerth's new ship, *Hessen* was a powerful if vulnerable ship with four eleven-inch guns in twin turrets fore and aft of the central superstructure, fourteen 6.7-inch guns and eighteen 3.45-inch quick-firing guns. She also had six eighteen-inch torpedo tubes submerged in her hull.[1] *Hessen* was a typical Tirpitz battleship, quickly made obsolete by Admiral Jackie Fisher's Royal Navy dreadnoughts, and coming to the end of its days.[2]

Gerth, in different roles, was to stay in the Baltic area for almost the entire war; he left for his Mediterranean posting in April 1918. His brother Georg overlapped in the period until June 1916 and one assumes they found some time to meet.

Gerth and the *Hessen* saw action if only from a distance. The ship provided background support for the bombardment of English towns Scarborough, Hartlepool and Whitby on 16 December 1914. While Hartlepool was a legitimate target as a naval town, the attacks on the undefended watering holes of Scarborough and Whitby as the unsuspecting population sat down to breakfast was declared a war crime.[3] Winston Churchill, in full hyperbolic flight, proclaimed that the 'stigma of the baby-killers of Scarborough will brand its officers and men while sailors sail the seas'.

---

1     Gröner, *German Warships*, Vol. 1, pp. 18-20.

2     Massie, *Dreadnought*. Marder, *Dreadnought*, Vols. 1 & 2. Lambert, *Naval Revolution*.

3     Massie, *Castles of Steel*, pp. 319-27.

The British navy's lack of defensive preparedness or offensive reaction reflected badly. It was the first time for 247 years that foreign naval guns had 'spilled blood on English soil'.[4] In total, 105 men, women and children were killed and 525 wounded. There was no fleet engagement, although it almost happened: Admiral Friedrich von Ingenohl thought skirmishes between destroyer screens meant that the British Grand Fleet would shortly arrive and he ran for home.

In April the next year, German battlecruisers, with Gerth in the *Hessen* in attendance, bombarded Yarmouth and Lowestoft in a tip-and-run raid timed to coincide with the Irish Republican Army's (IRA) Easter Rising in Dublin.[5] Before the raid started, the German flagship, the battlecruiser *Seydlitz*, was damaged by a mine and had to return. At Lowestoft, the German fleet destroyed two shore batteries, 200 houses and killed three civilians and wounded twelve. Poor visibility constrained the operation and this was made worse when the attacking fleet commanded by Rear Admiral Friedrich Bödicker failed to press home a real advantage when engaged with weaker British forces and turned for home.

Gerth's principal ships did not fare well. After participating in the Battle of the Gulf of Riga in August 1915, *Bremen* returned there for a second attack and struck a pair of Russian mines off Windau, now Ventspils in Latvia, losing 250 men. The *Hans Woermann*, the ship that brought Gerth home from South America, was captured in 1914 by HMS *Cumberland*, renamed the *Gold Coast*, and transferred to the Elder Line of Liverpool. She was torpedoed in 1917 off the Irish Coast by *UC 47*, commander Paul Hundius, a close acquaintance of Erich's brother Georg. *Hessen* was withdrawn from active service in 1917, disarmed and her four large guns were sent to the western front and mounted on rail trucks. *Hessen* was used as a depot ship, allowed to stay in Germany after the war under the Treaty of Versailles, and became an ice-breaker and a remote-controlled target ship. After the second world war, she was ceded to Russia where she acted as a target ship until scrapped in 1960.

The commander of *Hessen*, Kapitän Rudolph Bartels, felt Gerth was 'suited for employment in staff offices and also suitable for the position of submarine

---

4    On 8/6/1667, a Dutch fleet attacked Sheerness Naval Fort in the Thames Estuary, and landed troops. Four days later the Dutch sailed up the River Medway and towed back to Holland the eighty-gun *Royal Charles*, the Navy's largest ship.

5    Massie, *Castles of Steel*, pp. 555-59. Marder, *Dreadnought*, pp. 424-27.

commander'.[6] Early in February 1916, Erich Gerth moved to Libau in Courland as director of the 'E-Stelle' where he stayed until the end of June the next year. Gerth explained that the admiralty staff 'made use of the experience which I gained in the aforesaid activities in America and deployed me until the Russian collapse for a special mission'.

Here we have Gerth again with another 'special mission'. If the mission followed experience in the Americas, as claimed, it would have involved setting up etappe stations in enemy territory of Russia or Finland, which, given the relative compactness of the Baltic, and the lack of Russian vessels travelling to Scandinavia, seems unlikely. There is no evidence of Gerth visiting Denmark, Finland, Norway or Sweden and he spoke no Baltic languages.

'E-Stelle', perhaps standing for *Erprobungsstelle*, a trial centre, was a German station monitoring enemy radio traffic. 'E-Stelle West' heard French reports and alerted the Flanders command that Erich's brother Georg had stranded his u-boat at Wissant, south of Calais, in 1917.[7] This activity would fit with Erich's work on the establishment of etappes, but nothing is known of Gerth's time at the centre.

What could be the truth of all of this? Gerth's timing seems a little out. He left his post in June 1917, but claimed that he stayed until the Russian 'collapse'. Could Gerth have been involved in some way?

There are some intriguing possibilities, particularly in March at Sassnitz on Rügen Island on the German Baltic coast. Originally, the Germans sought unsuccessfully to encourage non-Russian nationalities to rebel against the Tsar. When the Germans switched their support to internal social revolution, the effect was 'world-shaking'.[8] Certainly, in February 1917, female workers in the Russian capital of St Petersburg marched through the streets calling for food, the ousting of the tsar and an end to the war. The next day, a multitude of men and women joined them on the streets. Troops refused orders to fire on the protestors and mutinied. On 2 March, Tsar Nicholas II abdicated and a provisional government was formed.

Next month, the Germans aided thirty-two members of two opposing factions, Vladimir Lenin with his exiled Bolshevist supporters and a group of Julius Martov's Mensheviks, to journey from Zurich to St Petersburg. A

---

6   Löhr, 'Obituary'.
7   Heal, *Sound of Hunger*, p. 301.
8   Holborn, 'Introduction', in Fischer, *War Aims*, p. xiii.

sealed German train took the group to Sassnitz, where there would have been German military oversight, and from there by ferry and train to Trelleborg in Sweden, then Helsinki, and finally across the Finnish border into Russia.

In Russia, the Germans backed the Bolsheviks with substantial finances.[9] War minister Alexander Kerensky took over the short-lived provisional government in June. It was not until October, four months after Gerth had left, that Vladimir Lenin, after a period in hiding in Helsinki from early August, called for the successful Bolshevik *coup d'état* against the Kerensky government. Lenin returned from self-exile in October to demand action from the Bolshevik Central Committee. The *coup* in St Petersburg was led by Leon Trotsky and Josef Stalin and ended when the Winter Palace was occupied easily by a small group while the Kerensky cabinet was in session.[10]

However, from a German military perspective, the Russian 'collapse', when Gerth said he left his post, did not happen until the next year in March 1918. The German Army was then just eighty-five miles from St Petersburg. The Russians were beaten, the imperialist treaty of Brest-Litovsk was forced on 3 March and the fighting stopped.[11] A great swathe of land from the Baltic to the Crimea and the northern shores of the Black Sea was transferred to German control; the captured lands included Estonia and Latvia which were intended as fiefdoms for the Kaiser's close family. It had always been part of Chancellor Bethmann's plan to 'thrust back the Russian border as far as possible from Germany's eastern frontier' and to break her domination over the non-Russian vassal peoples.[12]

Freed by the collapse, the Germans moved substantial forces quickly to the western front to support Operation Michael, Hindenburg and Ludendorff's last-ditch spring offensive in 1918. The German Supreme Command also hoped against all logic to extract a million tons of grain from the 'unwilling population of the Ukraine'.[13] They were sadly disappointed. Conditions were

---

9    Fischer, *War Aims*, pp. 365-75.

10   Lenin died in Russia of a stroke 1923; Trotsky was murdered in Mexico on Stalin's orders in 1940; Stalin died of a cerebral haemorrhage in his dacha in Russia in 1953, but his chief of the NKVD, the secret police, Lavrentiy Beria claimed to have poisoned him; Kerensky died of heart disease in New York City in 1970 and, because the Russian Orthodox church would not bury him there, he was interred in Putney Vale Cemetery in London.

11   Kitchen, *Silent Dictatorship*, pp. 157-184. Hull, *Absolute Destruction*, p. 199.

12   Fischer, *War Aims*, pp. 103-6.

13   Arnold-Forster, *Blockade*, p. 27.

'utterly chaotic' and the puppet regime was incompetent. The truth had to be covered with propaganda.[14] Ukrainian peasants forcibly resisted German army requisitions by destroying their half-ripened crops.[15] Even when added to the 'ruthless draining' of supplies from Romania, Poland and the Baltic States, and the rape of the captured territories in the west, Germany still found herself far from self-sufficient.

Apart from the possibility of acting as a 'guard' for Lenin at Sassnitz, there are two other options for Gerth's 'secret mission' at Libau.

The first may have involved preparations for the German invasion of the Baltic islands of Dago, Moon and Ösel at the head of the Gulf of Riga, now Hiiumaa, Muhu and Saaremaa off the north-west coast of Estonia, in October 1917. This action finally ended the High Seas Fleet's inactivity since the Battle of Jutland over a year before.[16] Some 25,000 German soldiers, accompanied by ten dreadnoughts, 350 other vessels, a half-dozen Zeppelins, and eighty aircraft (possibly with Gerth's involvement), took the islands in the most successful amphibious operation of the war. The Gulf of Riga was opened to German warships and threatened Russian naval bases in the Gulf of Finland. An estimated 20,000 Russians were captured.

The second option is probably far-fetched and comes back to Canaris. After his promotion to Kapitänleutnant, he spent a few days with the Navy Inspectorate at Kiel in November, but transferred at the end of the month to the Intelligence Section of the Admiralty Staff. On 4 January 1916, under the cover name of 'Carl', Canaris arrived in Spain with a covert mission to set up an etappe system for the supply of German u-boats in the Atlantic and *en route* to the Mediterranean, and to create a network of informers to report the movement of enemy shipping.[17]

By the end of January, 'information centres' were installed in Santander, Seville, Cadiz, and Melilla while those at Algeciras, La Linea, Tripoli, Huelva, Tangiers, Barcelona, Vigo and Corunna were in preparation. Canaris was not acting alone, but his assistants are not named in the military record. For a while, Canaris went back to Germany suffering from a bout of malaria caught in South America. On his return, British naval intelligence in 'Room 40' in

14    Feldman, *Army, Industry and Labour*, p. 461.
15    Howard, 'Social and Political Consequences', p. 165.
16    Barrett, *Operation Albion*.
17    Mueller, *Canaris*, pp. 20-25.

London was on the case. It was clear to the Germans that there was also a source in their Spanish embassy leaking information to the French. In addition, the German codes were broken and the British and the French were reading radio traffic between Berlin and its three main espionage centres in Madrid, Barcelona and San Sebastian.

Late in February, Canaris left for Genoa using a Chilean passport in an attempt to get to Switzerland. He was held by the Italians and it took a month for him to get back to Spain. Canaris complained of a 'very harsh time under arrest', which included 'long interrogations and foul treatment'.[18]

By June, it was decided to get Canaris out of Spain as his life was thought to be in danger. Kapitänleutnant Lothar von Arnauld de la Perière, commander of *U 35*, missed Canaris during a twenty-four hour stop-over at Cartagena on 21 June as Canaris was forbidden to 'sneak aboard'. On 14 September, Canaris tried again to board the u-boat, but the attempt failed due to bad weather. Then, on 29 September at a rendezvous point off the Spanish coast at Salitrona Bay, Canaris was finally collected by Arnauld in *U 35* and taken to the Cattaro u-boat base in the Adriatic, arriving on 9 October 1916. The number of Allied trawlers and a submarine near the pick up strongly suggested the leaks from the embassy continued. Canaris returned to Germany and on 24 October, with the Kaiser's personal approval, received the Iron Cross 1st Class. He was then assigned to the Navy Staff Inspectorate of Submarines. On 11 September 1917, probably desperate for a return to action, he took up training as a u-boat commander.

Is there a possibility that Gerth could again have followed in Canaris's wake? Could the time as director of 'E-Stelle' have been a cover? Might he have been assisting Canaris in Spain as the obvious choice following their similar experiences in South America? Gerth claimed in 1922, as noted, to have served in Spain, Italy and Africa. There is no record of Gerth doing this, but Canaris served in all three during his Spanish mission, the last two in Genoa and in Tangiers and Tripoli.

It is always possible that one of Gerth's early large ships made stopovers in Africa: he spent seven months on SMS *Kaiser Karl der Grosse* at the ending of his sea cadetship in 1907 and 1908, but the pre-dreadnought battleship was a part of the High Seas Fleet and remained in the North and Baltic Seas; and

---

18    Mueller, *Canaris*, p. 22.

followed that with a year aboard the light cruiser *Königsberg* which was not sent to Africa until 1914. However, just as Canaris was in Spain, Italy and the north of Africa in 1914, so Gerth's brother Georg was stationed off West Africa in the gunboat *Panther* in 1912 and early in 1913.

If there was any imaginary credit claimed by Gerth by association, there were plenty of close sources.

There is one other element that gives pause. Canaris made royal contact during his time in Spain. A British agent jealously reported that Canaris was often seen in deep conversation with the king. When seeking to escape Spain, Canaris was threatened with kidnap by the French and British secret services. Discussions took place as to whether the Spanish king should be alerted to the need to keep a confidential watch on Canaris's safety.

In 1922, in his foreign office application, Gerth gave several surprising referees all of which would be contacted by a conscientious German ministry. In other words, a false referee would severely hinder the employment application. On Gerth's list of Prussian and Bavarian residents were Their Royal Highnesses Prince und Princess Ludwig Ferdinand von Bayern and Maria de la Paz de Bourbon, the Spanish infanta and daughter of Queen Isabella II; His Excellency Pablo Soler, ambassador to his Majesty the King of Spain; His Excellency Diego von Bergen, the Italian ambassador; and Monsignor Eugenio Maria Giuseppe Giovanni Pacelli, the papal envoy, later in 1939 to become Pope Pius XII. Clearly these contacts need further discussion, but for now they show an extraordinarily high level of political and religious intimacy with the upper echelons of Spanish and Italian Catholic society.

Gerth began his u-boat training in June 1917, a few months before Canaris. The physical criteria were higher than other branches of the service: no history of heart or vascular diseases, a muscular body with healthy skin, good teeth, and perfect ears, nose and throat, good hearing and no colour blindness.[19] Speech had to be without stutter. Gerth had to present a family history which showed no hereditary disease, particularly tuberculosis. The age limits were between eighteen and thirty years, but this was raised in 1917 to thirty-five years; Gerth was thirty-one and possibly the rule change was timely. Applicants needed to weigh between sixty and eighty kilograms and be no taller than 180 cm to move easily through a cramped submarine. Applicants also needed

---

19    Termote, *Krieg unter Wasser*, pp. 115-17.

to pass a psychological profile and to have no criminal record; any crime committed during u-boat service meant an immediate transfer.

*The best and most intelligent of our officers have been transferred to cruisers, torpedo boats and submarines … With few exceptions those who have remained behind don't have much on the ball … The fact that it was possible to select the supply of the needed personnel for our submarines … was largely due to the fact that the German fleet served as a means of training a reserve of personnel from which officers, petty officers and special enlisted ratings could be carefully selected.*[20]

The emphasis laid on preparing the submarine crews can be seen in the increase of the training establishment in the Kiel − Eckernförde Bay areas on the Baltic coast. They rose from 175 at the start of the war to nearly 900 by July 1916: their facilities included the mother ship *Vulcan*; three permanent target ships, including *Amazone* in which Erich's brother Georg recently served; a residential ship; nine submarines; seven torpedo boats; and a considerable number of training staff.

Emphasis was on u-boat familiarisation, engines, navigation, diving, secret documents, signals, radio and decoding, seamanship, gunnery, torpedo maintenance and firing … and many more. One of the, perhaps, unexpected subjects was training in role playing with captains and crew of investigated and destroyed ships, and the recommended behaviour in the event of capture. One u-boat directive instructed commanders to capture, when possible, captains and engineering officers of sunken ships to stop them returning to the Allied skill pool.[21]

Commanders were expected to have the 'ability to take quick decisions, stay calm and keep a clear head in critical situations where duty must be done in difficult circumstances'.[22] Training an officer for command could take up to seven months. Erich Gerth took ten months, but this may be because, by 23 September, he commissioned and was commander of a Kiel training boat,

---

20    Mulligan, *Neither Sharks*, p. 34.

21    Mulligan, *Neither Sharks*, p. 40. This instruction was repeated in 1942.

22    *BA-MA*, Freiburg, RM 27-XIII/214, Vol. 8.

*UB 76*, an appointment which lasted for five weeks and suggests that Gerth was accounted a success.[23]

On 1 December 1917, the long-term head of the Submarine Training School, Korvettenkapitän Theodor Eschenburg, wrote that on the course for submarine commanders Gerth showed 'keen interest, diligence and deep thoroughness. Also, his practical achievements were good; he navigated with good vision and great confidence below and above the water, calmly carried out the attack and remained mostly unseen even at close distance. His hit results including night shooting can be described as very good.'[24]

---

23    *UB 76* spent her life in the Training Flotilla in Kiel. She was handed over to the Allies in 1919 under the terms of the armistice and broken up in Rochester, USA, in 1922 (uboat.net).

24    Löhr, 'Obituary'.

Ernst Gerth and his three sons, Carl, Erich and Georg. Carl, the youngest, drowned, about age three, in a courtyard fountain while playing with his two brothers, briefly unsupervised, c. 1892. *Family archive*

Publicity picture of a horse-drawn tram from Ernst Gerth's company in Berlin in 1890. *Stiftung Deutsches Technikmuseum (VI.1.003 Foto-SLG, DTMB01574)*

If any writing caused the inflamed passions in Germany that led to war, it was these two: Alfred Thayer Mahan, The Influence of Sea Power upon History, 1660-1805 (1890) and Georg Wislicenus, Deutschlands Seemacht, sonst und jetzt (1895). *Author*

The German Imperial Naval Academy (Marineakademie) at Kiel about 1910.

Naval officer cadet Erich, about 1905, with his mother, Hedwig. *Family archive*

The two manuals which governed the Gerth boys' lives while cadets: Instructions for the replenishment of the naval officer corps with regulatory statutes, 1909, and Instructions for the training of naval cadets on the school ships, 1910. *Author*

Erich in junior naval officer's uniform, left, and Georg, a cadet, about 1910. *Family archive*

South American spy-ship for Wilhelm Canaris and Erich c.1910, the light cruiser SMS *Bremen.*

Wilhelm Canaris and Erich were among sixty cadets assigned in 1905 to the fully-rigged training ship SMS *Stein* where they lived cheek by jowl for almost a year.

The light cruiser, SMS *Dresden*, in the Kaiser Wilhelm (Kiel) Canal; sunk by the British with Wilhelm Canaris aboard in 1915 off the Chilean coast

The 'Black Tom' sabotage in New Jersey city, USA, in 1916 by German agents, perhaps a postscript to the pre-war work of Canaris and Erich?

Wilhelm Canaris, the man with a finger in every secret pie, pre-war spy, leader of the Abwehr, close friend of Erich, Spanish royalty, assassins, and plotters to kill Adolf Hitler.

Karl Dönitz, fellow u-boat commander to Erich in the Mediterranean, future German Führer, whose Berlin background closely mirrored that of the Gerth brothers.

# 3

# GERTH: U-BOATS IN THE ADRIATIC

During May 1918, Kapitänleutnant Gerth travelled overland by train through Vienna to the Mediterranean u-boat bases in the Adriatic and reported to the Führer der U-boots, Kapitän zur See Theodor Püllen.[1]

The Germans decided to start submarine warfare in the Mediterranean in 1915 to assist the Turkish forces being heavily shelled by Allied ships in the Dardanelles.[2] It was initially an offensive military operation. Several u-boats were sent to disrupt warships and the supplies to the Gallipoli front. Later, the German u-boats in the Adriatic fleet 'only received orders from the Austrian command for military missions which were rare as the Austrians never ventured further than the Ionian Sea'.[3] The German Admiralty directed all instructions for commercial warfare either through Püllen or directly to boats at sea.

Behind the immediate support for Turkey lay a much more extensive strategy that had its roots well before the start of the war. Germany's rise to become a world power, thwarted by the colonial land grabs outside of Europe of the previous centuries, was thought to be dependent on the disintegration of the British Empire.[4] The promotion of independence within large parts of the

---

1    The initial leader, Commander Kophamel, returned to Germany to take over the converted mercantile submarine *U 151* (Koerver, *Submarine Warfare*), p. 218.

2    Gayer, *Submarine Warfare*, pp. 5-6.

3    Laurens, *Histoire de la Guerre Sous-Marine Allemande*, p. 367.

4    Fischer, *War Aims*, pp. 120-22.

British empire was itself a long-term German war aim. In a famous speech in Damascus in November 1898, made the day after a speech in Jerusalem full of strong support for Christianity, the Kaiser declared himself the protector over all Muslims:

> *Deeply moved by this imposing spectacle [the Damascus reception] and likewise by the consciousness of standing on the spot where held sway one of the most chivalrous rulers of all times, the great Sultan Saladin, a knight sans peur et sans reproche, who often taught his adversaries the right conception of knighthood, I seize with joy the opportunity to render thanks, above all to the Sultan Abdul Hamid for his hospitality. May the Sultan rest assured, and also the three hundred million Mohammedans scattered over the globe and revering him as their caliph, that the German Emperor will be and remain at all times their friend.[5]*

'The British', the Kaiser wrote in 1906, 'had better understand that war with Germany means the loss of India and therefore a world war'.[6]

This was a theme to which he returned regularly. In 1914, before the start of the war, the Kaiser wrote to the German ambassador in St Petersburg, 'England ... must have the mask of Christian peacableness torn publicly off her face ... Our consuls in Turkey and India, agents, etc, must inflame the whole Mohammedan world to wild revolt against this hateful, lying, conscienceless people of hagglers, for if we are to be bled to death, at least England shall lose India.'

Setting the Islamic world afire was an integral part of Germany's official policy. As part of a continuation 'by other means' of this policy, the German-Turkish alliance of 2 August 1914 was concluded with an 'eye to unleashing a pan-Islamic movement, which was to lead off with a Holy War'. On the same day, the retired Freiherr Max von Oppenheim, the man who had inspired the Kaiser's Damascus speech, was recalled to the foreign ministry. 'Taking up his ideas of 1898, he recommended Holy War and pan-Islamic propaganda as the most effective weapons for revolutionising the Islamic world and, as a first step, he proposed that expeditionary forces should be sent to Persia and Egypt.'

---

5    Schierbrand, *Kaiser's Speeches*, p. 321.
6    Fischer, *War Aims*, pp. 120-24.

*While the German armies were trying to overrun France in their first onset, the German government, in collaboration with the general staff, was working out a far-reaching programme of revolution which was directed equally against the British Empire and imperial Russia. These activities began immediately on the outbreak of war. They were at first a means of strategic warfare; they were intended on the other hand, to delay the Russian deployment on Germany's eastern frontier and keep part of the Russian armies tied down by internal unrest, and on the other hand, to draw off part of the British fleet to overseas stations and make it difficult for France to raise recruits in her colonies. The most vulnerable points of Britain and France seemed to be among their colonial subjects while Russia offered fields for subversion among her non-Russian peoples.[7]*

The u-boat bases in the Adriatic added support to the strategic goals. They aided Turkey, first, by guarding the Gallipoli narrows and the Bosphorus so as to sever communications between the European allies in the Mediterranean and the Black Sea with its Russian ports and, second, as an advanced force by which Germany could attack Britain's empire at her two most vulnerable points, India and Egypt. For both these countries, the Suez Canal and its shipping was of supreme importance.

The delivery of Sir Roger Casement, with guns and ammunition for the IRA, was just another example of marrying national aspirations, in this case those of the Irish, with a weakening of the British Empire. Casement was landed by German submarine to facilitate a rebellion against British rule across Ireland during the Easter Rising of 1916.

The Mediterranean flotilla was headquartered in an old Austro-Hungarian cruiser *Maria Theresia* anchored in the main base at Pola, where they shared a shipyard with a large Austrian fleet. The town name was spelled 'Pola' in Italian but 'Pula' in Croatian. The town had a rich Illyrian and Roman history and, from 1813, had been part of the Hapsburg Empire. Its commercial and military language was German.

Gerth was to be in the Adriatic for less than six months and his immediate discussions would be with Austrian and German colleagues. This was not the time to achieve his claimed fluency in Italian through mixing with a minority Italian community.

---

7    Fischer, *War Aims*, pp. 120-154.

Cattaro, now Kotor, Montenegro, was the advance base with a repair ship from where all missions started and finished because of its proximity to the entrance to the main sea and the security of the one hundred fathom line.[8] The Austrians had taken the port from the Italians with little fight. Later, Fiume, now Rijeka, Croatia, and Trieste at the head of the gulf were added to the fleet anchorages to provide u-boats with more extensive facilities for three-monthly overhauls. All these ports on the eastern shore of the Adriatic are deep water harbours, 'resembling Norwegian fiords' and are protected for almost the 'whole length of the coast by a fringe of islands'. This is in sharp contrast to the Italian Adriatic coast where the limited ports are much exposed.

In three of those recurring connections in the small world of the German navy officer corps, the senior administration staff officer at Cattaro was Kapitänleutnant Hubert Aust, the second administrative staff officer at Pola was Kapitänleutnant Hermann von Fischel, and Oberleutnant Kurt Hartwig, commanding *U 32* and *U 63*, who had been on the *Dresden* with Canaris in Chile, were all class mates of Erich Gerth at the naval academy crew of 1905.[9]

*We merely added German personnel and material to these two plants in order to increase their efficiency, but unfortunately did not undertake to enlarge or extend them such as was done by the very energetic commander, Bartenbach, at Bruges and Ostend in Flanders. The result was that at the climax of the submarine activities in the Mediterranean, it took longer and longer to repair the boats. In 1918, this became really serious. The chief of the submarine division took energetic steps and ordered extensive improvements and enlargements to Pola and Cattaro as submarine bases. The repair shops, etc, at Trieste and Fiume were also enlarged and increased in efficiency through proper measures. As a result of the Austrian collapse, these measures unfortunately were never entirely carried out. It was tragic that we never succeeded in getting hold of Valona; the passage through the Otranto narrows would have then been considerably easier.*[10]

A new fixed barrage of mine nets was laid to 150 feet by the British in the Otranto Straits to block access by the u-boats to the Mediterranean. This was

---

8     Koerver, *Submarine Warfare*, pp. 218-20.
9     Fischel became at admiral. He died in a prison camp near Moscow five years after the end of WW2. His son, Unno, died commanding *U 374* in 1942 (uboat.net).
10    Gayer, *Submarine Warfare*, pp. 7, 29.

to enhance an inefficient first attempt at a barrier made in 1915 which had accounted for only one submarine.[11] The new work began in April 1918 and was not completed until September. It was an out-and-out failure. Between April and August, Adriatic u-boats made 121 passages by simply diving underneath or, occasionally, around the obstacle. The nets had the 'adverse effect of increasing the u-boats' offensive potential once they were out in the Mediterranean because the convoy escorts were denuded in order to increase the strength of the barrage patrol'. This resulted in the overall loss rate of Allied Mediterranean convoys being twice as high as those on the Atlantic, even though there the ships travelled out of convoy for much of the war.[12]

Another May arrival at Pola with Gerth was Oberleutnant Martin Niemöller, an old Adriatic hand, who noticed that the 'intimacy of 1916 had disappeared, but the spirit survived, as did the good custom that all German submarine officers should address one another as *Henry*, irrespective of rank and real name'.[13]

There were two other 'Henrys' who would become particularly famous in the second world war: Oberleutnant Karl Dönitz, the future leader of the u-boats; and, as one could expect, Canaris.

The history of the German Mediterranean Flotilla is 'largely the history of three or four conspicuously able commanders, who stand out among a number of quite mediocre performers'.[14] Most striking overall was the disproportionate success rates for a small number of u-boat aces: twenty-two of some 400 u-boat commanders in the Great War realised more than sixty per cent of all Allied merchant sinkings; only four per cent of all u-boats sank thirty per cent of all merchant shipping lost.[15]

Pola was at one end of, perhaps, the most humorous tale of the u-boats in the Mediterranean. It involved *UC 20* which was often employed in 1916 to transport rifles, machine guns and hand grenades to the Senussi, a religious sect resident in Libya and Egypt. The Germans and the Ottomans persuaded the Grand Senussi, Ahmed Sharif es Senussi, to declare jihad and to attack

---

11    Tarrant, *U-boat Offensive*, p. 63.
12    Mulligan, *Neither Sharks*, p. 38.
13    Niemöller, *From U-boat*, pp. 116-17.
14    Koerver, *Submarine Warfare*, pp. 218-19.
15    Mulligan, *Neither Sharks*, p. 40.

British-occupied Egypt from the west. This would divert British forces from a proposed Ottoman raid on the Suez Canal from Palestine.

On one of *UC 20*'s voyages the crew was presented by the grateful Grand Senussi with a camel. Pride challenged, the captain decided to ship the beast home. The submarine went as close inshore as possible while the camel was driven into the sea but, when released from its tether, it paddled off at full speed. 'The commanding officer carried out a faultless attack with a 90° track angle and blew as the bows were just under the camel's belly. The boat rose and the camel lay on the bows, forelegs to port and hindlegs to starboard.'[16] The beast was hauled onto the deck and made fast. The next morning the captain told his watch officer that, if the boat had to dive on the way back to Pola, 'it's all up for the camel'. The watch officer had an answer. 'We can dive quite well with the camel … With the boat at 4½ fathoms, the camel's head will just be sticking out above the surface. I have already marked it on the depth gauge.'

Twice during the crossing, *UC 20* dived to evade enemy ships and each time came the order, 'Go to camel depth.' Close to the entrance to Pola, *UC 20* passed through a fishing fleet and the captain could not resist diving once more.

'A frightful horror seized the fishermen, who only saw the head and hump approaching and consequently believed it to be some fearful sea-monster. Setting all sail, they fled hastily.'

There is, today, a herd of wild camel on the Pola peninsular where tales are told in the waterfront bars of a fearful creature of the deep.[17]

Chief among the able commanders in the Mediterranean was the leading u-boat ace, Arnauld de la Perière, who had rescued Canaris from Spain, and who sank 193 merchant ships with a total of 453,369 tons; two warships, 2,500 tons; and damaged eight ships, 34,312 tons.[18]

A close second was the entirely ruthless Kapitänleutnant Max Valentiner who sank over 140 ships and was the third ranking ace of the war. In November 1915, Valentiner torpedoed the Italian passenger liner *Ancona* without allowing

---

16    Hashagen, *Commander*, pp. 127-29. There are variations on the story elsewhere, but this one is preferred.

17    Other sources suggest three camels were eventually transferred, two by *UC 20* and one by *UC 73*; on one trip *UC 20*'s camel was accompanied by a sheep (1914-1918.invisionzone.com/forums/topic/96831-disposal-of-a-camel, accessed 10/2017).

18    uboat.net.

time for the passengers to abandon ship with the loss of 200 lives. Valentiner flew the Austro-Hungarian flag during the attack as, at that time, Germany was not at war with Italy. Rather than admit the truth and risk an Italian war, the Germans forced Austria-Hungary to admit falsely that it was one of their own submarines. Further, Austria-Hungary pretended to discipline a non-existent u-boat commander, and to pay reparations to Italy.

A month later, Valentiner was branded a war criminal after sinking the passenger liner *Persia* without warning, contrary to international law at that time, and killing 343 of the 519 people aboard.[19]

Both men survived the war. Arnauld was killed in 1941 in an aircraft accident at Le Bourget airport near Paris, France, while Valentiner died in 1949 in Sønderborg, Denmark.[20]

Gerth found Canaris had beaten him to the Adriatic by six months where he was appointed to the admiralty staff officer at Pola. He had also been acting Führer for two months. These quick promotions were unusual as Canaris had no u-boat leadership experience although his training record praised him highly. Perhaps, as the Mediterranean flotilla was under the direct command of naval staff in Berlin, they wished to have their own man in place.[21] Canaris was not in the Adriatic to greet Gerth as he had returned to Kiel in March to pick up a new boat, *UB 128*, and was much delayed in a traumatic return journey.[22]

Canaris had a poor start to his tour in the Adriatic. His first u-boat, *U 38*, was in constant repair for two months. In the replacement, *UC 27*, Canaris was sent in November to mine the entrances to the Algerian harbours used by the Allies.[23] There were technical problems: the gyro compass failed and engine sealing rings leaked. The sea was too rough for torpedo attacks.

---

19    At the time of sinking, *Persia* was carrying a large quantity of gold and jewels belonging to the Maharaja Jagatjit Singh. The wreck was located off Crete in 2003 at a depth of 3,000 metres and an attempt was made to salvage the treasure located in the bullion room. The salvage attempt met with limited success, retrieving artefacts and portions of the ship, and some jewels from the bullion room.

20    Bridgland, *Outrage*, Chapter 8, 'Max Valentiner Strikes Twice', pp. 121-135.

21    Robert Derencin, uboat.net.

22    Mueller, *Canaris*, pp. 29-30.

23    *BA-MA*, Freiburg, RM 97/1785, KTB, *UC 27*.

*The watch on the deck wore oilskins and were lashed to the rails in lifebelts, as every*
*other sea broke over us with full force, sweeping us right off our feet.*[24]

A December voyage nearly ended in disaster as two mines exploded
prematurely; torpedo attacks in January off Sardinia were unsuccessful; there
were more technical faults. That month, only five u-boats were operational
in the Adriatic, the other twenty-eight were in the dockyard or undergoing
maintenance. Extensive refits had to be taken 4,000 miles away in Germany.
'Mechanical breakdowns and the inability to put them right quickly were
probably as much responsible as convoying for eventually bringing down the
number of Allied ships lost to u-boats in the Mediterranean.'[25] This view was
endorsed by the later Vizeamiral Andreas Michelsen, commander of the High
Seas Fleet's submarines from June 1917 until the end of the war, who explained
that not much was done at Pola and even less at Cattaro.

'[This was] negligence for which they paid dearly. The German submarines
had need of big repair works and [not having them] reduced the gains in the
theatre of operations that the Mediterranean offered and which could have
been so profitable.'[26]

Canaris was moved to command *U 47* which was another dockyard case.
Then, at the start of 1918, he was concurrently given *U 34*, a hugely successful
boat with almost one hundred sinkings to her name. On his first trip with *U 34*,
the engine malfunctioned and Canaris had to return.[27] 'Finally, off the Algerian
coast on 28 January he sighted a heavily laden French steamer escorted by a
cruiser and a trawler.'[28] His first torpedo struck the *Djibouti* amidships and she
sank with her cargo of phosphate and case oil.[29]

---

24    Niemöller, *From U-boat*, p. 24.
25    Compton-Hall, *Submarines*, pp. 221-22.
26    Laurens, *Histoire de la Guerre Sous-Marine Allemande*, p. 367.
27    BA-MA, Freiburg, RM 97/753, KTB, *U 34*.
28    Mueller, *Canaris*, pp. 26-28.
29    uboat.net.

# 4

# GERTH: INTO THE
# MEDITERRANEAN

By the time Gerth got to sea in July, Canaris was already well ahead in the race for recognition. It was a depressing time to start active patrols as May had been the 'most disastrous' month for the flotilla which lost five submarines: three to armed patrols, *U 39* interned at Cartagena, and *UB 52* torpedoed by the British submarine *H 4*.[1]

Gerth's first operational u-boat was *U 47*, Canaris's cast off.[2] Gerth took it over on 18 June when it was under repair at Pola and he spent a frustrating three months dealing with a series of technical problems that mirrored Canaris's introduction. He had his first outing on 13 July with a trimming trial in the harbour and then moored alongside *Maria Theresia* to prepare for a test voyage.

Two days later, he sailed out with the torpedo boat *A 82* and fired eleven practice torpedoes near Cap Porer. After an engine test the next morning, and heavy leakage from a hatch, two torpedoes were fired at him by one or two enemy submarines; two periscopes were spotted nearby. More days of testing followed while the hatch still leaked. On one of the trips when he was trialling a new wire cutter, Gerth accidentally cut some Austrian telegraph cables.

Early in August, Gerth took the flotilla chief, Püllen, out for a final trial off Cap Porer. Getting the all clear, he took on provisions and equipment that

---

1    Gayer, *Submarine Warfare*, p. 7. Koerver, *Submarine Warfare*, p. 224.
2    *Deutsche U-Boot Museum*, Cuxhaven, KTB, *U 47*.

afternoon. The hatch started leaking again and the mission was postponed for twenty-four hours. Gerth took an Austrian pilot as he wound his way south through the channels inshore of the Adriatic islands. He met *UB 105*, Kapitänleutnant Wilhelm Marschall, and swopped stories, handed the pilot over to an Austrian torpedo boat, and continued above and below water to patrol off the Italian coast near Pelagosa Grande.[3]

> *The cook stretched up his arms to us in the conning tower with tin cups and a steaming plate of pea soup and pork in his hands. I put the plate on my knees and dipped out its contents. The moisture which forms in large drops on the ceiling during long trips underwater fell down on my head and into my plate and left small splotches of oil in the pea soup as a sign they were real drops of u-boat sweat.*[4]

On 6 August, a water cooling pipe broke in *U 47* which caused serious damage. With the starboard engine not working, Gerth headed back to Cattaro for repairs. He tried to get on patrol again on 10 August, sailing out with an Austro-Hungarian torpedo boat and *U 35*.[5] *U 35* was Arnauld de la Perière's worn-out boat which he commanded from November 1915 to March 1918. It was also the most successful u-boat of the war, active since 1914, with 236 ships sunk or damaged.

In the Straits of Otranto, Gerth sighted two ships, possibly older Italian cruisers, one of which steered towards him. Gerth dived to sixty metres. The port engine had to be switched off because of overheating and water began coming in through the long-faulty hatch. It was back to base again avoiding an enemy submarine which could not fire a torpedo because of the heavy swell. Gerth called in at Spalato, modern day Split, to fix a small engine fault, but workers at Cattaro could not handle the larger repairs so it needed a further retreat to Pola, where Gerth handed in his torpedoes and planned an optimistic

---

3    Wilhelm Marschall was a WWI u-boat ace with over forty ships sunk. From 1934, he captained the pocket battleship *Admiral Scheer*. During the Spanish Civil War, he commanded the German naval forces off the Spanish coast. Promoted admiral in 1939, he flew his flag in the battleship *Gneisenau* and led the German naval force which intercepted and sank the British auxiliary cruiser *Rawalpindi* off the Faroe Islands. In 1940, Marschall with *Gneisenau*, and her sister-ship *Scharnhorst*, sank in a two-hour action the British aircraft carrier *Glorious* and her accompanying destroyers, *Acasta* and *Ardent*, while *Scharnhorst* was badly hit by one of *Acasta's* torpedoes.

4    Spiegel, *U-202*, p. 48.

5    *Deutsche U-Boot Museum*, Cuxhaven, KTB, *UC 47*.

fourteen days in docks. In September, an additional two weeks of tests and repairs were needed.

With *U 47* seemingly beyond repair, Gerth was given command in September of another suspect boat, *UC 53*, of the same basic type as *UC 61*, his brother Georg's final command, and had just a week to prepare himself and his crew.[6] The boat had undergone extensive maintenance in Trieste throughout July and August.

Gerth was ordered to lay his eighteen mines north of Messina Strait and then sail to the Tyrrhenian Sea to look for merchant ships. It was a ferocious start to his operational u-boat career. He sailed from Cattaro on 19 September and the next day at South Adria was seen by three destroyers and survived twenty-two depth charges in his fully-mined boat.

*A pallid corpse-like countenance peered out at me from one of the bunks, and retched and retched. At this sight, my own stomach began to turn again, and I could barely contain myself. The atmosphere below was really beyond description. The damp, warm, almost stifling air, saturated as it was with oil, made me feel sicker than ever … I fled from this oil-reeking domain and tried to get some sleep on my bunk. Though hitherto it had been the cold that made me curse my fate, it was now the foul air that made breathing a torture and would not let me sleep. Sweat broke from all my pores; I tossed about and tried to wedge myself in every conceivable position so as not to be flung out by a sudden heave of the boat. Those five hours of rest, that were mere restlessness and torment, seemed eternal, and the summons to turn out came almost as a relief. Exhausted and shattered, without a wink of sleep, I hoisted myself out of my bunk and went to my post in the control-room.*[7]

When Gerth surfaced, a hot air balloon signalled with lanterns to some armed trawlers who presented him with another eighteen depth charges. The following evening in bright moonlight he passed the chain barricade at Otranto at periscope depth because of six armed trawlers ahead. He found his boat was down by the stern with a strong starboard list. The regulator flooded.

At dawn on 22 September, Gerth saw a laden steamer guarded by two armed trawlers travelling on the route from Malta to Corfu. He fired a torpedo

---

6    *Deutsche U-Boot Museum*, Cuxhaven, KTB, *UC 53*.

7    Leading Seaman Schlichting, 'Hurricane', Neureuther, *U-Boat Stories*, p. 99.

at 380 metres and hit the steamer's bow. Firing a torpedo from a u-boat laden with mines was a highly risky affair. Down at fifty metres, he endured ten depth charges from the escorts which left splinters on the deck of his boat. The steamer sank and armed trawlers closed on the site of the sinking while a French four-funnel destroyer dashed about at great speed.

After the escorts had picked up the full crew and left the area, Gerth found on papers among the lifeboats that he had sunk the English steamer *Gorsemore*, 3,079 tons, carrying coal from Barry in South Wales to the Italian port of Taranto. The life boats were in 'very good condition and well equipped' with emergency ration packs labelled 'For Army and Navy Use'. *UC 53* replenished its fresh provisions from a floating cooling cabinet.

> *[The ship] screamed and groaned like a fatally wounded beast, till the sea closed over her masts and funnel. Gurgling and bubbling, white eddies, boats and wreckage. Even some minutes afterwards great wooden beams, tearing themselves loose deep below, shot violently up and through the surface ... The ship's death agony stood long in my memory. The seaman, in his heart of hearts, is a good-humoured, generous fellow. For him each ship has a soul. But war turns hearts to steel. Had we not been attacked? Then draw swords! And forward with our u-boats, ruthless, against British trade, the life-nerve of the United Kingdom.*[8]

For the next few days, Gerth cruised the Malta Channel and Medina Bank in a strong sea, heavy rain and bad visibility. The boat was too heavy and low-lying. There were problems with the ventilation and leaks caused flooding. On 26 September, he ran into a small cargo steamer and an armed trawler which opened fire forcing an emergency dive.

> *'Diving stations!' The order suddenly rang out from the conning-tower. In an instant the deck was empty. Everyone jumped, climbed, or swung himself on to the conning-tower; and thence down the open hatchway. The tall periscope is soon in place. Quickly down the smooth iron greasy ladder; and don't let the great seaman's boots above you crash on to your fingers! And mind your head and your bones in this iron tube, plastered with iron plates, levers, screws, and wheels, and now crammed with scrambling men. In less time than it takes to describe, everyone from on deck has*

---

8    *Hashagen, Commander*, p. 66.

*dashed to his appointed place, inside the conning-tower, in the control-room, or in one of the other compartments of the vessel. Last of all the commander climbs into the conning-tower and the heavy hatch is fastened above his head. The oil-engines are switched off and the electric motors started. Just as the commander stands at the periscope in the conning-tower, the eye of the u-boat, so in the control-room, the brain of the vessel, the chief engineer stands at the centre periscope.*[9]

Thunderstorms after dark meant the radio had to be switched off; no radio messages were received the next day because of atmospheric disturbance. On 28 September, at the northern entrance of Messina Strait, Gerth entered the 'perilous currents and whirlpools of Scylla and Charybdis' and logged praise for his navigation officer, Oberleutnant S Peters, for his careful navigation. Near Faro, Gerth fired a second torpedo at a half-laden steamer. There was a loud detonation and Gerth speculated he had ignited a cargo of ammunition. It was the French steamer *Caraibe*, 2,976 tons. Six depth charges followed. Gerth went north submerged, but found the boat too heavy, sagging by the stern, so he surfaced, and spent the day sorting out his torpedoes, reloading, and recharging his batteries.

At this time, Gerth's torpedoes, and those of all the Mediterranean German and Austrian boats, were made by British armaments firms Vickers and Armstrong which each held a large proportion of the shares of Whitehead & Co, the torpedo manufacturer with works at Fiume. An ex-secretary to the Committee of Imperial Defence was also a director of Armstrong, Whitworth, and a director of Armstrong's Italian firm, Armstrong Pozzuoli, on the Italian coast.[10] Labour MP Philip Snowden was like a dog with a bone with the story and was unsparing with his criticism of the directors of these companies. His pursuit lasted well into the 1930s but, eventually, to no avail.[11]

*'Numerous individuals sitting in the warm comfort of Westminster or their exclusive London clubs of grand gothic cathedrals profited from the torpedoes that sent thousands of brave British seamen to cold graves. These men made untold fortunes on the products of death and misery.'*[12]

---

9    War artist Claus Bergen, 'My U-Boat Voyage', Neureuther, *U-Boat Stories*, p. 11.

10   Murray, *Krupp's International Armaments Ring*, p. 179.

11   Docherty & Macgregor, *Hidden History*, p. 142.

12   Interpreted from Labour MP Philip Snowden, *Hansard, House of Commons*, Debate, 5/5/1915, Vol.

A piston on *UC 53*'s portside engine disintegrated and put that engine out of order for several days reducing maximum speed to six knots.

Gerth then caused mayhem with a series of small Italian sailing vessels. On the morning of 30 September in the Gulf of Salerno, he used his machine gun to stop *Francesco Padre*, 101 tons, based in Palermo, travelling in ballast from Naples to Messina. Gerth sank her with explosive cartridges and released the crew in their tender.[13] Next in a group came *Francesco P*, seventy tons, travelling from Castellamare to Messina with a cargo of wood, sunk by cartridges following some gun practice after the crew were also released in their tender; then *Isanna I*, a mere five tons, with empty barrels for Salerno. The crew 'had no tender and the boat no value so released sailing boat after cutting its sails'.

Close to Capri, Gerth spotted three more sailing boats which he approached at dusk and stopped two of them with his machine gun, *Gabriele Costa*, 105 tons, and *Giovanni Costa*, 102 tons, and then sank them with cartridges. Both were sailing in ballast from Genoa to Messina. Gerth then chased the third sailing boat while towing the tender of *Gabriele Costa* and carrying her crew on the deck of *UC 53* when a destroyer moved swiftly toward them. The crew of *Gabriele Costa* were put into their tender and Gerth made an emergency dive to twenty-five metres.

> *It was a touching scene which, in spite of our inner joy, was hard on our nerves, as every true sailor regards the sailing-ship as a remnant of romance, dying out faster and faster in these days. This was truly the reason why now and at other times our hearts ached for each sailing ship which we had to sink.*[14]

Early the next morning, 1 October, Gerth stopped and repeated his routine with the sailing boat *San Giuseppi A*, fifty-six tons, travelling from Civitavechia to Trappani in ballast and, later that afternoon, the sailing boat *Giuseppino M*, thirty-nine tons, Trappani to Castellamare with a cargo of wood.

> *At 0900, I came across a bunch of large two-master schooners of the French deep-sea fleet. Once in their midst, I used their dories to ferry my prize crews from one schooner*

---

71, c1091; 8/11/1934, Vol. 293, ccl1293-1416. Murray, *Krupp's International Armaments Ring*, pp. xiii-xiv, 176-84.

13    Spindler's annotations on *UC 53*'s KTB, dated 11/2/1941.

14    Spiegel, *U-202*, p. 30.

*to the next, sinking them as they went. Within ninety minutes we had finished. Twelve large schooners, each with holds brimming with fish, lay wrecked on the sea bed. The loss of the fish, and more to the fishing boats, would make an impression on French food supplies.*[15]

The next day it rained and the radio was switched off because of storms. On 3 October, Gerth finally discharged his two rows of nine mines in the Strait of Messina unnoticed by Allied patrols.[16]

*We turned and began laying our mines. The after-compartment, which contained our main mine tubes, was the scene of hard and perspiring work ... The engineer officer had charge in the control room and maintained the boat at a uniform depth by admitting the correct volume of water to compensate for the weight of each mine as it was dropped, while standing by to dive at any moment.*[17]

From there on Gerth was dogged by more engine problems. On 4 October, he saw a hospital ship in a convoy of four steamers protected by six armed trawlers, but could not get into position because only one main engine was working and his maximum speed was only six knots.

Oil consumption was high and his range of operation was subsequently reduced. In the Messina Strait, *UC 53*'s periscope was seen by three armed trawlers as Gerth manoeuvred unsuccessfully for a torpedo shot at a 4,000-ton tanker. On 6 October, the crew worked to repair the starboard engine and its exhaust valve, the boat vulnerable and unable to dive. Lubrication oil consumption remained so high that Gerth decide to return while looking for opportunities to attack between Marritimo and Skerkibank, and off Syracuse. While both engines were running, that on the portside was restricted to four cylinders. Oil consumption was now excessive restricting him to one engine at a time and leaks were causing oil to burn in the cylinders.

---

15    Fürbringer, *Legendary*, p. 46.
16    Nine mines north-east of Capo Peloro, from 38°17'6N - 15°40'6E, course 58°; nine mines north of Capo Rasolcolmo, from 38°19'75N - 15°33'1E, course 1°; 3/10/1918 (Zu Minenkarte Nr. 22, KTB) p. 19.
17    Niemöller, *From U-boat*, p. 34. The mine tubes of *UC 53* were at the front of the boat.

*The only thing that we could not grow accustomed to was the fact that half the ship's company were sea-sick and the remainder had to clean up all day long.*[18]

It was now an emergency run home by the shortest route before the oil ran out. By 10 October, after passing Gozo and Malta, *UC 53* was limping through rain, hail storms, and zero visibility. On 12 October, in the Strait of Otranto, heading northward on a zig zag course, Gerth finally established radio contact with headquarters and reported his successes and forced return to 'Cleopatra'. The next day, *UC 53* sailed into the Bay of Cattaro and moored at the stone barracks.

*Who can understand the joy of a commander's heart when, sitting by his narrow writing table, he is carefully working out his report to his superiors? 'Have sunk X steamers, X sailing ships.' All around me were the happy faces of the crew. All were satisfied, every danger past and forgotten, thanks to the strength of youth and their stout hearts.*[19]

This was Gerth's sole operational patrol of the war. His eighteen mines had been laid and he had sunk one steamer and damaged another by torpedo, and six small sailing vessels sent to the bottom by thirty-eight cartridges, 6,509 tons altogether.

Perhaps sinking the clutch of Italian vessels was a trifle wanton at this very late stage of the war, but he had behaved meticulously to their crews. There were no injuries or deaths.

Canaris's total by war end was four largish steamers totalling 23,592 tons. Gerth had been plagued by mechanical problems. His flotilla commander was underwhelmed:

*First operation of new commander. Minelaying task completed successfully. A different route should have been selected for the journey both ways (via Adventure Bank) as there would probably have been opportunities to drop mines there. While navigating at periscope depth the boat accidentally brushed against the top link of a net of the buoy line Otranto-Fano. Criticism of reporting sailing-in via radio transmission message.*

---

18    Niemöller, *From U-boat*, p. 23.
19    Spiegel, *U 202*, p. 73.

*Flooding of the starboard regulator was the result of an operating error. The list of the boat during surface travel should have been identified as an indicator of an irregularity. The oil engine fault was caused by an error during the last maintenance works which now means further delays as all pistons will have to be replaced for checks. The cause for the boat's excessive lubricating oil consumption will have to be determined during repair works.*

One noticeable difference was manifested in the crews of the later u-boats: their proficiency deteriorated as a result of their hasty training and the inclusion of inexperienced hands in the complement. Many of the commanders of 1917-18, by their foolish or imprudent conduct, exhibited their inefficiency. During the last eighteen months of hostilities, submarines, when brought to combat and damaged, surrendered after a feeble resistance.[20]

Eighteen days later, *UC 53* was blown up and sunk by the Germans as one of ten unseaworthy boats in the Adriatic.[21]

Kapitän Püllen and his first officer Kapitänleutnant Otto Schulze witnessed the start of the collapse of their Austrian allies.[22] In January in Pola, Austrian naval shipyard workers with 'revolutionary sentiments' began a general strike demanding better living conditions and an end to the war. The Austrians were joined in the strike by some 1,500 German workers from Kiel who were helping to maintain the u-boats in the Adriatic. The strike was suppressed by the Austro-Hungarian Navy leadership backed by German land forces. However, on 1 February, sailors on the larger ships of the Austro-Hungarian fleet in Cattaro mutinied. Their commanders decided it would be better to sink the fleet before there was any chance that the sailors could take the ships to Italy. They asked Püllen and his u-boats to stand by. The situation was resolved temporarily, but remained tense throughout the summer with sporadic acts of severe indiscipline.[23]

---

20    Gibson, *Submarine War*, p. 183.
21    Destroyed: Cattaro: *U 72*, Hermann Bohm. Fiume: *UB 129*, Karl Neumann. Pola: *U 47*, Karl Bunte; *U 65*, Clemens Wickel; *U 73*, Fritz Saupe; *UB 48*, Wolfgang Steinbauer; *UC 25*, Karl Dönitz (Dönitz switched command to *UB 68* 2/7/1918); *UC 34*, Hans Schuler; *UC 53*, Erich Gerth. Trieste: *UC 54*, Otto Loycke. Two torpedo boats, *A 51* and *A 82*, were also destroyed.
22    Schultz became a grossadmiral in 1936 and was a career-long mentor to Dönitz (Padfield, *Dönitz*), pp. 96-97. His son, Heinz-Otto, died in command of *U 849* in the South Atlantic in 1943.
23    Niemöller, *From U-boat*, pp. 147-56.

Mutinies broke out again in October on the Austrian warships. Püllen realised that if the Austrians sued for a separate peace then his u-boats could become bargaining chips.[24] On 24 October, the Kaiser and Chancellor Price Max von Baden officially terminated unrestricted submarine warfare and four days later Read-Admiral Adolf von Trotha announced to the government that the u-boats were being recalled following the army's announcement that it was unable to continue the fight in France.[25]

Püllen sought permission to withdraw from the Adriatic and, sworn to secrecy, he received permission the next day [25 October]. Püllen felt bound to warn Admiral Miklos Horthy, the last commander-in-chief of the Austro-Hungarian Fleet, and later Regent of Hungary from 1920-1924, and also the senior Austrian officer at Cattaro, Linienschiffskapitän Seitz. Evacuation of the flotilla offices at Pola began on the 28th and at Cattaro on the 30th. Between the 29th and 31st thirteen [actually fourteen] u-boats all left for Germany while two more which were on patrol, *U 34*, Johannes Klasing, and *UC 73*, Franz Hagen, received orders to follow them immediately.[26] Püllen was concerned that a third, *UC 74*, Adelbert von der Luhe, [probably Hans Schüler] which was then off Asia Minor had insufficient fuel and her commander opted for internment in Spain.

At a day's notice, all seaworthy u-boats were to return forthwith to Germany to be available for a 'last stand'. No passengers were to be accommodated. Boats not ready to sail within twenty-four hours were to be scuttled.[27] At Pola, on 27 October, torpedo boat *A 51* and a dockyard tug towed out seven u-boats, including Gerth's two wrecks, *UC 53* and *U 47*, and they were sunk with explosives where their remains still lie. The bases at Cattaro and Pola were destroyed.

The flotilla staff and the crews of the scuttled boats, several hundred men including Gerth, left for home overland by railway via Vienna on 28 October. There were followed by the 1,500 German dock workers.

---

24    Wilson & Kemp, *Mediterranean Submarines*, pp. 185-86.

25    Herwig, *Naval Officer Corps*, pp. 240-41.

26    *U 33*, Gustav Siess; *U 35*, Heino von Heimburg; *U 38*, Clemens Wickel; *U 63*, Kurt Hartwig; *UB 49*, Adolf Ehrensberger; *UB 50*, Heinrich Kukat; *UB 51*, Ernst Krafft; *UB 105*, Rudolph Peterson; *UB 128*, Wilhelm Canaris; *UC 20*, Hermann Rohne; *UC 22*, Eberhard Weichold; *UC 27*, Otto Gerke; *UC 52*, Carl Heinrich Sass; and *UC 67*, Martin Niemöller.

27    Mueller, *Canaris*, pp. 30-31.

This was not a good time to travel. The Austro-Hungarian lines were disintegrating, especially towards Italy. The Bulgarian front had collapsed completely. Nationalist movements seized their chance to break away from the Hapsburg Empire and to try to set up their own governments in Albania, Bohemia, Bosnia, Croatia, the Czech and Hungarian lands, Moravia and Silesia. At the same time, 'a wave of Spanish influenza hit railroad personnel in Vienna, making idle 8,000 cars of rolling stock'.[28]

In a volatile situation, it was a dangerous trip home for Gerth and his colleagues.

Niemöller was uncertain to the last minute whether his boat, *UC 67*, would be seaworthy enough to make the return journey to the Baltic:

> *While the overland convoy, which included many ship's boats, crossed the inner harbour of Pola on its way to the railway station, we carried out our first diving trial after the refit and it proved quite successful. The only outstanding defect was the conning-tower hatch-cover joint, which was badly worn. The dockyard was empty and deserted, so that a new jointing ring was unobtainable. A new ring was cut out of a piece of asbestos sheet. We spent a night over the job and I cannot forget how, on that last evening in Pola, four young Austrian naval officers came aboard asking for a passage to Germany.*
>
> *'What for?'*
>
> *'We should like to fight for Germany to the end.'*
>
> *It was enough to make one weep, but I could not accede to their request. The boat was already heavy enough and it was impossible to compensate for the additional weight of four men with their provisions, water and baggage. We went to sea on 29 October in company with UC 22.*[29]

The mass return of the serviceable u-boats was one of the most poignant and heroic stories of the dying days of the war. Gibson, an early UK submarine historian, noted forcefully that the u-boat commanders remained steadfast to the last.[30] 'The nervous tension and physical discomforts; the terrible experiences of crews which had escaped death by a hair's breadth; the ever-increasing losses; the uncertainty as to the fate of those who never returned

---

28    Hollweg, *First World War*, p. 435.

29    Niemöller, *From U-boat*, pp. 149-50.

30    Gibson, *Submarine War*, p. 182.

– all such were factors which might be expected to sap endurance and self-confidence in the bravest. Companionship in danger, active service, adventure – all these things preserved and upheld discipline.'

These poorly maintained Adriatic boats needed to travel across the Mediterranean, through the Bay of Biscay, and all the way round Ireland and Scotland to Norway and then to the German coast. The Royal Navy had been forewarned of the flotilla's departure and was patrolling in considerable numbers. Special patrols were organised around Gibraltar from 29 October. At least five u-boats were spotted and probably three were engaged, but only one did not make it because of enemy action.[31]

*U 34*, Leutnant Johannes Klasing, was claimed sunk by the Q-ship HMS *Privet*. Waiting to approach the narrows, Canaris was forced to watch from a distance off Gibraltar while *U 34* was depth-charged to destruction.[32] Another observer was Dönitz who was on Gibraltar on his way to a prison camp in Britain. The month before, his *UB 68* had been forced to the surface by mechanical difficulties and the boat was sunk by shellfire.[33]

However, the loss of *U 34* at this date is disputed.[34] The Gibraltar Straits were passed at night by the scattered fleet at periscope depth with great difficulty. Here are the views of Canaris and Niemöller:

*From the Spanish side strong beams illuminated the waters to the North Africa coast throughout the night, creating a lit area patrolled by numerous small warships and a submarine lurking in the shadows.*

*Canaris wrote that 'under the Moroccan coast are many patrol boats. They present the greatest danger. Basically, they are large American motor boats and small torpedo boats that are very difficult to make out in the darkness'.*

*The situation was not promising … Canaris bet everything on a single card: he attempted to run submerged below the light barrier. A steamer followed him and seven depth charges tumbled down; both electric rudders failed. It was the most dangerous moment of his u-boat career. Now he got lucky; when the screws of the enemy ships*

31    Laurens, *Histoire de la Guerre Sous-Marine Allemande*, p. 386. Wilson & Kemp, *Mediterranean Submarines*, p. 186. Koerver, *Submarine Warfare*, p. 210. uboat.net.

32    Mueller, *Canaris*, p. 31.

33    Padfield, *Dönitz*, p. 90. uboat.net.

34    uboat.net: 'Likely lost well before that date', implying that this was an unsuccessful attack on another u-boat.

*became inaudible he surfaced; a destroyer was so close that it screened him from the patrol boats searching the waters. He remained unseen and in the early hours slipped unnoticed through the last light barrier.*[35]

*As we come up that night close to Ceuta and try to enter the straits, we observe that things are pretty sticky here. We come up against a line of patrolling drifters so close together that there is nothing for it but to turn east again and to attempt a passage on the north side, close under the Rock of Gibraltar. Here at 2200, we meet two torpedo boats carrying lights, so that we begin to wonder whether the war is over. They are, however, followed by darkened patrol vessels and we are quite glad when the wind increases to gale force, as it affords us concealment. A French destroyer even slides past within one hundred yards of us. By daybreak we are in the Atlantic and steering for the open sea.*[36]

On the way out of the Straits, on 9 November, two days before an unanticipated armistice, *UB 50*, Oberleutnant Heinrich Kukat, twice torpedoed the 16,350-ton British battleship *Britannia* on convoy duty at the western entrance to the Straits killing fifty-one - 'the last British warship to be sunk in the war'.[37]

The u-boats met on 15 November off Finisterre and held a commanding officers' meeting. Niemöller spent much of the next few days with Kukat on *UB 50*. They had to decide whether to seek internment in a Spanish port or to continue to Germany.

*We had heard a good deal about the conditions prevailing in Germany through the German wireless press reports and enemy reports and, as this information reached us en clair, it was, of course, known to the ships' companies. No trouble was experienced with any of them. The crews were absolutely unaffected ... The attitude of the ships' companies decided us to make for home as we did not want to miss the coming upheavals in the reformation of Germany ... We simply could not believe that the press accounts which kept coming to us gave us a true picture of the state of Germany*

35    Mueller, *Canaris*, p. 31.
36    Niemöller, *From U-boat*, p. 153.
37    Gayer, *Submarine Warfare*, p. 8. Niemöller, *From U-boat*, pp. 147-156. Kukat's brother Hans, also a
      WWI u-boat commander, *UC 78*, was rammed by the steamer *Queen Alexandra*, west of Cherbourg,
      on 9 May 1918, all twenty-nine crew were lost (uboat.net).

*and of the spirit of its people and we had vague hopes that, perhaps, very shortly, another political upheaval would efface the shame of the incidents of 9 November.*[38]

When the remaining u-boats reached Norway, they were given permission by radio to pass through the fjords. Niemöller was met at Bergan Fjord on 24 November by a Norwegian torpedo boat which escorted him to Lervik for a Mediterranean reunion. From there, a flotilla of eleven submarines made a short stop at Haugesund, then travelled through the Skagerrak and entered Kiel Harbour where they arrived on 29 November. There was no hero's welcome; the ports of Wilhelmshaven and Kiel were 'in the grip of mutiny'.[39] Perhaps Gerth, or at least some of his fellow commanders of the scuttled Adriatic u-boats, safely back in Berlin after their difficult train journey, travelled quickly to the Baltic to congratulate their comrades on their return?

Nine days before, the first of 172 u-boats to be surrendered under the terms of the Armistice had already been handed over to the British at Harwich.[40] The Pola boats followed over the next few weeks.

Gerth started the war earlier than most with his activities in South America in 1911. While his direct involvement in the war ended in its last weeks with his train journey from Pola through Austria to Germany, he left some bitter memories.

U-boat commanders in all waters were under orders to record carefully the position of mines that they laid in accordance with an international agreement against the day after the end of the conflict when unfound mines could be raised and the seas made safe. Clause 24 of the 11 November armistice gave the Allies the right to 'sweep up all mine fields and obstructions laid by Germany outside German territorial waters, and the positions of these are to be indicated'.[41]

Gerth had delivered his mine maps in Pola, but there was clearly not enough time for much, if any, work to be done before 20 November when the newly-built 3,116-ton British steamer *War Typhoon* hit one of his mines nine miles off

---

38    Niemöller, *From U-boat*, pp. 154-56.

39    Mueller, *Canaris*, p. 33.

40    uboat.net.

41    This responsibility was reinforced in the armistice agreement, 11/11/1918 (Appendix 6, 'Military Clauses on the Western Front').

the Cape of Rasolcolmo, north of Messina. There were no casualties and the ship made it safely to harbour.[42]

More might have been expected in mine clearance by next year when, on 15 January, another of Gerth's mines sank the French passenger and general cargo ship *Chaouia*, 4,334 tons.[43] The ship disappeared at night in just a few minutes with the loss of 476 troops, mainly Greek. There were 184 survivors and most of these were saved by the British steamer *Daghestan*.[44] *Chaouia* was hit in the Straits of Messina on her way from Marseille to Batoum, or Batumi, today one of the major port cities in Georgia. At that time, it was held by the British, whom the Greeks were to reinforce. The previous occupiers, the Turks under Kemal Atatürk, had ceded the town under the Treaty of Brest-Litovsk.

There were only two recorded losses to u-boats in 1919. The other was the torpedo boat *Torpilleur 325* sunk seven days after the *Chaouia* with eighteen casualties, also French and also mined in the Mediterranean. *Torpilleur 325*'s mine was laid by Otto Gerke from *UC 27*, Canaris's second boat.

The *Chaouia* was therefore the penultimate boat of the war to be lost to a u-boat. It accounted for the twenty-second largest loss of life. Naturally enough all thirty-four ships on this list of sinkings with over 250 casualties were warships, troopships and passenger ships.

Gerth knew about the men killed on the *Chaouia* after the war had ended, but denied it was his mine. He later told his wife, Eva, that the German admiralty 'had to hang the sinking on somebody and they decided to assign it to him'.[45]

One can understand why Erich or Eva Gerth might say that, but the facts do not agree. *Chaouia*'s approximate reported sinking was at 38°18'N, 15°41'E.[46] When compared with Erich's handwritten mine charts, this position is too close to where he laid his mines to suggest that any other u-boat might have been involved.

---

42    In 1956, *War Typhoon* was transferred to the Chinese flag for break up (teesbuiltships. co.uk/167528).

43    uboat.net.

44    *Daghestan* was sold on many times. In 1938, she was bombed and sunk at Alicante in a Spanish Nationalist air attack. She was raised and eventually sank at sea in 1951 (mariners-list.com).

45    Private email, 3/3/2018.

46    u-boat.net.

# 5

# GERTH: BALANCE SHEET

What had Erich Gerth's short u-boat career achieved?

His commands of *UB 76*, a Keil training boat, and *U 47*, a worn out wreck, had been brief, non-combative affairs. He had laboured without reward for three months trying to fix *U 47*. He had twice put to sea, but been forced to return each time for repairs. Gerth had dodged two torpedoes fired at him and had accidentally cut an Austrian underwater telegraph cable.

With *UC 53*, Gerth achieved one single operational patrol in the Mediterranean before this badly-maintained boat was scuttled in the Adriatic to save it from becoming a bargaining chip as the Austrian front imploded. He travelled 2,803 sea miles above water and 337 miles submerged. He had been in action against a hot air balloon, several destroyers and armed trawlers and escaped at least fifty-six depth charges in four separate attacks.

*UC 53* sank by torpedo the British steamer *Gorsemore*, 3,079 tons, carrying coal, and, also by torpedo, damaged the French steamer *Caraibe*, 2,976 tons, which made it back to port. Both attacks reported no casualties. The u-boat also sank six unarmed Italian sailing vessels, very small cargo boats, totalling a meagre 453 tons.[1] The crews, again without casualties, were released into their tenders. A seventh vessel of a mere five tons was released after its sails were cut.

---

1    There is a small difference in total tonnage according to the record used.

Gerth dropped his eighteen mines unseen in prime Allied shipping lanes north of the Messina Strait. Nine days after war ended, the British steamer *War Typhoon*, 3,116 tons, hit one of Gerth's mines. Damaged and again without casualties, the ship made port.

If it had all ended there, Gerth might have claimed a bloodless war. However, two months later, the Straits still unswept, a French passenger steamer, *Chaouia*, 4,334 tons, hit another of his mines at night and sank with the loss of 476 troops.

And the cost to the Pola Flotilla of the *Kaiserlichen Marine*? The balance sheet shows a lot of sweat and sickness, twenty-four days of u-boat running costs, eighteen mines, three torpedoes (one missed), thirty-eight bombs and several bursts from the boat's machine gun.

*One source carefully calculated that Britain's fight against the u-boats absorbed the efforts of 770,000 men (including naval and merchant crews, shipbuilders, dockyard workers, and naval ordnance manufacturers) and diverted from other use some 13,000 naval guns, 3,700 searchlights, nearly 46,000 tons of munitions, and 16,327 kilometre's worth of wire for submarine nets.*[2]

---

2    Mulligan, *Neither Sharks*, p. 40.

# 6

# GERTH: WELCOME HOME

*'To go to Berlin was the aspiration of the composer, the journalist, the actor; with its superb orchestras, its hundred and twenty newspapers, its forty theatres, Berlin was the place for the ambitious, the energetic, the talented. Wherever they started, it was in Berlin that they became, and Berlin made them, famous.' And yet there was something ungainly and sprawling and fermenting about it. It was a capital city that, like some horrible adolescent, had yet to grow into its role. In some ways it was even worse – a sort of golem – something that had been created for the purpose of existing, like Weimar, a bubble, and a hyperventilating bubble at that.*[1]

Erich Gerth left Pola in the Adriatic by train on 28 October 1918. With over a thousand kilometres to travel to Berlin, there were many reasons for possible delay. The Austrian fronts were collapsing to right and left. Vienna, particularly its railway system, was in the grip of the influenza epidemic.[2] Erich was part of a large party, the Adriatic naval staff of Kapitän zur See Theodor Püllen, perhaps 300 men and officers from ten scuttled u-boats and two torpedo boats, and about 1,500 maintenance workers who would return to Kiel. Logistics were complicated. One train would be insufficient and the fragmented regional nature of the Austrian and German railway systems might suggest changes at least at Vienna, Prague and Dresden.

---

1    Historian Gay quoted by Hofmann, 'Translator's Introduction' in Roth, *What I Saw*, pp. 12-13.
2    Hollweg, *First World War*, p. 435.

Officers might wish to move ahead of the main party in travel accommodation suitable to their status. All were anxious to return home at speed so as to support the Fatherland's last stand. The German call to President Wilson for an armistice was made at the beginning of October. Although nothing had yet been agreed, the war was likely to end soon, but not before, it was assumed, the army and navy had placed Germany in the best negotiating position either by a daring, aggressive stroke or by strengthening their defensive lines on foreign soil.

It would be another month before any of Erich's comrade u-boat commanders reached the Baltic. However, their heroic and marathon race home to bolster the fleet would be in vain as they would sail into a humiliating and dangerous rebellion. While Erich was on the train, the crews of the High Seas Fleet battleships refused to put to sea for Admiral Scheer's 'honour by suicide' naval battle and were in revolt, especially at Kiel. Ludendorff, self-proclaimed saviour of the nation, had just been dismissed by a frustrated Kaiser.

Erich bought, probably, an edition of *Berliner Tageblatt* and read the major stories which emphasised the worsening situation: official negotiations underway between Turkey and the Allies, separating its fate from Germany; reactions to Ludendorff's 'resignation' from The Hague, Geneva and London; a written constitution after the collapse of the military bureaucracy to transfer power to the people; declaration of the Czechoslovakian state; notes to and from President Wilson; u-boat successes; attacks by the English at Famars, south of the River Schelde, and by the French at the Rivers Aisne and Oise, all reportedly failing.[3]

*Berliners read newspapers. They read them so voraciously that the German capital emerged as the newspaper city par excellence with more papers than London. The media culture ... helped change the look and the feel of the city as newspaper kiosks sprang up at every major intersection and newspaper vendors prowled the streets shouting the day's headlines.*[4]

---

3    *Berliner Tageblatt*, morning and evening editions, 553-558, 29-31/10/1918.
4    Large, *Berlin*, p. 88.

Tired from the journey, only a few weeks away from sinking a clutch of Italian fishing vessels and dragging his ailing u-boat back to port, Erich had a personal choice. He could either travel to barracks with his fellow captains or bid them farewell and make his way onto the street to find a tram or taxi. As Erich was one of the few officers in his flotilla whose home was in Berlin, perhaps he received an overnight dispensation from Kapitän Püllen. His mother lived alone in a rented apartment in Keithstraße 22, a few minutes from Berlin Zoological Gardens, her home since 1908.[5]

The change during Erich's short trip would have been a shock. Berlin had a 'bedraggled appearance'; once the cleanest city in the world, it was now filthy and so were many of its people.[6] The shortage of soap spread disease and the poor lacked boots and warm clothing. Poverty was on the streets, with long queues for food, haggard faces, the disfigured and the maimed. A large number of the men wore a motley array of untidy uniforms and semi-military attire. There were no cats or dogs, all eaten and their skins used for leather.

> *The great cities remained, the railway lines were more or less intact, ports still functioned. It was not like the Second World War, when the very bricks and mortar were pulverised. The loss was human. Millions of combatants – for the time of the mass killing of civilians had not yet come – died in those four years: 1.8 million Germans, 1.7 million Russians, 1.4 million French (a quarter of French men between eighteen and thirty – twice as many again of its soldiers wounded), 1.3 Austro-Hungarians, 743,000 British and another 192,000 from the Empire. Children lost fathers, wives, husbands, young women the chance of marriage … but the tally of deaths does not include those who were left with one leg, one arm or eye, or whose lungs had been scarred by poison gas or whose nerves never recovered.[7]*

When Erich found Hedwig, his mother, his surprise presence should have done much to raise her depression; she was prone to 'melancholia'.[8] With her husband dead for twenty-five years, her life was wrapped in her two surviving sons, both serving in the most dangerous profession of all. Georg sent regular

---

5    Berliner Adressbücher, 1799-1943, zlb.de/besondere-angebote/Berliner-adressbuecher (accessed 3/2017).

6    *Economic Conditions Prevailing in Germany*, Berlin, pp. 61, 67, 75.

7    MacMillan, *Paris 1919*, pp. xxv-xxvi.

8    Email, Christa-Maria Gerth, 18/3/2017.

news from his prisoner-of-war camp in France. And, now, here was Erich, her eldest, home unexpectedly and, if the news was to be believed, increasingly likely to survive the war. She scrambled to make a meal. Had she sufficient money to escape the worst of the famine? Or was it a diet of half-rotten potatoes, adulterated flour and a few carefully guarded scraps? During these last weeks of the war, Germany suffered from almost as many civilian deaths as from military ones, but the famine did not affect the population equally. Urban citizens, like those in Berlin, Catholics, low social classes and the highly-integrated regions along the Rhine river and the North and Baltic seas were hit the hardest.[9] The famine 'exacerbated deep inequalities and a new food hierarchy emerged in Germany'.[10] The lowest groups were families of soldiers living without a male bread-winner, single older people, and inmates of institutions.

*The poor, the weak and the elderly were very badly hit,' wrote Professor Bergahn, an historian of German and modern European history, 'whereas the better-off who had savings were able to obtain supplies on the black market at exorbitant prices.'[11]*

Among the cheerfulness and thanksgiving, Hedwig found a son whose military world had collapsed. Erich reported to naval headquarters and was given work which eventually lasted until the end of November 1921, over three years of unexpected employment. When the armistice was signed on 11 November, two weeks after Erich's return, the imperial navy was ordered to be reduced and was later limited by the peace treaty to a force of 15,000 officers and men.[12] Nothing definite is known of Erich's work at the Admiralty except that he claimed to have spent some time on official duty in Spain and in Italy. His story here is built on scraps of concrete information and conjectural straws.

Admiral Adolf von Trotha was appointed head of the newly-created Admiralty in Berlin on 26 March 1919. He was a Tirpitz disciple and had under his command following the peace treaty six old battleships, six cruisers, twelve destroyers and twelve torpedo boats. There was an absolute ban on naval

---

9    Blum, 'Government decisions', pp. 565-66.
10   Teuteberg, 'Food Provisioning', Zweiniger-Bargielowska, *Food and War*, p. 68.
11   Tarrant, *U-Boat Offensive*, p. 45.
12   Wegener, *Naval Strategy*, p. xxxii, p. 207, fn. 4.

aircraft and, particularly, on u-boats to put a block on any future submarine arm.

Trotha began planning secretly and immediately for a fleet for when Germany regained her temporarily lost status as a great power. He told a staff member, 'I want to preserve the smallest seed so that when the time comes a useful tree will grow from it.'[13] 'Consequently [Trotha's] immediate aim was in the personnel field; discipline and pride had to be restored, a nucleus of dedicated officers formed who would be able to guide the later expansion.'[14] Trotha was allowed only 1,500 officers so 'only the best and most loyal need be selected'.

Erich was one of the 'seeds', a small, tight group chosen from among the available submarine commanders.

Trotha has been met before within this story, at the mutiny of the battleships, when he was noted for his 'marked antipathy toward democracy, parliamentary government, and the idea of a negotiated peace'. He had an 'absolute abhorrence for all those who stood opposed to militarism'. His disdain had flowered to include those he saw as chiefly responsible for the navy's present humiliation, the Allies in general, but specifically the Republican politicians 'who, by signing the armistice, had robbed the armed forces of victory'.

Trotha had a fruitful seam to mine as the naval officer corps was 'imbued from top to bottom with a thoroughly vengeful spirit against the Versailles treaty and the Allies, particularly against Britain, with a 'poisonous hatred' for their 'inconsiderate inhumanity, incitement to revolution and the hunger blockade'.

Trotha had also been Erich Gerth's commanding officer for about a year in 1910 aboard the light cruiser *Königsberg*, which had a small complement of fourteen officers, and therefore knew him well enough to write his annual review.

A service analysis of the 498 German and Austrian u-boat commanders who served during World War 1 produces almost-accurate numbers and they tell an interesting story.[15]

---

13    Herwig, *Naval Officer Corps*, p. 265.

14    Padfield, *Dönitz*, pp. 95-96.

15    These numbers vary understandably from source to source. Mulligan, *Sharks Not Wolves*, p. 40, cites 457 u-boat commanders in World War 1 of whom 152 were killed and thirty-three captured, for a total loss of over 40 per cent. Tennant, *U-Boat Offensive*, p. 77, records a loss of 178 u-boats, 511

The top figure can be quickly reduced by the 159 captains who died in the war and by sixty or so more: early deaths; Austrians who were not a part of the imperial navy and were not available to Trotha; others in exceptional circumstances like long-term illness and detainment in Allied prisoner of war camps; and a handful for whom today insufficient information is available to make an assessment of their service period. From the end of the war to the great cull demanded by the peace treaty, forty-one u-boat officers dribbled from the ranks at the rate of a few a month probably led by normal attrition, by firm suggestions that they leave, or they were men who had better places to go and therefore made individual decisions to resign.

The whole of these losses still left Trotha with about 230 officers, all of whom he kept on strength as he selected his cream. At the peace treaty signing in November 1919, ninety-one of the remaining u-boat captains immediately left naval service. They were followed over the next four months by fifty-five more and, principally in August and September 1920, by a final, smaller cull of twenty-seven.

Those remaining were the sixty chosen men. One of these was Erich Gerth who stayed with the service until the end of 1921 when he left to prepare his application for the Foreign Office. One can deduce that Erich as a 'chosen man' was strongly aligned to Trotha's views, got to know him well and left with his blessing. Trotha, many levels of rank Erich's senior, agreed to act as one of Erich's referees for his Foreign Office application the following year.

Generally, Trotha chose his sixty men well. Of the forty-six u-boat officers identified who stayed long-term in naval service after 1922, one half made admiral: eight konteradmirals; eight vizeadmirals, including Wilhelm Canaris; four admirals (Hermann von Fischel, Wilhelm Marschall, and Otto von Schrader, who was to be Georg Gerth's commanding officer in Norway in WW2); and four grossadmirals (Rolf Carls, Karl Dönitz, Alfred Saalwächter and Otto Schultze).[16]

Most u-boat commanders assumed power with relish and through right from their fathers' aristocratic titles, powerful business institutions or landed estates. As with their British and French counterparts, their prejudices and

---

officers and 4,576 men, 'an exchange rate of almost thirty ships of 69,000 tons per u-boat lost'. The most current and also the most respected listing is compiled by uboat.net and this is used as the principal source in these calculations.

16    Canaris, Dönitz, Erich Gerth, Marschall and Schultze served together in the Mediterranean.

confidence was reinforced by their training at the 'better schools' and in the naval officer corps. These young men were far from natural democrats. It is also clear that they loved their country, thirsted for revenge, believed in a future as a maritime merchant power and relished the chance to fight again. None of that ended with the Versailles Treaty. Memoirs and reminiscences confirm that the men, as personal servants of the Kaiser, were decisively loyal to the monarchy, despite abdication, and were reluctant republicans. The Imperial German Navy had been 'in peace and remained in war a federal German institution directly under the emperor'.[17]

A love of risk and danger surges through the pages of their many published reminiscences. Yet, for most of them, there was also a clear sense of day-to-day chivalry. The majority were committed, as far as possible, to a 'civilised' war and believed they fought by its rules. In most of these characteristics, they were little different from their Allied counterparts.

---

17    Herwig, *Dynamics*, p. 80.

# 7

# TROTHA: ILLEGAL U-BOATS

Preoccupations at the Admiralty in this immediate post-war period can be reasonably deduced. There was the much reduced fleet to manage and new rules and regulations suitable to a republican navy to develop. For the immediate future the remaining older capital ships were used principally for training. They were not about to go to sea to fight. There were detailed arrangements for the humiliating transfer of the modern fighting ships demanded by the terms of the armistice and peace treaty, but this was quickly concluded. For instance, on 20 November 1918, twenty u-boats were shepherded by Royal Navy destroyers into Harwich, the last twenty miles with British crews and with the White Ensign hoisted above the German flag.[1] Over the next eleven days, this main transfer took the total to 114 vessels; those boats under construction were broken up on the shipyard slipways in Germany.

In addition, the Admiralty had to play its part in developing both the obfuscation needed to protect the office corps from criticism for its role and decisions made during the war and the arguments to undermine the Allies' peace assumptions so that better terms dealing with reparations and rearmament could be demanded.

This political manoeuvring included defeating social democrat parliamentary investigations into the responsibility of the naval command in the mutiny of 1918, for which much blame lay at the door of Scheer and

---

1    Tarrant, *U-Boat Offensive*, p. 77.

Trotha, and supporting the spurious claim that the revolt was a carefully planned Communist conspiracy.

More immediately, covert assistance was given to the three naval paramilitary *Freikorps* formed to fight the revolutionaries. Specific arguments were needed to show that the Allies had started the war and that Germany was an innocent party forced onto the attack to defend herself against determined aggressors. Claims that unrestricted submarine warfare as a whole, and the conduct of individual u-boat captains in particular, were criminal actions which warranted trial, needed continual rebuttal.[2] In the case of the latter, captains that might be found guilty were spirited away to safety both before and after their trials.

Finally, continuous support was needed for Ludendorff's and Hindenburg's insistence that the military, and by inference the navy, and this meant the whole meritorious officer corps, had been stabbed in the back by a consortium of communists, lying Allied propaganda and weak and unpatriotic elements in the home front.

*After the war was lost the German public opinion of its navy was at an all-time low; the navy had caused the war with England in 1914; further, it had caused the war with America in 1917 leading to the revolution in Germany in 1918. The assorted failures led to the ignominious scuttling of the Imperial High Seas fleet at Scapa Flow in June, 1919.*[3]

Despite outward resignation, the leaders of the new Republican navy remained determinedly against the social democratic constitution. Individual officers had to wrestle with their monarchist, anti-democratic consciences to decide whether

---

2    The first step in reassessment was to assemble the facts and this was undertaken by Konteradmiral Albert Gayer's four-volume series *Die deutschen U-Boots* (1920). His books became standard works which were republished in 1930. Korvettenkapitän Friedrich Lützow followed in 1921 with *Unterseebootskrieg und Hungerblockade*. Lützow concluded that Germany had strictly observed international accords whereas England's blockade was in contravention of all international and humane convention. In 1925, Vizeadmiral Andreas Michelsen wrote *Der U-Bootskrieg 1914-1918* '... not only to show the Volk just what the u-boat war meant in reality, but because I have a need to set the deeds of the u-boat crews in the proper light and to protect the u-boat arm against undeserved disparagement'. The Navy produced its multi-volumed *The War at Sea*, 1914-1918, edited by the Naval Archives which included contributions from Arno Spindler and Erich Raeder. Spindler later produced his monumental five-volume *Der Handelskrieg mit U-booten*, the fifth volume of which was suppressed by the Nazis as in it Spindler argued that the u-boats had been responsible for drawing the United States into the war (Hadley, *Count Not the Dead*), pp. 48-50.

3    Koerver, *German Submarine Warfare*, p. x.

they wished to take the new oath of allegiance. For most that did take the oath, like Erich in 1920, it was usually no more than a fig leaf.[4] In 1922, Erich still declared himself as 'Prussian' rather than 'German'. Another prominent sailor who chose to remain on active duty, Vice Admiral Wolfgang Wegener, did so despite the fact that he viewed the Weimar Republic as an 'unloved façade', but primarily so that he could have a chance to lay the intellectual groundwork for the future 'unavoidable struggle against the sea power of England'.[5]

Article 191 of the Versailles Treaty banned Germany from building, acquiring or operating submarines of any description.

One further secret and most important task of the 'new' officer corps of the republican navy was to prepare for the next world war. That part of this work which is of interest here concerns rebuilding Germany's u-boat capability.

A team of knowledgeable u-boat managers and commanders were slowly assembled. The latest plans and components for the next series of u-boats had to disappear from dockyards and admiralty offices before Allied inspectors from the Inter-Allied Control Commission called. Overseas facilities were needed to evade the complete ban on any work by Germany on new submarines.

Naval strategists were immediately put to work. Among them was Kapitänleutnant Erwin Wassner of the naval high command in Berlin who in July 1922 published a paper suggesting that, in his war experience commanding five u-boats, surface attacks had been the most successful and that since lone u-boat operations were uneconomic against convoys 'in future it will be essential for convoys to be hunted by sizeable numbers of u-boats acting together'.[6]

Future admirals Wilhelm Marschall and Karl Dönitz, the Führer of the Nazi u-boats and the final Führer of the Third Reich, agreed. 'The coming war may or may not involve war against merchant shipping', but u-boat officers must be trained to attack convoys. This strategy was propounded by many of the u-boat and command memoirs which were sucked up by an eager public looking for heroes and hope among the ruins of the Kaiser's reign.

---

4     Erich Gerth's application to the Foreign Office, 30/12/1922.
5     Wegener, *Naval Strategy*, p. xxxii.
6     Padfield, *Dönitz*, pp. 101-103.

*Whether one looks back on the Weimar years from the perspective of the late 1930s or forward from the 1920s toward the Nazi era, the idea that the Second World War had been 'implicit since the moment the first war ended' is simplistic.*[7]

Much of the clandestine operations formally came into operation after a few years, but the groundwork was laid while Erich was at the admiralty. When Dönitz arrived back in Kiel in July 1918 after his spell in a British prisoner-of-war camp, he was met by the adjutant of the navy station, Otto Schultze, his u-boat flotilla chief from Pola. Dönitz asked whether they would ever see u-boats again and Schultze said he thought it would take two years.[8]

Leading the work was the chief of the submarine department, Karl Bartenbach. Bartenbach, it will be remembered, was the long-serving Flanders u-boat chief, responsible for the establishment of the Bruges u-boat base, and was then Georg Gerth's senior officer. By the end of the war, Bartenbach was 'without doubt the leading German submarine expert'. Before Flanders, he commanded the Germany Navy's first submarine, *U 1*; was the first chief of the new German *U-Boots-Abnahmekommission*, co-ordinating submarine construction; and then head of the submarine school. Importantly, a strong *Kamaradenschaft* was formed aboard *U 1*, between Bartenbach, his second officer Ulrich Blum and his chief engineer Heinrich Papenberg.[9]

The German Navy 'began cheating on the Treaty of Versailles in June 1919', one month after its ratification, when Blum, still a serving naval officer, proposed by letter to Krupp's managers the founding of a submarine construction office at the Krupp Germaniawerft shipyard in Kiel.[10] The object was to use former u-boat officers to market German submarine plans and knowledge to other nations and thereby keep the German u-boat flame alive. Krupp agreed and Blum along with Bartenbach and a number of other former German naval officers, began trying to interest other nations in their wares.

7    Marks, '1918 and After', p. 40, commenting on Taylor, *Origins of the Second World War*, p. 267.
8    Padfield, *Dönitz*, p. 96.
9    Forsén and Forsén, 'Secret Submarine Exports', Stoker, *Girding for Battle*, pp. 114-15.
10   The following section on the early u-boat rearmament is a composite account taken from a number of sources including Forsén and Forsén, 'Secret Submarine Exports', pp. 113-33; Mueller, *Canaris*, Chapter 9; Mulligan, *Sharks Not Wolves*, pp. 139-40; Padfield, *Dönitz*, p. 102; Saville, 'Development of German U-boat Arm'; Stoker, *Naval Arms Trade*, pp. 124, 145-49; Ten Cate, 'Das U-Boot als geistige Exportware'; Tennant, *U-Boat Offensive*, p. 77.

Bartenbach began his overseas post-war career in Costa Rica in 1920, 'probably conducting negotiations with Japan from there', or with Argentina, where he moved in 1921.[11] Canaris did similar work in Italy and in his old stamping ground in Spain and it was to these two countries that Erich travelled on undisclosed 'missions' while working for Trotha, probably under Canaris's direction. Canaris re-established the *Etappendienst* in Spain, work that he and Erich had also undertaken in South America. Canaris found his old colleagues and friends from the war and he also 'recruited some new agents all around the world'.[12]

Here also, there is the answer to a small puzzle. In his foreign office application of 1922, Erich did not mention his time as commander of the Kiel training u-boat, *UB 76*, nor his operational u-boat experience in the Adriatic, nor what his most recent function had been in the *Marineleitung*, the naval high command in Berlin. Erich was no shrinking violet when it came to demonstrating his achievements. The likely reason was that Erich's most recent work was highly sensitive and this need for continued secrecy extended well into the 1930s, at least until the bombshell of the Lohmann Affair, described later.

Under the auspices of the newly-formed Reichsmarine, Bartenbach was closely involved in the German Navy's negotiations with Krupp and two other German firms to set up a covert Dutch puppet company, *Ingenieurskantoor voor Scheepsbouw* (or Scheepsvaart), known as IvS.[13] Blum became the commercial director. This drawing office in a shipyard in The Hague was ordered to stay on the cutting edge by offering comprehensive expertise in submarine development and construction to aspirant naval powers. The principal clients consulting IvS were Argentina, Finland, Italy, Japan, Russia (at various times), Spain, Sweden and Turkey. IvS's technical director was the former chief constructor at the Germaniawerft at Kiel, Hans Techel, who shipped a large amount of submarine plans and components over the Dutch border to begin operations. Germaniawerft also controlled the Ing Fijenoord shipbuilding yard in Rotterdam. The link between IvS and the German Admiralty was

---

11    Details of Karl Bartenbach's post-war career were partly supplied by Gisella Bartenbach, his niece, in an interview with Forsén and Forsén in 1999.

12    Derencin, u-boat.net.

13    Other German armaments firms that used Holland included the aircraft maker Fokker from 1919, Carl Zeiss Optical Works of Jena (*Nederlandsche Instrumenten Compagnie NV*) and Siemens, fire control equipment (F Hazemeyer's *Fabriek von Electrische Signal-Apparaten NV*) (Forsén and Forsén, 'Secret Submarine Exports'), p. 127, fn. 17.

provided by *Mentor Bilanz*, a dummy Berlin company, directed by former *U 64* commander Robert Moraht, who officially left the navy service in July 1920 and was one of Trotha's chosen men.[14]

The *Marineleitung* became a 'powerhouse of rearmament'. Among its senior members dealing with u-boats were Arno Spindler, naval chief of staff and future u-boat official historian, Canaris, Dönitz, Wilhelm von Löwenfeld, who had been commander of the Kurland naval installations on the Baltic while Erich was there for his secret mission in 1917 and who had led one of the most infamous *Freikorps*, Kapitän zur See Werth, and their leader, Rear Admiral Adolph Pfeiffer.[15]

The German Navy backed IvS with one million Reichsmark and promised an additional 120,000 per year, if needed. The money came from a secret slush fund, the *Sonderfond*, that the navy created at the end of the war. Initial funds, amounting to at least twenty-five million dollars, came from the sale of warships and u-boats scrapped in 1919 and 1920 under the Allies' direction. Unfinished u-boats must have been a large contributor to the fund; at the end of the war, 226 boats were being built with a further 212 projected.[16]

Additional support for navy 'black projects' came from 'Weimar officials, who colluded to vastly overcharge for navy equipment and then diverted the profits to what they considered more worthy causes'.

Funding was managed from perhaps as early as 1920 by Kapitän Walter Lohmann of the Naval Transportation Division who was given full charge by early 1923 of the disbursement of the navy's 'black' funds for clandestine purposes with the 'complete trust' of the navy's commander-in-chief, Admiral Paul Behnke.[17] Most of this money was transmitted to recipients, including IvS, through a middleman, a Lohmann-supported bank, the *Berliner Bankverein*. In 1927, this illicit operation was exposed in the 'Lohmann Affair' and crashed with disastrous and humiliating results for the Navy and the Weimar Republic, discussed in the next chapter (when a few more important characters have

---

14    Tarrant, *U-boat Offensive*, pp. 77-78.

15    Padfield, *Dönitz*, p. 111, 145. Padfield, *Dönitz*, p. 26. Löwenfeld had also been cadet Dönitz's navigating officer aboard the training ship, *Hertha*.

16    Compton-Hall, *Submarines*, p. 300.

17    Lohmann came to the fore through his work on negotiations concerning the Allies' appropriation of the German merchant fleet after the armistice and for his direction of emergency food supplies to Germany. Lohmann also managed the return from overseas of German war prisoners.

been introduced), and latterly came under review by the American Central Intelligence Agency from whose report details are taken.[18]

The best documented examples of the reach of IvS concerns their contracts with Finland and Turkey. Bartenbach moved in May 1924 to become naval advisor to the Finnish government on the recommendation of retired Admiral Tirpitz. He worked 'unostentatiously behind the scenes', principally on submarine projects, and was generally referred to by the Finns as 'our expert'. Dealing easily with competition from French and British firms, Bartenbach ensured that Finnish u-boat contracts went to IvS or to an associated Finnish business, Crichton-Vulcan of Åbo (a part-British company before the war). Crichton-Vulcan was roundly criticised in the Estonian press as being covertly German-owned at the time which was true, but which was denied by the Finns. The company was taken up by Krupp to build torpedo boats for the Russian Navy. Later, ownership had been transferred to Dutch and Swedish hands to camouflage the firm's German control. Contracts awarded to Crichton-Vulcan were secretly re-signed with IvS.

In March 1927, following complaints from the British and the French, the Conference of Ambassadors ruled that it was not possible to invoke Article 191 of the Treaty of Versailles to prevent the Dutch firm from constructing components for the Finnish submarines. The conference stated that Article 191 was only applicable to Germany itself and could not be invoked against a foreign German-controlled firm.[19]

Two u-boats, one of 250-tons at Åbo for the Finnish Navy and the other of 500-tons at Cadiz for the Turks, were built for the private account of IvS.

At one stage the Russians, alarmed at developments in Finland 'instigated and financed a metalworkers strike at Crichton-Vulcan' through the Red International of Labour Unions, *Profintern*, which lasted for nine months.

In 1927, an agreement was concluded with the King of Spain, with the assistance of Canaris, for the technical section of *Mentor Bilanz* to build a 750-ton u-boat in Cadiz. That same year, the British identified twenty Germans working in the Finnish Navy alongside Bartenbach who were actually in the employ of the German military.

---

18    cia.gov/library/center-for-the-study-of-intelligence/kent-csi/vol4no2/html/v04i2a08p_0001. htm, accessed 15/10/2017.

19    Stoker, *Naval Arms Trade*, p. 144.

One of these men was multiple u-boat commander Werner Fürbringer, who worked with IvS, and was to write Erich's obituary. Fürbringer also acted in an advisory capacity when in 1926 Turkey placed a large order for submarines to be built at Rotterdam. Before delivery in 1928, German crews gained useful experience by putting the boats through extensive trials. The boats created the need for a training school in Turkey and in due course German crews, including Fürbringer, were shipped out to lead clandestine courses.

In 1930, the first practical u-boat training on active service, as distinct from retired officers like Fürbringer, took place. The Germans were disguised at civilian tourists and carried out trials on a 500-ton Finnish submarine from July to September.

*The very re-birth of the German u-boat service owed its greatest debt to such First World War veterans as Hans Schottky, watch officer on UB 19 and UB 117, Kurt Slevogt, U 71, and Werner Fürbringer, commander of six u-boats. These men laid the foundations for the future campaign of 1939-1945 from the selection and development of basic submarine designs to the earliest tactical training in fleet and commerce operations.*[20]

In 1932, the Germans made a political decision to rebuild their submarine arm. Still bound by the restriction of the Versailles Treaty, the German navy decided in 1933 and 1934 to collect all of the components for sixteen u-boats, ordered initially through IvS, in guarded sheds in German shipyards. Fürbringer re-entered the German Navy in 1933 and was appointed senior instructor at the Kiel-Wik 'Anti-Submarine School' 'which was of course exactly the reverse of what its title stated'.[21] Designs for large 550-ton u-boats were drawn up in 1934, managed by an IvS subsidiary, *Schiffbaukontor*, in Bremen, and this vessel became Germany's most-produced submarine of the Second World War.

Hitler announced on 16 March 1935 that 'after the final collapse of our former enemy's disarmament charade we have taken our military sovereignty in our own hands'.[22]

An Anglo-German naval treaty allowing submarines construction was signed in June 1935. The first Nazi u-boat slid into the water eleven days later. That

20    Mulligan, *Sharks Not Wolves*, p. 25. Fürbringer, *Legendary*, p. ix.
21    Padfield, *Dönitz*, p. 119.
22    Hadley, *Count Not the Dead*, pp. 75-76, 80.

year, submarines *U 33* and *U 34* undertook illegal covert operations in Spanish waters, committing what many years later was deemed an act of piracy, by sinking Spanish submarine *C-3* on 12 December 1935.

As Admiral Wilhelm Marschall, who worked with Erich in the Adriatic, said in his book *Torpedo Achtung! Los!* in 1938, 'The seed is sown! We, the war-generation, see it rise with our own eyes; it's a magnificent feeling to be here and to be able to help it happen. Heil to our Fuhrer!'

On 17 November 1939, Kapitänleutnant Otto Schuhart, *U 29*, sank the British aircraft carrier HMS *Courageous* in the Western Approaches with the loss of 518 British lives.

*Britain's sleepy complacency in allowing Germany to re-acquire u-boats (which must also be set against the backdrop of political appeasement of the era) was a direct result of the Admiralty's belief, persisting since 1918, that the u-boat danger had been mastered, and that u-boats would never again be able to present Britain with the problem she had faced in 1917 ... a case, to paraphrase AJP Taylor, of men seeing the past when they peer into the future ... This confidence was reinforced when Germany denounced unrestricted u-boat warfare in 1936 [for which] Churchill accused the Admiralty of the 'acme of gullibility'.* [23]

---

23    Tennant, *U-boat Offensive*, pp. 79-80. Germany and other powers signed the London Protocol to this effect in November 1936. Churchill, *Second World War*, Vol. 1, p. 126.

# 8

# MARX: THE JEWISH COUNTESS

While still in the navy, Erich registered at the Friedrich-Wilhelms University in Berlin on 29 November 1918 as a student of law.[1] He was a youthful-looking thirty-two-year-old, sociable with an attractive personality, and a lover of parties.

He attended an eclectic series of lectures in his first semester over the winter of 1918/19: Mathematical Foundations of Natural Sciences, Contemporary Economics, Theory of Law and State in Modern Times, Origins of Man, World Harmony, History of Architecture and German and a further two dealing with Prostitution and Venereal Diseases. In the Spring seminars of 1919, his lectures seemed more germane: National Economy, 'Proseminar', Philosophy, Foundations of Logic, Modern Psychology and Modern History.

Were these subjects just a series of haphazard evening classes? Would this wide-spread selection have been made by a committed law student? How much time in any event would Erich have been allowed away from the Admiralty for study?

At the same time as he entered university, Erich met and fell in love with a wealthy, petite, vivacious, young widow, a countess, Gräfin Eva von Ahlefeldt, who was to provide the centre and the inadvertent ruination of his career.[2]

---

1    Humbold University, Berlin, archive, Erich Gerth, received 14/6/2017.
2    Interview, Christa Gerth, 15/11/2016.

The introduction was made by Wilhelm Canaris who had figured in so much of Erich's naval life since their years together as naval cadets.

Canaris was a frequent visitor to the home of Eva's father, Honorary Consul Salomon Marx, a banker and entrepreneur of considerable wealth who wielded much influence in Jewish, financial and political circles. Canaris, who came from Dortmund-Aplerbeck, less than thirty kilometres from Salomon Marx's birthplace of Schwerte, was 'an intimate family friend'.[3]

Marriage for a naval officer before and during the war had been a 'complicated business'.[4] From 1899, the groom needed Imperial marriage consent, *Allerhöchsten Konsens*, for reasons both financial and social. Officers needed enough money to support a family, lest they be overwhelmed with debt. Brides, too, had to have financial means, and a wife with low social status was considered unsuitable.

*Young officers searched for wealthy, socially acceptable young women so actively that, in 1894, the Marine Kabinett censured officers for advertising in the newspapers for a suitable match. Although there were no written rules, young officers were discouraged from seeking Jewish wives, even if the latter were financially and socially suitable. Marie Lipke [Tirpitz's wife] was wealthy and prominent enough to clear these hurdles. She was a baptised Protestant, born in West Prussia in 1860. [Her father,] Gustav Lipke was born in 1820 in Berlin to a wealthy assimilated Jewish banking and business family.*

There were evident similarities between Eva Marx and Marie Lipke, but, by the time of Eva's marriage to Erich Gerth, there was no Kaiser and the military world was upside down.

With his marriage, Erich now had three male mentors, Trotha, Canaris and Marx. All sought the replacement of the socialist-led Weimar Republic and were vehemently anti-communist, particularly in combatting the Spartacist League, formed by communists Karl Liebknecht and Rosa Luxembourg. This shared fanaticism led them into manipulations, plots, the *Freikorps* paramilitary groups and direct involvement in the murders of the two communist leaders. It is easy to see how Erich was seduced into their schemes.

---

3    Hintz, 'Salomon Marx', p. 103.
4    Kelly, *Tirpitz*, pp. 69-70.

Eva Marx was born on 29 August 1895 in Cologne, the third child of Salomon and Helene Clara Schirmacher.[5] With the birth of his children, Salomon joined his wife as a Lutheran Protestant.[6] Erich, a Protestant, married Eva in Berlin on 27 June 1919; she was nine years his junior. The year before her second marriage, Eva converted to Catholicism and took two additional suitable Christian names, Marie and Ignatia.[7] Eva's conversion was followed by Erich, her new husband, shortly afterwards and their subsequent enthusiastic support to the Catholic cause, discussed later, was a central and important part of their future private and working lives.[8]

There were two witnesses at the wedding, both from Berlin. The first was Eva's father, Salomon, aged fifty-three, of Brückenallee 29, Berlin, a fourteen-room villa with domestic staff in the up-market quarter of Tiergarten. The second was coroner and doctor of medicine Hugo Marx, forty-four years, of Alt Moabit 12A. Hugo was no doubt close family having travelled to New York from Hamburg with Salomon and his wife Helene aboard the *Kaiserin Augusta Victoria* in 1911.[9] There is no doubt that the marriage had Salomon's blessing. The records show that he fought hard over many years to secure his son-in-law's future career.

Eva's first marriage was to Leutnant der Reserve Graf Karl-Christian von Ahlefeldt-Eschelsmark; he was twenty-three, she nineteen, and the wedding took place in the Garrison Church at Stettin on the Baltic coast on 3 August 1914.[10] It seems to have been a rushed affair, the certificate carries no ages, places of birth or parents' names. No family was present. This may easily be

---

5    Salomon and Helene married in the Free State of Danzig on 27/2/1892. Eva's two siblings were born in Danzig: Eduard, 23 November 1898, and Eleonore, 29/10/1903. Salomon was the son of businessman Eduard Marx and Bertha Hecht; Helene, was the daughter of businessman Richard Schirmacher and Clara Scharloch.

6    Interview, Christa-Maria Gerth, 15/11/2016.

7    Foreign Office file, Berlin. Eva's conversion to Catholicism confirmed in the records of the Campo Santo, Rome.

8    Erich Gerth converted to Catholicism after his marriage to Eva Marx, 6/1919, and before his application to the Foreign Office 12/1922.

9    The year before, 1910, Marx took his wife Helene, aged forty, and two children, Eduard and Eva, on a holiday to Tenerife aboard the *Eleonore Woermann*, sailing from Hamburg. Tourists began visiting Tenerife from Spain, the United Kingdom, and northern Europe in large numbers in the 1890s. They were attracted to the northern towns of Puerto de la Cruz and Santa Cruz de Tenerife.

10    The hyphen in Graf Karl-Christian was added eighteen years after his birth on the Kaiser's birthday in 1909, when the certificate was amended by court order.

explained as a love match brought forward by the call for mobilisation the day before. There was a pressing need for Ahlefeldt to get from Stettin to Flensburg in Schleswig-Holstein on the Danish border where his regiment, Füsilier Regiment 'Queen' 86, was based.

*Officers and men were quietly recalled from furlough, mobilisation rosters appeared overnight in every newspaper and were posted on public buildings in every hamlet, village and city of the German empire, while heralds went round the towns blowing trumpets to summon reservists to the colours.*[11]

Ahlefeldt's regiment was appropriately connected as its commander-in-chief was Augusta Victoria of Schleswig-Holstein, the Kaiser's wife and second cousin. The Danish and Mecklenburg royal connections of the noble family of Ahlefeldt-Eschelsmark extended to the eleventh century.[12] On 8 August, Ahlefeldt left for the invasion of Belgium.[13]

*Crimes of excess began almost immediately: human shields, punitive destruction of buildings, mass execution of non-combatants began on 5 August 1914, the first day of the real shooting war. They were widespread. Half of all German regiments in the western theatre of operations committed such acts. In the first two months of the war there were 129 major incidents of execution involving ten or more civilians. The acts were committed by common soldiers or low-ranking officers.*[14]

The regiment suffered heavy casualties while fighting at Liege and the Marne, before falling back and settling into trenches in 1915 at Moulin, Quennevières Farm, Dreslincourt and Pimprez.

'Fear of the franc-tireur, civilian marksmen, was ubiquitous.'[15] Every one of the thirteen regiments taking part in the initial *Handstreich*, 'surprise attack', against Liège was 'involved in action against alleged *francs-tireurs*'.

---

11    Asprey, *German High Command*, p. 47.

12    Private letters and emails from Heiko von Ahlefeld, 9/2017. Also 'Ahlefeld', *Wikipedia*, accessed 4/3/2017.

13    War Diaries of Dieter Finzen, www.war-diary.com/dieter_finzen.htm, accessed, 19/12/2016. 'Ahlefeld' is a simple, but close, variant of 'Ahlefeldt'.

14    Hull, *Absolute Destruction*, p. 209.

15    Horne and Kramer, 'War between Soldiers', p. 187.

At this time, because of heavy losses, a demand for junior officers as air crew existed which was directly comparable to the call by the navy for u-boat commanders. Ahlefeldt volunteered and served as an observer in Kagohl 2, a unit of the *Luftstreitkräfte*, renowned for its 'aces', including the contemporary 'ace of aces' Freiherr Manfred von Richtofen, the 'Red Baron' with over eighty combat victories.

Ahlefeldt was shot down and killed while flying in an 'LGV C' on a photo reconnaissance mission over Douaumont Fort on 1 April 1916 during the Battle of Verdun.[16] His victor was Sergeant Lucien Jailler of Escadrille N 15 who was flying, probably, a Nieuport 11. Ahlefeldt's body was recovered and a picture of his battlefield grave exists. The Kagohl's Staffelführer, Hauptmann Claes, reported in his letter to Ahlefeldt's mother that he died in air combat with three French biplanes by a shot to the head. However, this was a common report to cover a more likely and more terrifying death.

Karl-Christian von Ahlefeldt's line is extinct in Europe since 1964; Graf Friedrich Karl of the only surviving branch emigrated in 1890 from Denmark to Argentine, married Maria Ramona Mendez and their descendants live in Buenos Aires.

At first view, Erich's initial meeting with Eva might be thought to have been made by Erich's class mate of '05, Kapitänleutnant Wilhelm von Ahlefeld, later of the Flanders torpedo boat service. However, the current family chronicler, Heiko von Ahlefeld, is confident that the two branches of the Ahlefeldt/Ahlefeld family were distant with no opportunity for an introduction. Similarly, he feels that there is no evidence that the noble Ahlefeldts discouraged Eva Marx's first marriage because she was a half-Jewish commoner, but who counted herself a Protestant. Heiko von Ahlefeld also suggests that, at the re-marriage to Erich, Eva should have relinquished her use of her noble title.

The Ahlefeldts made considerable sacrifice for the fatherland. One branch stemmed from Vizeadmiral Hunold von Ahlefeld, who died in 1919, and who was one of the first of the 'modern' sailors, joining the Prussian Navy in 1867. Three of his sons were killed and one, Oberleutnant zur See Paul-Friedrich, a crew member of *U 27*, was shot, most would say murdered, by British sailors in the infamous *Baralong* affair in August 1915 – 'a British disgrace'.[17] His eldest

---

16    Forum correspondence: 1914-1918.invisionzone.com and www.theaerodrome.com, accessed
      12/2016. Also, Franks, Bailey, Duiven, *Casualties of the German Air Service 1914-1920.*
17    Coles, *Slaughter at Sea, The Truth Behind a Naval War Crime.* Cole's book is a detailed indictment

son, Wilhelm was the fellow cadet of Erich in the Class '05. He served on torpedo boats in the Flanders Flotilla, re-joined the navy in World War 2, fell out with the Nazis, was dismissed, and shot himself in 1941 at the family seat at Gut Ludwigsburg near Eckernförde. Another von Ahlefeld, distantly-related to the above, Karl Gustav, was an officer on board the SMS *Prinz Adalbert* when its ammunition store was hit by a British torpedo in 1915 leaving just three survivors from a crew of 675, the worst German naval loss in the Baltic in WWI.

There is an interesting u-boat connection: Karl-Christian von Ahlefeldt's mother was Franziska Eugenie Elisabeth Katharina Adelaide Carola von Dresky, a member of another long-lived noble family which contained at least one admiral and four Prussian generals.[18] Franziska's nephew (or second cousin) was Hans-Wilhelm von Dresky, commander of *U 33* from Wilhelmshaven, who was drowned in the Clyde off the Isle of Arran in 1940 while on a daring mine-laying mission. The intention was to place mines far inside the extended Clyde naval base and cause havoc in what the Allies considered 'safe' waters.

The voyage was thought so dangerous that Hitler and Dönitz, now u-boat Führer, came in person to see the boat away after the crew enjoyed a sex and drink party send off in a wooden hut in the middle of a forest.[19] *U 33* was detected by the minesweeper HMS *Gleaner* and was badly damaged in three separate depth charge attacks in shallow water. Dresky brought his boat to the surface to allow his crew to escape and then scuttled. Only seventeen men survived; twenty-five including Dresky died from hypothermia in the freezing water.

---

of British conduct by the Baralong's captain and crew. For original material, *HMSO*, London, 'Memorandum of the German Government in regard to Incidents Alleged to have Attended the Destruction of a German Submarine and its Crew … and Reply of His Majesty's Government', Cd. 8144, 7/1916. Also, for alterative views: Newbolt, *Naval History*, p. 94; and Chatterton, *Q-ships*, pp. 20-23. A third of Hunold von Ahlefeld's sons, Leutnant Heinrich, an observer in the German air force, was shot down over Italy on 12/2/1918 (Heiko von Ahlefeldt). Five other von Ahlefeldts died and their names are recorded on a family-held roll of honour. See also, Schoenermarck, 'The Eight Heroes of Ahlefeldt', *Helden-Gedenkmappe des deutschen Adels*.

18    Erich von Dresky, 1850–1918, Vizeadmiral; Eugen von Dresky, 1831–1892, Prussian Generalmajor; Gotthardt von Dresky, 1844–1912, Prussian Generalleutnant; Rudolf von Dresky, 1776–1852, Prussian Generalmajor; Justus von Dresky und Merzdorf, 1818–1899, Prussian General der Artillerie.

19    Hadley, *Count Not the Dead*, has a picture following p. 78 of Hitler and Dönitz wishing Dresky good luck.

What makes the tale from another war worth telling here is that the sinking brought the first break-through in the attempt to read the Enigma code and happened far away from the British cryptographers at their secret intelligence base at Bletchley Park.[20] Dresky gave orders for the *U 33*'s Enigma machine's code wheels to be distributed among some of the men and to be dropped into the water once clear of the u-boat. One set of three wheels was collected by the British and taken to Alan Turing and his code-breaking team.

Perhaps it is not surprising that Erich's interest in his university course quickly dwindled. Within six months, Erich was married to a most eligible and wealthy widow, a countess, who was able quickly to raise him above the fray and to introduce him to a very different sort of world. He attended just one course on the Philosophy of Art in the Winter Semester of 1920/21. Erich then took complete leave of every other semester until, in July 1923, the University cancelled his registration because of his non-attendance. His final report of August 1925 noted that, 'Nothing negative has been reported about his behaviour.'

Something or someone persuaded Erich on a career in the Foreign Office. Optimistically, in his formal application in December 1922, Erich explained that had had 'not yet' received his doctorate, but that he had attended eight semesters between 1919 and 1922 studying Law, Political Sciences, Philosophy and History as well as one course at the High School for Political Sciences in Berlin.[21]

In the year, between first missing lectures at the university and applying to the Foreign Office, Erich worked in Berlin in Salomon Marx's *Internationale Handelsbank*, which concentrated on real estate, 'participating in the management of the business and thereby gained practical commercial knowledge', and in the telegraphy company *Vox Maschinen*.

The Vox-Haus, near Potsdamer Platz in Berlin-Tiergarten, was bought in 1920 by the *Vox* record company and, in 1921, a broadcasting studio was installed in the attic. The new medium of radio became hugely popular. One of the first transmissions was the Christmas speech by Chancellor Wilhelm Marx in December 1923; a photograph, dated 1924, shows guests at the Vox-

20    Sebag-Montefiore, *Enigma*, pp. 67-77, has a blow-by-blow account of the mission, the on-board confusion, and the sinking.
21    Foreign Office application 30/12/1922.

Haus including the papal nuncio Eugenio Pacelli. Both these men were to contribute significantly to Erich's career.

Perhaps the benefits and hard work of a doctorate were now not necessary for Erich's future. One other speculative thought: Berlin's universities at this time were a hotbed of student politics: republicanism, socialism, communism and anarchism. Could it be that Erich attended partly to gather information on dissidents for the Admiralty or directly for Canaris?

The idea is not so far-fetched as later events show. The period around Erich and Eva's wedding was a time of revolution and there was death on the streets, particularly in Berlin where the Gerth and Marx families lived. Erich was taking tentative, and quickly unsuccessful, steps towards a legal doctorate. He was still in the employ of the Admiralty, most probably working with Canaris and others on some aspect of the early stages of rebuilding the u-boat fleet. He was already deeply involved with leading anti-Republican, anti-communist militarists like von Trotha, Canaris, and his other colleagues among the commanders of the u-boat flotillas. Salomon Marx, Erich's father-in-law, was cut from the same stamp and, as one of the richest men in Germany, had the money to encourage extreme action. Eva would also have enjoyed a private income and Erich entered into a whirl of new contacts: Catholic leaders delighted with Eva as a high profile and attractive 'catch'; far-right activists; and senior commercial, political and industrial giants of the time who formed Salomon Marx's daily contacts. One can assume that many of these introductions took place at Salomon's home, particularly over dinner with the young couple in attendance. Kessler noted in his diaries in December 1918, presumably during the courtship,

> *The Christmas Fair carried on throughout the blood-letting. Hurdy-gurdies played in the Freidrichstraße while street vendors sold indoor fireworks, gingerbread, and silver tinsel. Jewellers' shops in Unter den Linden remained unconcernedly open, their windows brightly lit and glittering. In the Liepzigerstraße, the usual Christmas crowd thronged the big stores. In thousands of homes the Christmas tree was lit and the children played around it with their presents from Daddy, Mummy and Auntie dear. In the Imperial Stables lay the dead, and the wounds freshly inflicted on the Palace and on Germany gaped into the Christmas night.*[22]

---

22    Kessler, *Diaries*, 24/12/1918, pp. 41-42.

After Germany's defeat, Marx was instrumental in setting up a bourgeois citizens´ council for Berlin as a focus for opposition to revolutionary groups of soldiers, workers and the communist *Spartakusbund*. It was founded on 18 November 1918 as the *Bürgerrat von Gross-Berlin* with Marx as deputy chairman and chairman of the finance committee and one of the five members of the managing committee. Later, he became the *Bürgerrat*'s leader and also of the *Landesbürgerrat* of the Province of Brandenburg. On 5 January 1919, the *Reichsbürgerrat*, the national umbrella organisation comprising 300 citizens' councils countrywide was founded. 'The clear-sighted and energetic chairman of the Berlin *Bürgerrat*, Consul Marx was credited with this achievement.'

The *Bürgerrat of Gross Berlin* actively supported two causes at opposite ends of the spectrum – the fight against the peace conditions the Allies set out at Versailles and the provision of fuel and food to the city's population. Marx organised public protests against the demands of the Entente and against the lack of food, especially meat and fat and heating materials as a result of the continuing blockade. One of his initiatives, the *Holzhilfe GmbH*, provided the poorer population of Berlin with firewood.

Martin Niemöller, another of the Mediterranean u-boat commanders with Erich, became a pacifist, a pastor, and was sent to Sachsenhausen concentration camp.

Salomon Marx and his children, Eduard (in his sailor suit) and Eva, about 1911. *Family archive*

Graf Karl-Christian von Ahlefeldt-Eschelsmark, a member of the Red Baron's squadron, Eva Marx's first husband, killed on air patrol over Verdun in 1916.

Gott strafe England, 'May God Punish England' [for the hunger blockade], was a ubiquitous motto, daubed on buildings, on cufflinks, and imprinted on brown coal bricks. *Brockhaus family archive*

Sergeant Lucien Jailler of Escadrille N 15 who claimed Ahlefeldt's aircraft's destruction.

Erich, left, in an officers' mess, with his 'best friend' Rudi Seuffer, who went down with his u-boat crew in 1918, probably on his way to rescue brother Georg from his French island prison. *Family archive*

Erich, centre, with fellow officers in the Adriatic in 1918. *Family archive*

A hatch had to be totally opened to be able to lower a torpedo inside the boat. The crew of UC 64, sister ship to Erich and Georg's uc-boats, is busy at the task in Bruges docks. *Tomas Termote*

Adolph von Trotha, Tirpitz disciple, Erich's mentor, already co-leader in 1918 of covert plans for Germany's fleet for the 'next war'

Karl Bartenbach, founder of the Flanders u-boat bases with a 'fanatical following' from his captains; by war end Germany's leading submarine expert in charge of secret development overseas of the replacement fleet.

Erich and Eva, widowed Countess von Ahlefeldt, on their wedding day, 1919. *Family archive*

*Chaouia*, sunk by one of Erich's mines from *UC 53* in 1919, well after war end, with a loss of 476 men.

Was will Spartakus?

Neuer Militarismus

Junkertum

Kapitalismus

·K·P·D·
(Spartakusbund)

'What does Spartakus want?' The young Communist wields a sword against a six-headed establishment serpent. Two of the heads, Charles I of Austria and Wilhelm II of Germany, have fallen; four remain, capitalism, new militarism, the Catholic church and the Prussian aristocracy. German Communist Party poster, 1919

**Arbeiter, Bürger!**

Das Vaterland ist dem Untergang nahe.
Rettet es!
Es wird nicht bedroht von außen, sondern von innen:

Von der Spartakusgruppe.

## Schlagt ihre Führer tot!
# Tötet Liebknecht!

Dann werdet ihr Frieden, Arbeit und Brot haben!

Die Frontsoldaten

The infamous anti-communist poster, believed directly funded by Salomon Marx and pasted around Berlin early in 1919: 'Beat them to death! Kill Liebknecht'.

Karl Liebknecht, a 'lonely, essentially likeable man', anti-war campaigner, Reichstag member, political prisoner, Communist, murdered by the Freikorps in 1919

Rosa Luxemburg, an educated Polish Jew, mentored by Vladimir Lenin, murdered minutes after Karl Liebknecht in 1919, found in the Landwehr Canal, Berlin, four months later.

Walther Rathenau, head of electrical giant AEG, advisor to the Kaiser, friend to Salomon Marx, raised five million Reichsmarks for the Freikorps, Foreign Minister, machine-gunned to death in 1922.

There is only one photograph of Erich in his personal file in the Berlin Foreign Office, stuck firmly onto the bottom of his application of 1922, except that the top half, the half showing his face, has been torn off. Staff searching the archive as research for this book thought that the picture had been deliberately defaced.

# 9

# MARX: FREIKORPS AND EASY MURDER

*Karl Liebknecht and Rosa Luxemburg have met with a dreadful and fantastic end.*[1]

There is one further strand, the development of the *Freikorps*, to follow before events and protagonists come together with the murder of the Communist leaders Karl Liebknecht and Rosa Luxemburg.

The murder date of 15 January had a particular significance for Erich Gerth, but it would be some days, if ever, before he realised it. One of the mines he laid with *UC 53* in the Straits of Messina the previous October hit the French passenger and general cargo ship *Chaouia* on the same day. She quickly sank and 476 men, mostly Greek troops, lost their lives.

As war ended and the men came home, many to desert, where was armed authority to be found?

Kurt von Schleicher, protégé of General Wilhelm Gröner, one-time organiser of Germany's economic warfare and the last chancellor of the Weimar Republic before Hitler took over the government in 1932-33, had 'devised a secret plan to combat the disintegration of the old regiments'.[2]

In mid-December 1918, the Army Supreme Command approved Schleicher's plan and assigned an infantry commander, General Ludwig von Maercker,

---

1    Kessler, *Diaries*, 16/1/1919, pp. 41-42.
2    Friedrich, *Before the Deluge*, pp. 38-39. Schleicher and his wife Elizabeth were murdered at their home on Hitler's orders on the 'Night of the Long Knives' in 1934.

to organise an entirely new kind of volunteer force known as the *Freikorps*. Schleicher wanted only the 'most loyal and disciplined veterans, who could be organised into highly mobile storm battalions, each with its own trucks and artillery, signed on month by month'. The generals 'circumvented the problem of unreliable reservists and with the support of the skittish Social Democratic government organised the first *Freikorps* or freelance units, ostensibly to protect the Fatherland from subversion and plunder, but, in fact, to crush the radical left'.[3]

A dozen early corps were formed, each of several thousand men, including three corps from the navy: the Hermann Ehrhardt Brigade; the Colonel von Roden's 'Iron Brigade', loyal to Gustav Noske, who represented the government in negotiations during the Kiel naval mutiny; and the Löwenfeld Corps, 'the largest group, organised in Kiel, which included many former u-boat captains and crewmen among its ranks'.[4]

In something of an irony, it was these three corps of angry naval officers and reactionary leaders who were to define the fight against socialism in the capital. It was ironic because it was the sailors from the Baltic who precipitated the revolution in 1918 by standing up to their weak and ill-led officers of the High Seas Fleet, perhaps stiffened by the u-boat commanders, and it was these self-same officers who, over the next year, broke the revolution's back and crushed its temporary successes.

*Within a rather short time, [the Freikorps] were to become a collection of some 200 piratical bands, merciless in their attacks on civilians and loyal only to their unit commanders and seen as the only force able to stand up to the Communists.*[5]

There is a Gerth family memory, a story told many years later by Erich to his son Marco, in which Erich claimed to have played his part as a member of one of the naval *Freikorps* and to have 'manned the barricades in Berlin against the Bolsheviks'.[6] If true, and there is already a suspicion that Erich inclined to slight embellishment, then it is likely that he followed the lead of his Adriatic

3    Waite, *Vanguard of Nazism*, pp. 12-16, 35-37.
4    Mulligan, *Sharks Not Wolves*, p. 220. Jones, *Birth of the Nazis*, p. 64, Appendix A. Horn, *Mutiny*, p. 248.
5    Friedrich, *Before the Deluge*, p. 39.
6    Telephone conversation with Marc Gerth, 14/1/2018.

comrades, Arnauld de la Perière, Canaris, Kukat and Niemoller, all known *Freikorps* members of the Löwenfeld Corps, formed in December 1918.[7]

The story also adds credence to a possibly subversive role for Erich at his university which he joined the month before. The Corps disbanded in June 1920 and this coincided with his loss of interest in his studies. There is no record of Erich in the lists of naval *Freikorps*, but these are far from complete. His absence does, at least, suggest that he was not a prominent member.

Löwenfeld was one of those with Dönitz and others who were identified as leading the covert u-boat programme. Löwenfeld's assault battalion was commanded by the legendary u-boat ace, Lothar von Arnauld de la Perière, who had rescued Canaris from Spain in 1916, and the corps contained 'probably every naval officer in the vicinity' of Kiel.[8] Canaris was one of Löwenfeld's 'first and closest collaborators' and it was within this corps' organisation that Canaris began the 'outstanding intelligence bureau' that later led him to senior power in the Nazi government.[9]

In December, Canaris was sent from the Baltic to Berlin by Löwenfeld, to contact groups 'possibly preparing a kind of counter-revolution'. The Admiralty was ostensibly not interested, but one can imagine that Trotha, another eventual member of the Ehrhardt Brigade, gave him close attention. However, Canaris was successful with the Garde-Kavallerie Schützen Division (GKSD), a 'royal elite troop'.

In March 1918, on Ludendorff's order, Hauptmann Heinrich Waldemar Pabst had joined GKSD as its chief of general staff to convert it from a cavalry to a rifle division.

*Under Pabst, GKSD became the strongest counter-revolutionary unit in Germany, the 'backbone of all troops deployed' ... Pabst's main aim was to overthrow the Republic and its socialist leaders. He gathered like-minded men around him and, amongst the GKSD staff, were Kapitänleutnant Horst von Pflugk-Hartungg and his younger brother, Heinz. All were fanatical militarists, anti-communists and enemies of the Republic.*

7     Jones, *Birth of the Nazis*, p. 284.
8     Mulligan, *Sharks Not Wolves*, pp. 220-21. Mueller, *Canaris*, pp. 38-39.
9     Mueller, *Canaris*, p. 52.

Horst von Pflugk was a cadet member of the Crew of '07, and therefore a close contemporary of Georg Gerth, currently languishing in a French prison hospital recovering from influenza.

Several of the Gerths' fellow u-boat commanders were at the forefront of the *Freikorps*. Personal comrades were killed in action. Communism left the u-boat crews largely unaffected, and they were still prepared to fight on 'beyond the end of the war'.[10] Wilhelm Werner, a classmate of Erich Gerth, sank sixty-five ships with *U 7* in the Mediterranean and *U 55* around Britain. He was an unconvicted war criminal and later joined the *Freikorps* of Paul von Lettow-Vorbeck before fleeing to Brazil. Lettow-Vorbeck, who commanded the German troops in East Africa, ended the Spartacist uprising in Hamburg without the use of force.[11] Two men of the Adriatic flotilla, Heinrich Kukat and Martin Niemöller, were involved in 'one of the most bloody and savage episodes of the whole German revolution'.[12]

Kukat was killed fighting pro-communist forces in the Ruhr uprising in 1920; Niemöller commanded his own Academic Defence Corps of the *Freikorps* in the same action. Niemöller briefly became a farmer before studying Protestant theology and became a pastor in 1924 in Dahlem, a suburb of Berlin. He was an early supporter of Hitler until his seizure of power in 1933. Niemöller claimed that Hitler's writings on Aryan supremacy contradicted 'Christian charity values'. In 1936, Niemöller signed a petition along with a group of Protestant churchmen, calling for opposition to the Nazis' state control of the churches, an action that prompted the mass arrest of nearly 800 men. After a trial for 'activities against the state' he was eventually imprisoned in Sachsenhausen and Dachau concentration camps from 1938 to 1945, narrowly escaping execution. He later became an ardent pacifist.[13]

*The u-boat men who headed for Kiel Harbour [on their way home from the Adriatic] were neither potential pacifists nor future democrats. Neither Niemöller nor Canaris had the least desire to be welcomed home to red flags and solders' councils. The eleven*

---

10    Compton-Hall, *Submarines*, p. 300.
11    Jones, *Birth of the Nazis*, pp. 88-89, 173-74.
12    Jones, *Birth of the Nazis*, p. 192.
13    Niemöller, *From U-boat to Pulpit*.

*commanders agreed to enter harbour flying the Imperial ensign and the home-coming*
*pennant, and swore that the red flag would never be hoisted on their boats.*[14]

It was a further irony that the German general staff provided Lenin's 'sealed train' that took Lenin and his followers home after the Russian Revolution in the hope that he would sow disaffection among the Russian soldiery.[15] 'The seeds were scattered beyond Russian borders' and came back to haunt Germany's rulers. Lenin was a long-term, personal mentor of Rosa Luxemburg and a supporter of Karl Liebknecht.

Karl Liebknecht had always been a 'lonely, high-strung and essentially likeable man'. His father, William, was one of the founders of German Socialism, a friend of Karl Marx, who 'combined Marxist revolutionary theory with practical, legal, political activity'.[16]

In 1904, Liebknecht told the SPD party conference, 'Militarism is our most deadly enemy and the best way of waging the struggle against it is to increase the number of social democrats among the soldiers.' In 1907, he published a fierce attack on Germany's military and served an eighteen-month sentence for treason.[17] Liebknecht broke ranks from his party at the end of 1914 to vote against war credits, the socialists accepting that it was a defensive war.[18] It was only when the SPD became convinced that the German government was conducting a war of conquest that they declined to pass further credits. Despite Liebknecht's parliamentary immunity, the army retaliated by putting him in a punishment battalion on the eastern front where he refused to fight and served by burying the dead. Because of his deteriorating health, he returned to Germany in October 1915.

*As a Reichstag deputy, however, he had the right to attend each session and he*
*repeatedly asked embarrassing questions about the shooting of Belgian hostages and*
*about the specific causes of the war – greeted with cries from other deputies of*
*'Nonsense' and 'Madness'.*[19]

---

14   Mueller, *Canaris*, pp. 31-33.
15   Compton-Hall, *Submarines*, p. 300.
16   Friedrich, *Before the Deluge*, pp. 18-19.
17   Liebknecht, *Militarismus and Anti-Militarismus*.
18   Rosenberg, *Imperial Germany*, p. 73.
19   Harmer, *Luxemburg*, p. 101.

Expelled by the SPD in 1916 for his previous lone stand against war credits, Liebknecht began publishing a radical newspaper under the name of Spartakus, a small affair with only about 500 copies printed.[20] Liebknecht and Luxemburg developed the USPD, the Independent Social Democratic Party of Germany which briefly shared power with the SPD late in 1918. The USPD led in turn to the founding of the communist party and its attendant Spartacus League. In May 1916, while Liebknecht was giving an anti-war speech, mounted police charged the crowd and Liebknecht received a four-year prison sentence for high treason and 'contumacy to the authority of the state'.[21]

In October 1918, the Spartacus group was active with appeals and their first national conference for nearly two years. 'The spontaneous mutinies among the soldiers must be supported by all means and be led towards an armed uprising for the struggle to gain the entire power for the workers and soldiers.' In other words, the working class could only be relied on to invoke the weapon of the strike. The move to a revolution required the leadership of the intelligentsia.

*The whole process was intended as a continual raising of revolutionary sights so that the ponderous and reluctant dragon of the German working class could finally be induced to snort and move.*[22]

As the old order crumbled, Liebknecht was one of the first to be released under a general amnesty. He returned to Berlin on 23 October as a 'prophet vindicated' and with Lenin's full support. He was 'welcomed by huge crowds and carried shoulder-high by soldiers decorated with the Iron Cross'.

Rosa Luxemburg's relations with Liebknecht were politically close, but they were 'never personal friends'. She 'admired his courage and despised his slapdash existence'.[23] Luxemburg was an educated Polish Jew who moved to Zurich in 1889 where she met the founders of the first Russian Marxist party and received a doctorate in law and political science. It was also where she began her unusual love affair with Leo Jogiches, who became a stalwart if flaky

20    Named after the Thracian gladiator Spartacus, the leader of the slave revolt against the Roman Empire in the Third Servile War in the last century before the birth of Christ.
21    Nettl, *Luxemburg*, pp. 388-89.
22    Nettl, *Luxemburg*, p. 439.
23    Harmer, *Luxemburg*, pp. 10, 22, 28, 79, 94.

party member. Jogiches lived next door to Luxemburg because he wished to keep their relationship secret.

Luxemburg moved to Berlin in 1898 and, though women were not allowed to join political parties, offered her services to the SPD as a writer and speaker. In Berlin, she was 'confronted by a double prejudice' among Prussians who saw both Poles and Jews as 'irredeemably inferior'. She thought 'Berlin the most repulsive place: cold, ugly, massive – a real barracks, and the charming Prussians with their arrogance as if each one of them had been made to swallow the very stick with which he got his daily beating.'

On a holiday in Finland, she met again with Lenin whom she found a pleasure to talk to. 'He is sophisticated, knowledgeable, with the kind of ugly mug I like so much.'

Quickly becoming an activist, she roused a pre-war crowd of 6,000 SPD members. 'We are the millions of those whose work makes society possible … we can show our reactionary rulers once and for all that the world can go on without Junkers and Earls, without councillors, and at a pitch even without the police, but that it cannot exist for twenty-four hours if one day the workers withdraw their labour.'

She joined Liebknecht in condemnation of war. 'Once the majority of working people come to the conclusion … that wars are nothing but a barbaric, unsocial, reactionary phenomenon, entirely against the interests of the people, then war will have become impossible even if the soldiers obey their commanders. We think that wars can only come about so long as the working classes either supports them enthusiastically because it considers them justified and necessary, or a least accepts them passively.'

In July 1916, Luxemburg was suddenly arrested, a police decision unresolved as to whether to place her on trial or just to keep her in custody.[24] She remained incarcerated until November 1918, mostly in the city jail in Breslau. She missed the amnesty that freed Liebknecht because it was thought to apply only to those serving specific sentences. After addressing an expectant crowd in Breslau's central square, she hastened in the afternoon to Berlin where she was 'greeted with joy by her old friends, but also with concealed sadness, for

---

24    Nettl, *Luxemburg*, p. 401.

they suddenly realised what the years in prison had done to her. She had aged terribly and her black hair was gone quite white. She was a sick woman.'[25]

From 4 January 1918, more than 100,000 soldiers and civilians demonstrated against the government in what became known as the Spartacist uprising. The revolutionary committee of the Communist Party, the KPD, called for a general strike which led to street battles between its supporters and the moderate Social Democrats (SPD), whose government was led by Friedrich Ebert, Phillip Scheidemann and Gustav Bauer. Luxemburg considered any revolt at that time would be a catastrophe and spoke out against it. The SPD newspaper building and other publishing houses were occupied by the Spartacus League.

Schreiner, the author, captured the mood of long-repressed discontent, 'The Peoples of Europe are at one another's throat today because one set of capitalists is afraid that it is to lose a part of its dividend to another. The only way we have of getting even with them is to turn socialist and put the curb on our masters. The men in the trenches knew very well what they were fighting for. They realised that, now the struggle was on, they had to continue with it, but they had also made up their mind to be heard from later on.'[26]

Two of Erich Gerth's later referees, the Prince and Princess Ludwig of Bavaria, were warned to take care as 'Luxemburg and company were looking for new hostages, people with names, officers of the old army, princes ...'[27] These descendants of the Spanish royal family saw Luxemburg as 'drunk with blood lust and hideous', the ringleader whose 'ferocity gave her an uncanny power over the lowest elements of the mob'.

The Police Headquarters was in the hands of the Spartacists where ...

*Liebknecht was addressing a large crowd. He speaks with unctuous solemnity, like a parson, intoning his words slowly and expressively ... Only a part of his words were intelligible, but his sing-song inflexion carried over the heads of the silent and attentive crowd. When he ended there was a roar of approval, red flags were flourished, and thousands of hands and hats rose in the air. He was like an invisible priest of the revolution, a mysterious and sonorous symbol to which the people raised their eyes.*[28]

25    Nettl, *Luxemburg*, p. 442.
26    Schreiner, *Iron Ration*, p. 66.
27    Princess Ludwig, *Through Four Revolutions*, p. 317.
28    Kessler, *Diaries*, 5/1/1919, p. 52.

At the Reich Chancellery, it was Defence Minister Noske who suggested using military force against the insurrectionists and he was given wide-ranging powers by Chancellor Ebert to restore order.[29] Noske immediately set up his headquarters at Berlin Dahlem. One of the 'most active' officers was Pabst, whose adjutant was Canaris. Noske asked Kiel for help and within a few days a force of 1,200 men of the 'Iron Brigade' left for the capital. Canaris arranged for the distribution of weapons, uniforms, equipment and rations. After a bombardment of several hours, the Spartacists vacated the SPD Vorwärts newspaper building.[30] 'Five intermediaries, who had negotiated the surrender of the building, were summarily tried and executed; three couriers were murdered.' Over 150 insurgents and seventeen *Freikorps* soldiers died.

> On 13 January, the Freikorps were now mopping up the final doomed resistance in bloody and pitiless street-fighting in which deaths rose to over 1,000. Luxemburg, her cheeks sunken, her eyes dark with tiredness, wrote her final article. 'The leadership failed. But the leadership can and must be created anew by the masses and out of the masses ... 'Order reigns in Berlin!' You stupid Lackeys! Your 'order' is built on sand. The revolution will 'raise itself up again clashing', and to your horror it will proclaim to the sound of trumpets: I was, I am, I shall be.[31]

Noske 'marched 3,000 men through the city and government district to demonstrate their military strength and the resolve of the government'. There was no resistance. Liebknecht and Luxemburg went into hiding. Luxemburg wrote on 25 December that she had 'received urgent warning from official sources' that the assassins were looking for them both and 'we shouldn't sleep at home'.[32]

On 9 January 1919, Salomon Marx, the most influential man of the *Bürgerrat Gross-Berlin*, called upon 'every man capable of bearing arms who had previously done military service to join the Republican civic militia at once'. Bands of citizens armed themselves to fight against the Spartakusbund with the rallying cry, 'Shoot down the red dogs!' Bourgeois businessmen like

---

29    Mueller, *Canaris*, pp. 41-42.
30    Nettl, *Luxemburg*, p. 483.
31    Harmer, *Luxemburg*, pp. 134-35, citing the *Die Rote Fahne*, the *Red Flag*, 14/1/1919. For other
      extracts, Nettl, *Luxemburg*, p. 485.
32    Nettl, *Luxemburg*, p. 473.

Marx initially financed the *Freikorps* troops under whose protection many armed vigilante groups consisting of bourgeois voluntary fighters were formed. Walther Rathenau, heir to AEG, the leading electrical company, reputedly personally raised five million Reichsmark to support the *Freikorps*.[33] The same day, Eduard Stadtler gave a speech at Berlin University where Erich Gerth studied and called upon all students to take up arms.

On 10 January, Salomon Marx organised a meeting of fifty representatives of banks, industry and trade, including Ernst von Borsig, Friedrich von Siemens and Hugo Stinnes. Eduard Stadtler who had just returned from Russian captivity and had become one of the leading anti-communist agitators gave a talk entitled 'Bolshevism as a world danger'. Following this meeting, the attendees from industry and banks set up a fund worth 500 million Reichsmark with the aim of putting down the revolution. Historian Hintz questions this sum, but suggests an amount of twenty million Reichsmark. The next day an organisation of academics demanded that all men in professional occupations joined forces to fight against Bolshevism.

*A strong anti-Bolshevist propaganda is being carried out by the Government and Berlin is placarded with a variety of posters on the subject. One of the commonest represents a huge skull holding a dripping dagger in its teeth, the poster being in lurid colours and headed 'Die Gefahr des Bolshevismus'. Berlin in itself is a fair representation of the people at the moment. Dirt, disorder, dancing and death. The traffic is chaotic. Every dancing hall is filled to overflowing and, almost with the sound of their orchestras, Spartacists and Government troops shoot each other dead every day.*[34]

Erich's father-in-law, Salomon Marx, chaired daily meetings in the back room of a 'well-known' inn in the Unter den Linden where the *Bürgerrat* and *Freikorps* leaders exchanged information and plotted the arrest of Karl Radek, an Austro-Hungarian Jew and prominent Bolshevik who travelled with Lenin in the sealed train the year before. Radek had recently crossed into Germany illegally, arriving in Berlin a few weeks earlier. Marx also called for the killing of Liebknecht and Luxemburg on whose heads a reward of 100,000 Reichsmark,

33    Friedrich, *Deluge*, pp. 28-29, 102.
34    *Economic Conditions Prevailing in Germany*, Berlin, pp. 61, 67, 75.

at least unofficially, had been placed by right-wing private enterprise, with the probable backing of Phillip Scheidemann at the top of government.[35]

A poster appeared across Berlin:

*Workers, Citizens!*
*The fatherland is close to its downfall.*
*Save it!*
*It is not threatened from outside, but from the inside:*
*The Spartacus Group.*
*Strike their leaders dead!*
*Kill Liebknecht!*
*Then you will have peace, work and bread!*
*The Front-line Soldiers*[36]

Writer Engelmann credits the 'man behind the scenes', Salomon Marx, with the financing and authorship of this propaganda poster.[37] The German Historical Museum, *Deutsches Historisches Museum*, however, argues that the pamphlets in their data base which can be directly linked to the *Bürgerrat Gross-Berlin* and Salomon Marx show a different line of attack, for example, calls for the speedy foundation of a national assembly or to promote a future co-operation with Austria.[38]

On 16 January 1919, a day after the murders of Liebknecht and Luxemburg, the *Dresdner Bank, Deutsche Bank* and *Disconto-Gesellschaft* each transferred donations of 50,000 Reichsmark into the account of Salomon Marx at *Bürgerrat Gross-Berlin*.

*The street fighting in Berlin between 10-15 January culminated in an attack on an*
*ill-considered and chaotic demonstration of extreme left socialists and communists and*
*the deaths of the Communist party leaders, Karl Liebknecht and Rosa Luxembourg,*
*on 15 January. The crushing of the so-called 'Spartacus revolt', in no way deserving*
*of the name, and the 'white terror' that followed was a shattering defeat for the left-*
*wing radicals. Strikes and armed conflicts took place in February and March, and*

---

35    Nettl, *Luxemburg*, p. 485.
36    Stadtgeschichtliches Museum, Leipzig, PLA 487, GOS-Nr. p0006819.
37    Engelmann, *Germany Without Jews*, pp. 243-44.
38    Letter, German Historical Museum to Alfred Hintz, 17/5/2010.

*for a brief period, 4 April – 1 May, a Soviet republic was established in Bavaria. All were suppressed.*[39]

The murders themselves are well covered in many publications although, as always, there are long-lasting queries as to the complete facts.[40]

'From the early days of the revolution, shortly after they had both been released from the Kaiser's jails, Liebknecht and Luxemburg were targeted for destruction.' The murders were 'politically vital' as they removed the 'two most able and charismatic leaders of the German left'. They also exposed the 'guilt of the SPD' in agreeing to the elimination of their former party comrades and this left 'a legacy of bitterness that was to divide and fatally weaken the forces of German socialism for more than a generation'.

In brief, Pabst and the GKSD had their headquarters at the Hotel Eden in Berlin under the local command of Heinz von Pflugk-Harttung; his brother Horst, the cadet contemporary of Georg Gerth, was in the unit and present. Pabst had 'often met with Liebknecht and considered him a dangerous enemy'.[41]

Civilian militia at Wilmersdorf arrested Liebknecht and Luxemburg at a safe house, possibly as a result of tip-off by a 'friend' and took them separately to the Eden where they were reportedly separately tortured. The government was informed of the arrests and private instructions were passed and understood. Late that evening, Liebknecht was taken to the rear of a waiting open car to a 'barrage of insults from soldiers and hotel guests'. Once seated, flanked by the Pflugk-Harttung brothers, Rifleman Otto Runge, on guard at the hotel revolving door, ran forward and hit Liebknecht with a 'savage blow' with the butt of his rifle.

Faking a puncture near Berlin Zoo, Horst Pflugk-Harttung took Liebknecht by the arm, released him and then shot him several times from behind as if he was trying to escape. The 'unknown' body was later taken to the city morgue where it was identified.

---

39    Steiner, *Lights That Failed*, p. 10.

40    Mueller, *Canaris*, pp. 43-44. Jones, *Birth of the Nazis*, Chapter 6, 'The Twin Murders: Liebknecht and Luxemburg', pp. 70-83. Bouton, *Kaiser Abdicates*, pp. 225-36. Harmer, *Luxemburg*, pp. 135-37. Nettl, *Luxemburg*, pp. 486-94.

41    Mueller, *Canaris*, p. 40.

Luxemburg was interviewed by Pabst, who had also met her several times. She darned the hem of her coat and read *Faust* in the toilet. When word was received that Liebknecht was dead, Luxemburg was taken outside where Runge struck her twice on the head with his rifle and she was thrown into the waiting car. About forty metres from the hotel, Oberleutnant Kurt Vogel jumped onto the running board and shot her dead. The body was thrown into the Landwehr Canal where it was found near sluice gates four months later and identified only by clothing.

> *In the early hours of 8 May 1919, the Landgericht courthouse at Berlin Moabit resembled an army depot. Units of GKSD was stationed at all entrances, on the streets patrols broke up large gatherings; the whole east wing of the courthouse swarmed with soldiers and visitors; reporters and witnesses were searched for weapons. Hundreds wanted to watch the trial ... British and American visitors were offering up to 5,000 Reichsmark on the black market for a ticket.*[42]

All of the men on trial had previously been released from custody. Only Vogel was charged with Luxemburg's murder. Liebknecht's accused were Otto Runge, Heinz and Horst Pflugk-Harttung and four others.[43] The chairman of the GKSD panel of military judges was Hermann Ehrhardt, the brigade commander of the men on trial. He was assisted by three lay judges, one of whom was Canaris who had role-played the evidence with the defendants, especially that of his two personal friends, the Pflugk-Harttungs.

Unsurprisingly, there was 'ever-growing criticism' from Press, politicians and the workers' and soldiers' councils. All except two were acquitted: Vogel was cleared of murder, but found guilty of a number of minor disciplinary matters and sentenced to twenty-eight months imprisonment; Runge, who was brought back for trial from the Danish border where he had been smuggled personally by Pabst, was sentenced to two years imprisonment.

Three days after sentencing, a 'Leutnant Lindemann' arrived at Moabit prison with authority to remove Vogel to Tegel penitentiary. 'Lindemann' and Vogel drove off and disappeared, Vogel to Holland.

---

42    Mueller, *Canaris*, pp. 45-46.
43    Ulrich Ritgen, Heinrich Stiege, Bruno Schulze and Rudolf Liepmann.

'Lindemann' was Canaris. In a trial in 1933, Canaris's involvement was uncovered, including 30,000 Reichsmark made available for the Pflugk-Harttung brothers to flee. Heinz was blown up in his car in Berlin in 1920 and died the same day of wounds.[44] It was a retribution bombing by Polish communists, Luxemburg's native comrades.

In a later career that has all the hallmarks of Canaris's involvement, Horst Pflugk-Harttung co-ordinated the Fascist movement in Sweden. He became the leading German spy in Denmark where he set up a ring that operated secret broadcasting stations that dealt with nautical and hydrographical material.[45] At the same time, he worked for General Franco arranging the sinking of Spanish Republican fishing boats and was instrumental in the sinking of the Spanish Republican freighter *Cantabria* ten miles off Dover by the Spanish nationalist cruiser *Nadir* in 1938

In 1944, Pflugk-Harttung commanded the Germany Navy docks in Bordeaux. He was arrested by the Americans and taken to Arizona for questioning and eventually released because he was not seen to be a Nazi, and returned to Germany in 1947.

Luxemburg's long-term lover, Jogiches, did not have long to live. On 10 March, he was arrested and identified at once. At police headquarters, one of the detectives in charge was an ex-Sergeant-Major Tamschick, a 'notorious bully'. He knew Jogiches as one of the leaders of Spartakus and shot him in cold blood at the first opportunity. No attempt to punish him was ever made.[46]

Demands from the military mounted on Noske to seize power and reject the peace treaty. Borsig-director Benningsen-Förde wrote on 12 February 1919 to Ernst Borsig that, 'The soul of the citizen councils is Consul Marx.' He has close links to the government.

Marx's influence, and that of his family friend, Canaris, was ubiquitous. Marx belonged to the financial committee of the *Ausschuss Deutscher Verbände zur Schaff Ung eider Einheitsfront zur Bekämpfung der Schuldlüge*, 'Committee for the Creation of a United Front to Fight against the Guilt Lie'. This committee

---

44    Heinz Pflugk-Harttung had had an interesting war career in the Prussian infantry (severely wounded), joined the air force (the same path as Salomon Marx's daughter's first husband, Karl-Christian von Ahlefeldt), and flew over 300 bombing missions, including the first in 1915 on Paris (forum.axishistory.com, accessed 3/2017).

45    Gollomb, *Army of Spies*, pp. 88-89.

46    Nettle, *Luxemburg*, p. 493.

became one of the biggest and most influential propaganda organisations of the Weimar Republic. Further, during the socialist March revolts, the Berlin *Bürgerrat* could be credited with setting up a regiment of 1,200 volunteers in Berlin at short notice, thus boosting the regular army troops.

It seems as if Salomon Marx's conscience was pricking him, particularly as a Jew, despite his conversion to Christianity. He asked the President of the Central Association of German Citizens of Jewish Faith, Dr Ludwig Holländer, for his views on Judaism and Revolution or Socialism.

Holländer confirmed that Judaism 'strictly condemned subversive actions and that Jewish life was by its nature conservative'. Another prominent Jewish representative of the time, Dr Cäsar Hirsch, stated that 'revolutionary Jews were behaving contrary to the teachings of Judaism and had therefore stopped being Jewish'. Hintz believes that the motive for Salomon's role as a counter-revolutionary was the fact that he was deeply rooted in the traditionally conservative milieu of the educated and wealthy German-Jewish upper classes. Of course, there were Jewish protagonists on both sides of the political divide, revolutionaries and radical conservatives.

Under pressure to leave from the Swedish government and attracted by the rise of the *Freikorps*, Ludendorff returned to Germany in February 1919 to free rooms at the Adlon Hotel in Berlin.[47] He was given a private entrance to keep him away from the Allied Disarmament Commission, meeting in the same hotel, who wanted Ludendorff as a war criminal.

Ludendorff plotted and met with, for instance, General Walther von Lüttwitz, commander of the troops in Berlin, including all of the *Freikorps* and who had helped suppress the Spartakists uprising; Pabst; and Wolfgang Kapp, the co-founder with Tirpitz of the short-lived Fatherland Party. In August 1919, Pabst founded the *Nationale Vereinigung*, an anti-republican organisation, in order to 'prepare the counter-revolution'.[48] Membership included von Lüttwitz, Ludendorff, Max Bauer, the former chief of staff, *Freikorps* leader Ehrhardt, Kapp, and, of course, Canaris.

In May 1919, leading figures involved in the eventual 'Kapp-Lüttwitz Putsch' to depose the government met at Marx's Brückenallee address to discuss plans. The *Reichsbürgerrat*, headed by Marx, published a pamphlet calling for the

---

47    Friedrich, *Before the Deluge*, pp. 58-59.
48    Mueller, *Canaris*, pp. 51-52.

revision of the Versailles Treaty because its demands could not be met. Marx used a recent book by the British political economist John Maynard Keynes, *The Economic Consequences of the Peace*, to further his arguments.

Marx gained widespread public attention by an event he organised in June on the day of the scuttling of the German fleet at Scapa Flow. The commander of the German fleet had been instructed to hoist the British flag above the German one during the transfer of the ships, a command that was seen as an humiliation by large parts of the German population. The German government had guaranteed that French flags seized during the war would be returned. In response, members of the *Freikorps* entered the Berlin arsenal and forced the guards to hand them over for burning at the memorial for Friedrich the Great. Many university students, perhaps including Erich Gerth six days before his wedding, were involved in the protest.

In the spring of 1919, the *Freikorps* were greeted as liberators by burghers in the cities where they smashed the general strikes of militant workers and the Spartakist uprising in Brunswick. They marched to Munich to lead the suppression of the Communist government in Bavaria, then moved to Silesia in search of Polish guerrillas. Once the *Freikorps* had 'murdered their way across Germany and finally disbanded', they left behind a loose confederacy of secret organisations, veterans' clubs, and rifle clubs which included Hitler's nascent *Sturmabteilung*.[49]

At the same time, regional governments promoted the creation of local citizens' or home guards, *Einwohnerwehren*, to maintain law and order, so that more than one million men were enrolled in paramilitary activities in 1919 and 1920 with local armouries, veterans back in uniform, and rifles under the floorboards – all attesting to the deadly mobilisation that had taken place in hundreds of communities across the Reich.

On 29 February 1920, Defence Minister Noske ordered the disbandment of two of the most powerful *Freikorps*, the naval brigades of Löwenfeld and Ehrhardt. Ehrhardt refused to disband and staged a parade where Lüttwitz backed the unit. Noske then removed the brigade from Lüttwitz's command. Lüttwitz ignored the order, but agreed to a meeting with President Ebert. On 10 March, Lüttwitz, Ebert and Noske met. Lüttwitz reiterated that he

49    Fritzsche, *Germans into Nazis*, pp. 105, 122-24.

would rather 'bring down the government' than disband.[50] He demanded the immediate dissolution of the National Assembly, new elections for the Reichstag, the appointment of technocrat *Fachministers* as Secretaries for Foreign Affairs, Economics and Finance, his own appointment as supreme commander of the regular military and the revocation of the orders of dissolution for the naval brigades.

One particular dispute where the public at large agreed with an infuriated Lüttwitz was the matter of war criminals.

The Allies had just 'heightened the tension' by publishing a list of nearly 900 war criminals and demanded that they be surrendered to stand trial.[51] Civilian and military resistance to the charges were prominently made. Atrocities and war crimes included many types of incidents: behaviour to wounded soldiers and prisoners, the treatment of occupied or even home populations, aerial bombardment, economic blockade and unrestricted submarine warfare. 'These lay behind articles 227-230 of the Treaty of Versailles and the subsequent Allied attempts to bring German war criminals to trial in 1921.'[52]

The list included the Kaiser and his entourage, Hindenburg, Ludendorff, Falkenhayn, Tirpitz, Scheer, von Trotha and eighteen u-boat commanders.[53]

---

50   Mueller, *Canaris*, p. 52.
51   Yarnall, *Barbed Wire Disease*, 'Leipzig: The Aftermath'.
52   Horne and Kramer, 'War Between Soldiers', p. 153.
53   Proposed list of those to be tried as war criminals (Bridgland, *Outrage*), pp. 193-94, corrected from uboat.net: Hans Adam, *U 82*, Galway Castle (actually sunk by Heinrich Middendorff, *U 82*); Hubert Aust, *UC 45*, *Golden Hope*; Thorwald von Bothmer, *U 66*, *Mariston* (actually sunk by Erich Sittenfeld, *U 45*); Otto Dröscher, *U 20*, *Ikaria*, *Tokomaru* (both actually sunk by Walter Schweiger, who also sank the *Lusitania*, which was not on the list); Konrad Gansser, *U 33*, *U 156*, *Clan Macleod*, *Belle of France* (actually sunk by Otto Hersing, *U 21*), *WC McKay*, *Artesia*; Carl-Siegfried Ritter von Georg, *U 57*, *U 101*, *Refugio*, *Jersey* City (actually sunk by Leo Hillebrand, *U 46*), *Teal*, *Richard de Larrinaga*, *Glenford*, *Trinidad*, *John G Walker*, *Lough Fisher*; Alfred von Glassenapp, *U 91*, *Haileybury*, *Birchleaf* (damaged), *Landonia*, *Baron Herries*, *Ethel*; Heinrich Jess, *U 96*, *U 90*, *Apapa*, *Destro*, *Inkosi*; Wilhelm Kiesewetter, *UC 56*, *Glenart Castle* (a hospital ship, his only sinking); Constantin Kolbe, *U 152*, *Clan Murray* (actually sunk by Theodor Schultz, *UC 55*), *Ellaston*, *Elsie Birdett*; Heinrich von Nostitz und Jänkendorf, *U 152*, *Dwinsk*; Karl Neumann, *UC 67*, *Dover Castle* (a hospital ship); Helmut Patzig, *U 86*, *Llandovery Castle*; Claus Rücker, *U 103*, *Victoria*; (Rücker did sink a *Victoria* in 1915, two years earlier than claimed; there were four *Victorias* sunk in 1917 by other commanders); Otto von Schrader, *UB 64*, *Dartmoor* (actually sunk by Rudolf Seuffer, *UC 50*, who was the captain lost on his way to rescue Georg Gerth from Boyardville); Max Valentiner, *U 38*, *Glenby*, *Persia*, *Clan Macfarlane*; Erwin Wassner, *UC 69*, *Addah*; Wilhelm Werner, *U 55*, *Clearfield*, *Artist*, *Trevone*, *Toro*, *Torrington*, *Rewa*, *Guildford Castle* (the last two were hospital ships; his technique was to load survivors without lifebelts on his u-boat deck having wrecked their lifeboats, then submerge. Werner fled to Brazil, worked on a coffee plantation rather than stand trial, and returned in

After much negotiation, the Allies agreed that the Germans could themselves conduct the trials of a much-reduced list of forty-five persons, including Ludwig von Schröder for the murder of Captain Fryatt, the captain of an unarmed steamer which attempted to ram a u-boat in the North Sea.[54] In the end, only twelve people were tried in February 1921 in Leipzig and of these two were u-boat captains, Karl Neumann, promoted Kapitänleutnant in 1918, who travelled home to Berlin from Pola with Erich Gerth, and Helmut Patzig.[55] Most of the twelve were found not guilty or given short prison sentences. Lowell, a u-boat historian, has a particular view:

> But how about all of those atrocities which were so liberally attributed to the u-boats? Here, as with the subject of atrocities in general, it is difficult to find any sound evidence, anything more than rumour. The two particular crimes attributed to the u-boats were the sinking of hospital ships and the firing on lifeboats. In the first instance, the Germans cite the fact that ships often struck mines and were thought to be torpedoed. There are two authenticated instances where hospital ships appear to have been sunk deliberately. In the second instance, I ran across cases where lifeboats were said to have been fired upon. The Germans reply to this by pointing out at least one instance where a seemingly innocent lifeboat tried to sink a submarine with a sudden throwing of bombs, and it was scarcely more than human for the u-boat to open fire.[56]

U-boat commanders routinely asserted that the Allies deliberately used hospital ships as troop carriers, abusing the Red Cross Convention. While

---

1924 to join the NSDAP and later the staff of SS Reichsführer Heinrich Himmler. Werner was a classmate of Erich Gerth.

54    Heal, *The War of The Raven*, for Georg Gerth's involvement.

55    Bridgland, *Outrage*, pp. 193-200. MacMillan, *Paris 1919*, pp. 164-65. Neumann sank the hospital ship *Dover Castle* off Algiers in 1917 (Bridgland, *Outrage*), pp. 151-56. *UC 67* was 'brought home' by Martin Niemöller when Pola was closed at war end. Neumann was found not guilty because he was 'following orders'. One of the worst atrocities of the naval war, which gathered the longest sentences, happened on 27 June 1918 when Oberleutnant Helmut Patzig, *U 86*, sank the Canadian hospital ship *Llandovery Castle* off Fastnet while travelling from Halifax in Canada to Liverpool (Bridgland, *Outrage*), pp. 176-92. Patzig ordered his u-boat to ram the life boats and shot at the survivors. Of a crew of 258, only twenty-four survived; another report in uboat.net claims 146 casualties. Patzig's senior officers, Ludwig Dithmar and John Boldt, were given four years imprisonment. Patzig could not be found (he was in hiding in the Free City of Leipzig) and his officers 'escaped' on the way to their labour camp (Newbolt, *Submarine and Anti-submarine*), p. 125.

56    Lowell, *Raiders*, pp. 6-7.

returning from a voyage in February 1915, *U 20* attempted unsuccessfully to torpedo a hospital ship approaching Le Havre, her decks and rails crowded with armed British troops bound for the front. Werner Fürbringer, then one of commander Walther Schwieger's officers, said he could hardly believe his eyes and 'confirmed Schwieger's own observation through the periscope before the attack was made'.[57]

> *The ship which was safe under the holy flag of humanity and mercy [the Red Cross] was loaded from bow to stern with artillery supplies and amongst the guns and ammunition there was crowded an army of soldiers and horses. Under the protection of the colours of the flags which they were so atrociously misusing they were proceeding in daylight on the way to the front.*[58]

No Allied war criminals were tried which is, perhaps, the right of the victor. The Germans certainly had a list of Allied war criminals with Churchill and Haig right at the top. Allied hypocrisy and ruthlessness was an ever-present in high strategy.[59] British Cabinet Secretary Maurice Hankey was fond of quoting Machiavelli on the subject:

> *When the entire safety of our country is at stake, no consideration of what is just or unjust, merciful or cruel, praiseworthy or shameful, must intervene. On the contrary, every other consideration being set aside, that course alone must be taken which reserves the existence of the country and maintains its liberty.*[60]

As usual British admiral Jackie Fisher was more blunt. Hankey quotes him thus:

> *As Fisher used to say, 'You can no more tame war than you can tame hell!' The only laws of war that are of any value are those which are mutually beneficial, such as arrangements for the Red Cross, flags of truce, and for the treatment of prisoners. Even these are apt to break down. To attempt more than this is certain to lead to*

---

57    Fürbringer, *Legendary*, p. 6.
58    Spiegel, *U-202*, p. 58.
59    Peterson, *Propaganda*, pp. 78-79.
60    Machiavelli, *Discorsi*, cited in Hankey, *Supreme Command*, I, p. 352 onwards, Chapter 'Belligerent Rights'.

*mutual recrimination, where compromises fail and rules are broken, to prolong and embitter the war by exasperating public opinion on both sides, and to bring the whole fabric of international law into disrepute.*[61]

Ebert and Noske rejected Lüttwitz's demands and told him that they expected his resignation the next day. Instead of resigning, Lüttwitz went to Ehrhardt and asked whether he would be able to occupy Berlin that evening. Ehrhardt said he needed another day, but in the morning of 13 March he could be in the centre of Berlin with his men.[62] Lüttwitz gave the order, and Ehrhardt began his preparations. At this point, Lüttwitz brought Pabst's *Nationale Vereinigung* into the plot, and included Kapp and Ludendorff.

*On the day of the Kapp Putsch, a new movie was playing at the Marmorhaus on the Kurfürstendamm. It was a story of murder and madness. And it was to become immensely popular. It was called 'The Cabinet of Dr Cagliari'. All through the war, there had been a growing interest in the new medium of moving pictures. The number of German theatres showing these novelties grew from 28 in 1913 to 245 in 1919 The German government saw political possibilities in the phenomenon ... and agreed to establish the powerful Universum Film A. G. (Ufa) for the creation of propaganda films.*[63]

On the morning of 13 March, the Ehrhardt Brigade reached the Brandenburg Gate, where it was met by Lüttwitz, Ludendorff, Kapp and their followers.[64] Ludendorff claimed later that the meeting was accidental and that he was just out for a walk. The Reich Chancellery and the government quarter was occupied. Kapp declared himself *Reichskanzler* and formed a provisional government. Lüttwitz served as commander of the armed forces and Minister of Defence; von Trotha cabled naval stations to say that he had placed himself

---

61    Hankey, *Supreme Command*, I, p. 101. In 1911, a slightly penitent Fisher wrote, 'Perhaps I went a little too far when I said I would boil the prisoners in oil and murder the innocent in cold blood, etc, etc. But, it's quite silly not to make war damnable to the whole mass of your enemy's population, which of course is the secret of maintaining the right of capture of private property at sea ...'

62    Padfield, Dönitz, pp. 97-98. Friedrich, *Before the Deluge*, pp. 63-64.

63    Friedrich, *Before the Deluge*, pp. 64-65.

64    Waite, *Vanguard of Nazism*, Chapter VI, 'In The Service of Reaction', pp. 140-167.

at Kapp's disposal and expected that the 'Navy will continue to obey my orders'.[65]

*Kapp, founder of the Fatherland Party, an anonymous pamphleteer and unstable adventurer, has put himself at the head of [the government] as Chancellor. General Lüttwitz has treasonably gone over to him with the troops under his command and been rewarded with the appointment of Defence Minister ... It smacks more of farce than history. Berlin has evidently been taken over by the counter-revolutionary forces and the old Government has disappeared. Where to, nobody knows. The Social Democrats have proclaimed a general strike. That, it is to be hoped, will wring this gang's neck. Else the position would become extremely grave. If these people were to stay in the saddle, civil war, foreign intervention, and chaos would be almost inevitable.*[66]

The strike proclaimed by the fleeing government was 'more effective than anyone anticipated' and paralysed the country making it impossible for Kapp to govern. The Army refused to support the government, but all of the serving men, particularly in Kiel, were 'torn between their service duty and sympathy with family and friends supporting the strike'.[67] Kapp resigned on 17 March and fled to Sweden. He proved to be a 'leader of almost absurd incompetence, promulgating and rescinded instructions every day of this short five-day reign'.[68]

In Kiel, communist groups stormed the naval arsenal, killing the commanding officer and fighting broke out between them and the men of the torpedo boats until von Löwenfeld's brigade went into action. Lüttwitz tried to hold on for another day as head of a military dictatorship, but then resigned. He was offered an amnesty, a false passport and money to leave the country. Ehrhard was allowed to march his brigade out of Berlin. A boy in the crowd laughed as they passed and was attacked with rifle buts. Several bursts of machine guns were fired into the crowd.

At the same time, many *Freikorps* brigades marched to the Ruhr to put down a full-scale Communist revolution. The troops of the 'Red Ruhr' were well

---

65    Mueller, *Canaris*, p. 54.
66    Kessler, *Diaries*, 13/3/1920, pp. 41-42.
67    Padfield, *Dönitz*, p. 98.
68    Friedrich, *Before the Deluge*, p. 72.

organised and, at first, beat back the *Freikorps* and took Duisburg, Düsseldorf, Hamborn and Mülheim. There were ferocious battles at Chemnitz, Dresden, Gera, Gotha, Jena, Leipzig and Weimar. The insurrection was seen by the Right as heralding union with Russia and providing a 'springboard for world revolution and world socialism'. Red Army recruitment offices were opened on the streets.

> *The atrocities accompanying and following the campaign … matched previous patterns of behaviour that made the Freikorps so feared in Berlin, the Baltic and Bavaria the year before. Hundreds of Red Army captives were 'shot while attempting to escape'. Scores of civilians who had played no part in the uprising, but were merely Trade Union officials or thought to have leftist affiliations were rounded up and shot after appearing before illegal Freikorps courts-martial … The total casualties were never counted, but some indication of their scale can be estimated by the fact that Freikorps historian von Oertzen admitted that one thousand 'Reds' were shot in the first two days of the campaign. This, the last and most bloody full-scale military campaign waged by the Freikorps against fellow Germans, left an enduring legacy of hatred.*[69]

A special committee of the Reichstag was set up to investigate the navy's complicity in the Lüttwitz-Kapp putsch and 'some 172 officers, including von Trotha, either retired or were discharged, but on 31 May those officers deemed to have taken no part were reinstated'.[70]

In 1922, 2,500 veterans of the *Freikorps von Löwenfeld* were integrated into the grand total of 15,000 navy personnel allowed under the Treaty of Versailles, that is every sixth man in the Reichsmarine which meant the 'incorporation of strongly nationalistic and anti-republican attitudes in the inter-war navy'.[71]

The same legacy can be seen in the WW2 appellation *Freikorps Dönitz* for the entire submarine service of Nazi Germany.

---

69    Jones, *Birth of the Nazis*, Chapter 14, 'The Red Army of the Ruhr', pp. 192-202. Friedrich Wilhelm von Oertzen, *Die Deutschen Freikorps, 1918-1928.*

70    Padfield, *Dönitz*, p. 99.

71    Mulligan, *Sharks not Wolves*, pp. 220-21.

# 10

# MARX: POWER BEHIND THE THRONE

*[Marx was] the forgotten or the unknown man who was pulling the strings behind the scenes. A skilful diplomatic mediator with excellent links to the most influential men of his time in German business, politics, Jewry, and society. Marx was one of the best known and respected Berlin private bankers, with an active mind, full of vitality and energy, who enjoyed the highest esteem in the world of art and literature. Marx's annual income from thirteen positions on the supervisory boards of different companies and his own private bank was more than 250,000 Reichsmark.*[1]

Salomon Marx, a 'small chubby man', played a large part in the story of Erich Gerth, his son-in-law from 1919.[2] Salomon came from a wide-spread and successful Jewish business family. He was born in Schwerte near Dortmund in 1866, attended grammar school in Höxter and Soest, and studied law at

---

1    Alfred Hintz, 'Salomon Marx (1866-1936) - Industrieller, Bankier und Politiker', *Berlin in Geschichte und Gegenwart, Jahrbuch des Landesarchivs Berlin*, 2011, pp. 101-130.

2    The following material comes from four principal sources: [1] Erich Gerth's personnel files at the Berlin Foreign Ministry and kindly retrieved by Martina Nibbeling-Wriessnig following the good offices of Emanuele Ojetti of Rome (Auswärtiges Amt, Politisches Archiv, Gz: 117-251.09: IH 004386-7, Personalia, Vols. 1-2; IB 004388, Personnel Finances 'Persönliche Geldangelegenheiten', Vol. 1; IBV 004389, Personalia, Vol. 2) with additional material from Matthias Löhr, also of the Foreign Office; [2] LABO Entschädigungsamt, Berlin, Restitution File, Salomon Marx, 1956, researched by Renate Rüb, archivservice-berlin; [3] Hintz, above; and [4] 'Salomon Marx', Deutsches Biographisches Archiv (Neue Folge), Microfiche NE 859, p. 207. Translations from the German are by Cathrin Brockhaus-Clark.

Freiburg, Berlin and Marburg universities. He worked for the Deutsche Bank, partly in London.

There are two occupations for Salomon Marx in the Cologne address book at Ehrenfeld for 1896: one as a director of *Ehrenfelder Terraingesellschaft*, a real estate company; and another as an owner with Wilhelm Oldemeyer of *Oldemeyer, Marx and Company* factory which produced *papier maché* goods, folded boxes, packages for sugar cubes, and technical articles made from paper, cardboard and wrapping paper.

Marx sought to deliver cardboard articles to the military and to try to begin an export business into Russia. To facilitate this he opened a branch of Oldemeyer in Danzig, current Gdansk, his wife's home town, where he had family ties to a timber company, *Münsterberg*. These plans failed through a lack of skilled manpower and slow orders.

One of the political aims of the German empire at that time was the industrialisation of West Prussia and of the cities Danzig and Posen, current Poznań. In the midst of Marx's struggles, one of the leading Prussian politicians and civil servants, Gustav von Gossler, recognised a 'young, ideal candidate' to further the state policy. Gossler approached other industrialists in the Rhineland and, with an invested capital of 400,000 Reichsmark, Marx founded the company *Ostdeutsche Industriewerke Marx & Co.*

In April 1897, the *Nordische Elektrizitäts-Aktiengesellschaft* was founded in Gdansk with Marx as general director with a brief to build and operate electrical light and power plants, steel and roller mills. The company was successful, paying a five per cent dividend in 1897 and eight per cent in 1898. In the summer of 1897, the *Norddeutsche Elektrizitäts* bought the *Ostdeutsche Industriewerke* and, in 1898, the two companies merged under Marx´s leadership to form the *Nordische Elektrizitäts und Stahlwerke AG*.

After two successful years, one of its electricity subsidiaries collapsed threatening bankruptcy. Because of the political importance of Marx´s enterprises, Gossler and several Prussian politicians, including the Lord Mayor of Danzig, Clemens von Delbrück, and the Prussian Finance Minister, Count Georg von Rheinbaben, decided to support the business by raising a further two and a half million Reichsmark from the Prussian State Bank.

The Kaiser asked Fürst Henckel von Donnersmarck, the magnate of the Upper Silesian heavy industry, for his views about the Danzig recovery plan. Donnersmarck criticised Marx and the other businessmen from the Rhineland involved in the project for their lack of understanding of local conditions. However, others like Maximilian Harden, the Jewish intellectual, publisher, journalist, actor and critic, praised Marx's achievements. In correspondence between Harden and Walther Rathenau, heir to AEG, the leading electrical company, and later Foreign Minister, Marx was repeatedly mentioned positively.

Harden said, 'the little Marx is *in summa* a jolly good fellow'; Marx is 'very good, tough and calm'. Rathenau said he was 'full of personal respect' and was pleased that 'the little one', 'the capital little fellow', had managed to secure the deal with the government to save his company.

In 1906, Marx became a member of the industrial council of the *Darmstädter Bank* in Berlin. He set up as an independent banker in 1912, founding *Salomon Marx*. By 1910, Marx was travelling as 'Consul Marx'. On 21 February 1913, he was appointed Honorary Consul to Berlin representing the Grand Duchy of Oldenburg, a town in Lower Saxony in North-West Germany near Bremen. He was also one of twelve recipients of the Leopold Order of the Principality of Lippe which he received for 'special merits'.[3]

Marx changed the name and status of his bank in 1920 to *S Marx & Co* and then in 1923 with a Jewish business partner, Alexander Elfer, to the *Internationale Handelsbank KGaA*, situated at Jägerstraße 20 in Berlin. The chairman of the supervisory board of the *Handelsbank* was Minister of State Friedrich Wilhelm von Loebell who became a 'big-name' referee for Erich Gerth's application to the Foreign Office.[4]

'Consul Marx' belonged to numerous supervisory boards of German companies including *Deutsche Bank*, founded in 1870 as a specialist bank in foreign trade to combat British and French dominance in the world at large; the major *Engelhardt Brewery*, founded in Berlin in 1860; *Groterjan & Co*, banking and insurance; the *Portland-Cement-Werke AG* in Schwanebeck, and *Carl Lindström*, a Berlin-based record company, the forerunner of Parlophone, later recording label for *The Beatles*.

---

3    ordensmuseum.de/historische-oe/der-furstlich-lippischer-leopold-orden, accessed 10/2017.

4    Loebell had one loose connection with Erich's past. Erich's father, Ernst, was a pioneer of Berlin's horse-drawn trams. Loebell was the driving force behind the construction of the Brandenburg urban railway with its five radial, networked routes into Berlin.Ihm zu Ehren erhielt auch eine Lokomotive den Namen „Landrat von Loebell", die am 25. März 1904 den Eröffnungszug der Strecke zog. In Loebell's honour, a locomotive was named 'District of Loebell', which in 1904 pulled the opening train. From 1901 to 1912, Loebell was chairman of the railway company (wikipedia).

The firm of Lindström, together with *Deutsche Bank* which was always close to Marx's investments, three private banks, and the heavy industry concern of Fürst von Donnersmarck, and Robert Bosch, controlled the majority of shares of Ufa, *Universum Film*, headquartered in Babelsberg.[5] The board of directors also contained a 'respectable cross-section of the Wilhemite *haute bourgeoisie* with especially strong representation from Prusso-German financial and industrial capital'.

Ufa was founded in 1917 with Ludendorff's direct involvement as a patriotic propaganda tool for the army command and the imperial government. Ludendorff's strategy was to establish German control over film supply in Central Europe, as well as in large parts of eastern and south-eastern Europe, and to influence the 'volatile mood of the people'. The directors of Ufa bought the 'Haus Vaterland' at the Potsdamer Platz in Berlin, a six-storey, pleasure dome with bars, restaurants and entertainment venue, 'a beacon of commercial kitsch'. Salomon Marx was seen as the 'founder' of the Haus Vaterland because of his considerable financial investment.

During the 1914 war, as a financial expert, Marx concerned himself with how the costs of war could be met and published his conclusions.[6] On 17 December 1917, he addressed a group of business leaders in Rhineland Westphalia and recommended that the repayment of war debts be postponed. On 30 October 1918, leading representatives of German finance capital, led by representatives of the *Deutsche Bank*, met at the Hotel Adlon in Berlin and issued a statement welcoming political reforms and calling for an immediate peace.[7]

Can one doubt that Marx attended?

In his memoirs, Eduard Stadtler, founder of the Anti-Bolshevik party, described a dinner party on 24 October 1918 at the 'elegant upper middle class mansion of Consul Salomon Marx'. Stadtler had advocated that year the creation of a national socialist dictatorship; Anton Drexler, the founder of the Nazi Party, attended Stadtler's lectures in Berlin.[8] Among those attending

---

5    Kreimeier, *UFA Story*, pp. 1, 30.
6    Marx, *Die Deckung unserer Kriegskosten*, 'The Coverage of our War Costs' (Berlin 1917), copy. National Library.
7    Kitchen, *Silent Dictatorship*, p. 266.
8    Stadtler claimed to have encouraged Waldemar Pabst in the murder of Karl Liebknecht and Rosa Luxemburg (Stadtler, *Life Memories*, Vol. 3), pp. 46-49.

was Kurt von Kleefeld, a baptised Jew like Salomon Marx, founder of the *Hansabund*, an economic organisation for German merchants and industrialists based in Berlin, and brother-in-law of Gustav Stresemann, briefly Weimar Chancellor in 1923, Foreign Minister for six years, and winner of the Nobel Peace Prize.[9]

After dinner, the men withdrew for political talks to the gentlemen's parlour where Marx explained how the progressive wing of the conservatives should merge with the progressive powers of the national liberals with the aim of forming a new political movement to carry out state reforms.

Stadtler, however, pleaded to marry conservative Prussian militaristic ideals with the acceptable socialist content of the revolution. Marx was impressed with Stadtler's views and asked him if he would write down his thoughts in a speech. Stadtler agreed, gave Marx the manuscript eight days later and received a fee of 200 Reichsmark. At the beginning of November 1918, Marx gave the speech written by Stadtler at the packed Aeroclub and later printed the lecture as a brochure titled 'The organic principle of the state' under his own name.[10]

'The main task of the new party would be to help restore and strengthen German nationalism … In the fight against Anglo-Saxon capitalism and imperialism and the Bolshevism of the East, Germany would emerge as the power of culture based on a true people's state … Despite the defeat [in WW1], Germany would be politically ahead of its peers in the world.'

Salomon Marx was a member of the small initial founding group of the German National People's Party, the *Deutschnationale Volkspartei* (DNVP).[11] Before the rise of Hitler's National Socialist German Workers' Party (NSDAP), the DNVP was the major conservative and nationalist party in Weimar Germany, an alliance of nationalists, reactionary monarchists, anti-Semitic elements and the völkisch groups, and supported by the Pan-German League.[12] The party's right-wing diversity was both its strength and, eventually, as a disparate coalition, its weakness. Marx joined the executive committee of the party in

---

9    The Peace Prize of 1926 was received jointly with the French politician Aristide Briand for work on reconciliation between Germany and France which resulted in the Locarno agreements of October 1925.

10   Marx, *Das organische Staatsprinzip*, 1919, Deutsche National Bibliothek.

11   Hertzman, 'Founding of the DNVP', p. 26, fn. 9.

12   Walker, 'Nationalist People's Party', p. 627.

December 1918, promising to finance the party with several hundred thousand Reichsmark of his own money and was suggested as the party's treasurer. Marx decided to leave the DNVP in February 1919 because of the anti-Semitic propaganda supported by some its members and also an insulting letter by party leader Oskar Hergt addressing 'the gentlemen of Jewish descent in the party'.

It is worth reflecting on the extent of Salomon Marx's known contacts in the 1920s. Salomon kept close contact with Wilhelm Marx, German lawyer, Catholic politician and a member of the Centre Party who was twice Chancellor from 1923 to 1925 and again from 1926 to 1928. Salomon Marx was cousin to Wilhelm Marx's father and this explains how Wilhelm came to be another referee later offered by Erich Gerth.[13] Marx was closely associated with the industrial and Jewish giants of the day: Fürst Henckel von Donnersmarck, Gustav von Gossler, Maximilian Harden, Friedrich Wilhelm von Loebell, Walther Rathenau of AEG, and the scions of the household-name-firms Bosch, Henckel, Krupp and Siemens and the leading figures of heavy industry in Rhineland-Westphalia like Hugo Stinnes, owner of the Woermann and East German shipping lines, who organised the coal production in Belgium after the invasion at the request of Ludendorff; Emil Kirdorf, known as the 'Chimney Baron' for having Europe's largest coal mine enterprise; Ernst and Conrad Borsig, railway and locomotive magnates.[14]

Through long-term friendship, Salomon was close to Wilhelm Canaris, also an intimate friend of Erich Gerth, and established as a leading figure in the murky world of naval and national politics, and, through Erich, Admiral Adolf von Trotha, head of the post-war naval office in Berlin. These anti-republican, anti-socialist figures, introduced Salomon to Philipp Scheidermann of the SDP, to Prince Otto II of Salm-Horstmann, the anti-Semitic president of the Navy Association, the *Flottenverein*, and leading Pan-German, and to Kurt von

---

13    *LABO*, Berlin, file Salomon Marx/304.641, pp. C4-6, 'Duplicate of prosecution papers against Walter Firnhaber and Dr. Eduard Marx, Berlin 28/7/1942.

14    In 1910, August Borsig, father of Ernst and Conrad, was one of the sixty richest men in Prussia. After the war, he financially supported the *Freikorps* Ehrhardt Brigade, helped found the Anti-Bolshevik League, and promoted Hitler and National Socialism. Stinnes was known as the *Inflationskönig*, 'Inflation King', for borrowing vast sums in Reichsmark and repaying them when the currency collapsed. At the time of his early death in 1924, his empire held about 4,500 companies and 3,000 manufacturing plants. The company collapsed in 1930 and merged with AEG.

Kleefeld, Gustav Stresemann, and the radical-conservative agitator Eduard Stadtler.

Marx's same-street neighbours at Brückenallee 29 in Berlin included Leo Arons, physicist and social democratic politician at number nine; Dietrich Bonhoeffer, the theologian later persecuted by the Nazis at number five; Botho zu Eulenberg, Prussian Minister President and Interior Minister, number two; Walter de Gruyter, publisher, number nine, Else Lasker-Schüler, writer and artist, at number sixteen with her studio at number twenty-two. The quarter was home to many other wealthy Jewish bankers and merchants, politicians and intellectuals.

In December 1921, Helene, Salomon Marx's wife and Eva Gerth's mother, died in Berlin.[15] No details are known, but just over a year later, Salomon must have caused a stir when he remarried to Charlotte Mayer-Schalburg, twenty years his junior, only three weeks after her divorce to her first husband became effective.[16] Charlotte, known as Lotte, was just ten years older than Marx's own daughter, Eva. Lotte's husband was Robert Mayer, a Royal Lieutenant, son of Royal General Lieutenant August Mayer. Robert and Charlotte married in 1906 and, in 1920, hyphenated their surname to include his mother's maiden name.

In 1928, Salomon Marx took over the Nordische Bank in Berlin. In 1931, the Marxes moved home five miles in the south of Berlin from Brückenallee 29 to Lessingstraße 31, where they were joined by Eva's brother, Salomon's unmarried son, Dr. Eduard Marx.

---

15    Helene Marx, née Schirmacher, born Danzig, 13/1/1869, died 5/12/1921, Berlin (Einwohnermeldekartei StA XIII a, Nr. 1977).

16    Charlotte Sommer, age twenty, married Robert Rolf Friedrich Ludwig Mayer, born 25/3/1883, died 1976, 15/10/1906, Berlin Charlottenburg. Surname change to Mayer-Schalburg 6/1920. Divorced 13/1/1923, registered 11/2/1923, five days after Charlotte's remarriage to Salomon Marx (Einwohnermeldekartei StA XIII a, Nr. 1977).

# 11

# CANARIS: REARMAMENT

Wilhelm Canaris continued his u-boat trade missions. In 1924, he shipped aboard the steamer *Rhineland* for Japan. His instructions were to bring to fruition previous sales to the Japanese of sketches of u-cruisers and minelaying u-boats and to secure construction orders that would be supervised by German naval architects. The next year, and the following, Canaris was back in Spain on a similar task where he took time to meet Max Bauer, who fled there after the Kapp Putsch and was now military adviser to King Alphonso XIII.

*The long-term value of Spanish-German co-operation cannot be underestimated. The Spanish Navy placed modern submarines at the disposal of the German naval forces for testing and manoeuvres. For the future German production of u-boats, these preliminary steps and the fact that Spain helped Germany keep up with new developments in submarine technology would prove of decisive importance.*[1]

On 8 and 9 August 1927, Kurt Wenkel, financial editor of *Berliner Tageblatt*, investigating the bankruptcy affairs of the film company Phoebus, stumbled on and published details of an extraordinary clandestine network of companies funded since 1923 through Kapitänleutnant Walter Lohmann's office at the Navy High Command.[2]

---

1    Mueller, *Canaris*, pp. 63-71.
2    Padfield, *Dönitz*, pp. 117-18.

Kreimeier, the biographer of Ufa, estimated that ten million Reichsmark were transferred from Lohmann's secret fund to Phoebus to be used for rearmament.[3] 'The reach of these funds was considerable covering the naval intelligence service; submarine development with a bubble-free torpedo, aided by IvS and secret funds from Krupp in Kiel, Wesser in Bremen and the Vulcan Shipyard in Hamburg; aircraft and small boat production; and pilot and future officer training.[4]

The background was straightforward. Lohmann was 'imbued with a mixture of too much zeal, arrogance and false patriotism, had become involved in a number of madcap schemes … He continued to expand his armaments empire and had so lost sight of what he was doing that it finally collapsed'.[5]

Shortly before the Lohmann Affair broke, Canaris warned his superiors that matters were out of control. Undeterred, at the height of the ensuing uproar, Pfeiffer, Canaris and Spindler held a meeting on the funding necessary for Canaris' Spanish u-boat project and four million Reichsmark were signed off from the Navy's own construction budget. The following spring, ex-u-boat commander Werner Fürbringer and his men, having carried out trials on a second German-designed submarine built for Turkey by Krupp's Rotterdam yard, delivered the boats to Constantinople, and both Fürbringer and his chief engineer stayed on to guide the Turkish u-boat school.

The cover-up mounted, first by the navy and then by the government, was extensive and to some degree successful in that the full extent and reach of the rearmament funding was not discovered.

The government through Chancellor Wilhelm Marx tried to suppress knowledge of the government's involvement. Dönitz was involved in preparing the Navy's defence for the Reichstag. The German navy's dummy company, *Mentor Bilanz*, was liquidated in 1928 and a new covert operator 'Igewit', *Ingenieurbüro für Wirtschaft und Tecknik*, was formed as the Admiralty's u-boat technical section in such a way that the Navy and Government would not be compromised.

Lohmann was sacrificed, as previously agreed with him, but was never prosecuted for fear the whole story would come out. He died, impoverished,

---

3    Kreimeier, *UFA Story*, p. 166.

4    *CIA Report*: 'The Lohmann Affair', Studies in Intelligence 4, Heft 2, Spring 1960: A31-A38. RG059.

5    Mueller, *Canaris*, pp. 73-74.

shortly afterwards. Other famous heads to roll, most mentioned previously in this book, were Defence Minister Otto Gessler, Pfeiffer, Werth, von Löwenfeld and the navy chief, Admiral Hans Zenker.

'What is clear is that these were cosmetic changes.'

# 12

# MARX: FILMS FOR PROPAGANDA

In 1927, with Phoebus bankrupt, government-owned *Universum Film A. G.* (Ufa) also experienced financial difficulties and had to borrow money from the American film companies, Paramount and Metro-Goldwin-Meyer (MGM). It was Lohmann's concern about America's fifty per cent ownership of Ufa that had led him to support Phoebus in order to maintain a major German-controlled presence in film production.

Salomon Marx's pet project, Haus Vaterland, was used as a guarantee for a four million dollar loan. Marx was instrumental in negotiating the purchase of Ufa by Alfred Hugenberg, the mega industrialist from the steel and armament firm, Krupp, in Essen.[1] Only five of the original founders of Ufa continued as members of the supervisory board under Hugenberg´s chairmanship. Salomon Marx was one of them, taking responsibility for finance and for maintaining relations with the Americans.[2]

In the early 1930s, Salomon and Lotte Marx, travelled several times to the United States on Ufa's business, and to holiday in Funchal, the latter also a holiday destination of Salomon and his first wife, Helene, and their two children in 1910 aboard the *Eleonore Woermann*. In 1928, Phoebus, its business

---

1    Hintz, 'Salomon Marx', pp. 111-13. Walker, 'Nationalist People's Party', p. 632.
2    Kreimeier, *UFA Story*, pp. 160-61.

mortally wounded, became dependent on United Artists (UA) and, as with Ufa, on MGM.[3]

It was only a matter of time before the film industry would attract a German national front 'much given to chauvinist rhetoric to do battle against the omnipotence of the dollar'.

The overlap between Ufa and Phoebus, albeit fierce competitors at the production and distribution level, can now be seen with joint backing from senior industrialists, German banks and American film dollars.

Hugenberg, together with Hugo Stinnes, Emil Kirdorf and, significantly, Wilhelm Beukenberg of Phoenix, formed the *Wirtschaftliche Gesellschaft*, 'The Economic Society', as a private association to administer a trust fund derived from the Ruhr industrialists' discretionary accounts to 'countermand threatening dangers in the economic and social fields'.[4] In January 1928, Ernst Hugo Correll, formerly sole executive of the politically and economically destroyed Phoebus, was appointed Ufa's production chief.[5]

Two years later, Ufa, now the greatest German motion film company, produced one of Germany's greatest films, *The Blue Angel*, starring Marlene Dietrich. Correll identified totally with the nationalistic principles of Ufa's senior executives and co-operated with the National Socialists after 1933.

*Alfred Hugenberg who became Ufa's master in March 1927 is integral to the wider story of Germany's political direction, as is Marx as his financial right arm.*[6]

When still an unknown young attorney, Hugenberg founded the *Allgemeine Deutsche Verband*, the 'Universal German Union', which in 1894 changed its name to the *Alldeutsche Verband*, the 'Pan-German League', the great protagonist for Tirpitz's navy and aggressive world economic expansion. In 1909, he made a big step up when he became chief executive of Krupp after its owner, Friedrich Krupp, committed suicide when his letters to his Italian lovers were published. Krupp left the company to his daughter, Bertha, but the Kaiser felt that Bertha, as a woman, could not be up to the job.

---

3    Kreimeier, *UFA Story*, p. 129.
4    Leopold, *Hugenberg*, pp. 7-8.
5    Kreimeier, *UFA Story*, p. 129.
6    Kreimeier, *UFA Story*, p. 158.

Hugenberg had a long-term grudge against the communist Karl Liebknecht, the Social Democrat Reichstag member.[7] Liebknecht exposed industrial espionage by Hugenberg at Krupp in October 1912. A civil servant at the war ministry and four arsenal lieutenants supplied Krupp with extracts from contracts by competing firms. The firm's management did not 'even try to deny the allegations of bribery and industrial espionage with Krupp arguing in a press article that any attack on the firm of Krupp was an attack on the ability of the German state to wage war'. Several junior employees were convicted of corruption, but Hugenberg was never indicted. The sentences that were handed down were 'very lenient'.[8]

Krupp was also charged at this time with orchestrating an international armaments ring from 1901, called the Harvey United Steel Company, which was designed to 'remove all excuse for competition between the major international armament firms in their united aim of encouraging the growth of jingoism, that the jingoism of one nation react on the jingoism of another to the profit of the armament manufacturer'.[9]

Harvey's directors included representatives from Germany: Krupp, Dillingen; Britain: Vickers & Maxim, Beardmore, Coventry Ordnance, Armstrong Whitworth, Cammell Laird; France: St Chamond Steel, Chantillon-Commentry; Schneider, Cresuot; and Italy: Societa Degli Alti Forni Fondiere ed Acciaiene de Terni.

As the industry's trade journal commented, 'It is the idlest of delusions to imagine that any nation is going to forego a quarter of a century of preparation and expenditure without trying whether it can recover in war something of what it has spent in peace.'[10]

In September 1914, Hugenberg dusted off the aims of the Pan-German League and, in collaboration with its then chairman Heinrich Class, prepared an extensive memorandum delivered to the Kaiser suggesting concrete war aims:

*The ultimate goal was the security of the German people, security from future attacks and security for internal development. Germany needed a colonial empire to supply*

---

7    Leopold, *Hugenberg*, p. 4.
8    Murray, *Krupp's International Armaments Ring*, p. 182.
9    Murray, *Krupp's International Armaments Ring*, Preface, pp. xiii, 174-75.
10   *Arms and Explosives*, 2/1894.

*her with raw materials, a market for surplus products, and also a war indemnity to subsidise a system of rural colonisation and urban improvement. Belgium would have to remain under German control by right of conquest; France would have to cede valuable territory from the Swiss border to the channel coast; British sea power would have to be broken; and Russia would have to be confined to the boundaries existing at the time of Peter the Great. In addition to expanding its African colonies, Germany would have to unite central Europe (including Scandinavia, Finland, Rumania and Bulgaria) into a single economic unit.*[11]

Salomon Marx aided, one could say led, but undoubtedly under Hugenberg's direct instruction, the taking of the German film industry into ultimately Nazi control. The 'Spiro Plan' of 1932, drafted primarily by Marx, cemented the centralisation of the film industry and 'asserted the priority of production over distribution, and argued for a state-controlled economy that would work against the forces of free competition'.[12] The plan favoured large premiere theatres owned by the big companies to the detriment of small theatres obliged to book films 'blind' for allocated times. It was a 'seamless transition from a media industry based on private capital to an essentially state-owned one that remained committed to the profit principle'.

The combination of Hugenberg's preference for, and trust in, Marx at Ufa, and from Marx's delivery under direction of a 'Nazi-ready film industry', suggests that the two men's politics were similar. Hugenberg was notoriously intolerant of alternative views. There was a noticeable overlap between their business partners and dinner guests like Kirdorf, Stinnes, Albert Vögler and Freiherr Hans von und zu Löwenstein.[13]

Hugenberg 'concentrated the financial resources of the Ruhr and made his office a central clearing house for the distribution of immense political funds'. Hugenberg, and by implication Marx, sought the total elimination of democracy and socialism.[14]

---

11    Leopold, *Hugenberg*, p. 6, citing extensive correspondence between Hugenberg and Class and, particularly, '*Denkschrift betreffend die national und sozialpolitischen Ziele des deutschen Volkes im gegenwärtigen Kriege*', (Als Handschrift Gedruckt).

12    'Spiro', *Spitzenorganisation der Deutschen Filmwirtschaft*, the 'Council of the German Film Industry' (Kreimeier, *UFA Story*), pp. 184, 193-94.

13    Leopold, *Hugenberg*, pp. 4-5.

14    Leopold, *Hugenberg*, pp. xv-xvi.

'Hugenberg had always been an outspoken nationalist and was resolutely opposed to any move that might be interpreted as a gesture of reconciliation to the hated Weimar Republic'.[15] He believed that only a patriarchal approach that 'viewed the corporation and the state as extended families could prosper the nation'. In industry, the entrepreneur as lord of his house had to have ultimate authority. In government, the Kaiser had to be a 'strong and determined leader who would decree the best for his subjects and rule with an iron hand'.

Hugenberg initially tried to work out of the limelight. During the inter-war period, he became the country's leading media proprietor. He patronised the radical masses who believed fervently in the nation state through his direction of regional newspapers, news agencies and film. He was a dominant figure in nationalist politics as leader of the National People's Party (DNVP) which, while never taking power in its own right, at least joined coalitions, briefly in 1925, but principally to join the cabinet in 1927 under Chancellor Wilhelm Marx.[16] The DNVP reached a peak of seats in 1924 with 103 places in the Reichstag, second only to the Social Democrats. The party's lists contained many famous names, including from among these pages, Karl Helfferich, Paul von Lettow-Vorbeck, Freiherr Hans von und zu Löwenstein, Eduard Stadler and Alfred von Tirpitz.

Hugenberg pursued policies through his business and private life that considerably eased Adolf Hitler's rise to power and he served briefly in Hitler's first cabinet in 1933.

'The national opposition which ultimately triumphed was the tragic result of such tactics'.[17] The DNVP viewed the Versailles Treaty as a national disgrace, signed by traitors, which should be repealed; wished to restore the monarchy; and sought the reacquisition of all lost territories and colonies.

15    Jones , 'Greatest Stupidity', p. 64.
16    Walker, 'Nationalist People's Party', p. 628.
17    Leopold, *Hugenberg*, p. xvi.

# 13

# MARX: MURDER, MURDER, EVERYWHERE

There was a wider background of murder and secret conspiracies to this period of which the killing of Liebknecht and Luxemburg was but a part. Many of these deaths had close links to Salomon Marx, and sometimes Erich and Eva Gerth, not as perpetrators, but in the loss of social, religious and business contacts.

If the Weimar Republic failed through a lack of leadership, it was partly because the assassins 'cut down so many of the men who might have provided that leadership'.[1]

A month after Liebknecht and Luxemburg's killing by the *Freikorps*, Kurt Eisner was shot in the back while on his way to the Bavarian parliament building in Munich to resign as prime minister.[2] Bavarian nationalist Anton Graf von Arco auf Valley drew the short straw in a lottery with colleagues for the honour of the task.[3] Valley 'was so covered in wounds inflicted by the infuriated mob and the red guards that he was left for dead', but recovered.

Eisner was a journalist who organised the socialist revolution that overthrew the Wittelsbach monarchy in Bavaria, and declared a free state and a republic. He had spent spells in prison for criticising the Kaiser and for inciting strikes.

---

1    Friedrich, *Before the Deluge*, pp. 117-18.
2    Murdered 21/2/1919.
3    Princess Ferdinand, *Through Four Revolutions*, pp. 312-13.

He was also editor of *Vorwärts* after the death of Karl Liebknecht's father, Wilhelm.[4] After Eisner's death, a short-lived Bavarian Soviet Republic followed until ruthlessly suppressed by the *Freikorps*.

In the winter of the same year, Hugo Hasse was shot and severely injured on the steps of the Reichstag by Johann Voss, a deranged leather worker, and died a month later.[5] Hasse and Friedrich Ebert co-chaired the Council of the People's Deputies after the German revolution of 1918-1919; Hasse was later leader of the Independent Socialist Party. He defended social democrats in many legal cases including Karl Liebknecht after he published *Militarismus und Anti-Militarismus* in 1907. Hasse organised the anti-war rallies of the SPD in 1914, and with Liebknecht argued against war credits.

A year after the *Freikorps*-managed Kapp putsch misfired in March 1920, Matthias Erzberger, finance minister, was shot to death while walking in the Black Forest.[6] His greatest and most tragic legacy would always be his signature on the armistice for which he was never forgiven by the extreme right.

The murder was master-minded by Manfred von Killinger who recruited two members of the ultra-nationalist death squad, 'Operation Consul', Heinrich Tillessen and Heinrich Schulz, former navy officers and members of the disbanded Ehrhardt Brigade.

Erzberger had a varied career, leader of the Catholic Centrum Party, pre-dating future Chancellor Wilhelm Marx, and confidant of previous chancellor Bethmann.[7] It was always Erzberger's plan to use a German victory to gain control of the European continent 'for all time'. Tuchman called him a 'shrewd and able opportunist who represented whatever opinion was dominant ... a political flexibility unseen in Europe since Talleyrand'. He had 'no convictions, only appetites'. Erzberger served as chairman of the Armistice Commission and achieved other important legacies including new taxation measures heralding a redistribution of the tax burden in favour of the less-well-off. This particularly upset the political right-wing. Erzberger also stabilised the national

---

4    Liebknecht's family descended from Martin Luther. While Wilhelm Liebknecht lived in exile in London through the 1850s, he joined the Communist League and became an intimate friend of the family of Karl Marx (Roth, *Social Democrats*), p. 49.

5    Shot 8/10/1919, died 7/11/1919.

6    Murdered 26/8/1921.

7    Tuchman, *August 1914*, pp. 360-61.

finances and nationalised the railways which began, as a result and for the first time, to make a profit.

Within a few weeks in the summer of 1922, three close associates of Salomon Marx were attacked and one of them killed. The first was Philipp Scheidemann, joint chairman of the SDP parliamentary group with Hugo Hasse, who was killed the previous winter. It was Scheidemann who made the impromptu speech from a Reichstag balcony after the abdication of the Kaiser.

'The old and rotten, the monarchy has collapsed. The new may live. Long live the German Republic.'

Scheidemann formed the first democratically elected government, but resigned a few months later because of the harsh terms of the Versailles Treaty. He was the purported quiet support of Salomon Marx's poster calling for the murder of Liebknecht. Scheidemann was hated by the right who coined the term *Scheidemanner* as a derogatory terms for Weimar supporters.

In June 1922, Scheidemann was attacked with prussic acid in a blinding attempt.[8] 'He survived, but lived with his scars.'[9] In 1926, Scheidemann exposed the clandestine co-operation between the *Reichswehr*, the post-Kaiser central military organisation in Germany until 1935, and the Red Army which was in violation of the Treaty of Versailles; this negotiation brought down the third cabinet of chancellor Wilhelm Marx.

Maximilian Harden, was initially the crusading editor of *Zukunft*, 'Future', and became an influential Jewish intellectual. He was godfather to Salomon Marx's daughter Eleonore and publicly praised Marx's business achievements. At first a monarchist, elitist, anti-democrat, anti-egalitarianist, Harden became a fierce critic of the Kaiser and his entourage and made open accusations of homosexual behaviour, then a criminal offence in Germany. These charges led to numerous trials and did 'sustained damage to the House of Hohenzollern'.[10]

Harden supported the invasion of Belgium and demanded that Germany take over most of Europe after winning the war. 'Ibsen and Strindberg were his literary heroes; Nietzsche and the new prophets of Social Darwinism his philosophical guides.'

After the war, Harden became a pacifist and supported the republic. In July 1922, Harden was beaten half to death with a heavy steel rod; he died

8    Attacked 4/6/1922; died 29/11/1939.
9    Friedrich, *Before the Deluge*, p. 118.
10   Volkov, *Rathenau*, p. 44.

five years later.[11] His assailants were *Freikorps* members Bert Weichardt and Albert Wilhelm Grenz who claimed that they had been incensed by Harden's writings. Grenz was imprisoned for four years, Weichardt less.

The third attack shocked the country.

Foreign Minister Walther Rathenau was machine gunned as he was driven in his open-top car from his home to the Foreign Office in Wilhelmstraße.[12] His murderers then threw a hand grenade into the car for good measure. It was another murder by 'Operation Consul', led by Hermann Ehrhardt.[13] Rathenau had been warned many times about a pending attack, most significantly in May 1922 by Eugenio Pacelli, the papal nuncio, who had been tipped off by a priest.[14]

Rathenau's friend and biographer, Count Kessler, felt that 'not since the assassination of Abraham Lincoln has the death of a statesman so shaken a whole nation'.[15] Over a million people marched in Berlin in homage, 150,000 in Munich and Chemnitz, 100,000 in Hamburg, Breslau, Elberfeld and Essen.

As a regular dinner partner, one must assume that Rathenau also met Erich Gerth during his frequent visits to Brückenallee with Eva. Rathenau was killed in June 1922 and Gerth wrote his application to join the Foreign Office that December. Was Rathenau an inspiration for Gerth's choice of career, a mentor even? Foreign Office attachés, Gerth's designation next year, stood guard as Rathenau's coffin lay in state in the Reichstag.[16]

There was a possible slight personal reason for a close private discussion between the two. Gerth's father, Ernst, was a founding manager of Berlin's first horse-drawn tram. Rathenau, as a young man, superintended the introduction of electric trams in Genoa and his own conglomerate bought a streetcar firm in Madrid.[17]

Rathenau's father, Emil, bought the European rights to Edison's electric light patent in the first step to becoming one of Germany's most

11    Attacked 3/7/1922; died 30/10/1927.
12    Murdered 24/6/1922.
13    Martin Sabrow, 'Der Rathenaumord: Rekonstruktion einer Verschwörung gegen die Republik von Weimar', *Schriftenreihe der Vierteljahrshefte für Zeitgeschichte*, Issue 69, Munich, Oldenburg, 1994. Kessler, *Rathenau*, pp. 367-68.
14    Dalin, *Myth of Hitler's Pope*, p. 51.
15    Kessler, *Rathenau*, p. 380.
16    Kessler, *Rathenau*, p. 379.
17    Kessler, *Rathenau*, p. 360.

successful entrepreneurs, the renowned general manager of the *Allgemeine Elektrizitätsgesellschaft* (AEG), an innovator on a world scale, a system builder and an extremely rich and powerful man.[18] Maximilian Harden saw in him 'the Bismarck of Germany's industrial empire'. Walther Rathenau, the younger son and the least favoured by his father, was a student at the Wilhelm-Gymnasium in the wealthy Tiergarten district of Berlin, the classical sister of the Gerths' own school. After a shaky start in business, Walther came into his own. By 1904, he was officially involved on the boards of 107 companies, twenty-one of them foreign.

In 1907, Rathenau's growing commercial reputation saw him invited to join a team to visit Germany's African colonies.[19] His first report entitled 'The Development of the German East African Colony' was presented to the Kaiser in November and gave an overview of the chances for economic growth. It also discussed the failures and achievements of the German administration.

His second report on South West Africa was much less well received and was banned from publication. Lieutenant-General Lothar von Trotha was sent to South West Africa with a military force to deal with the Herrero tribe who were protesting against the theft of cattle lands by German settlers. Trotha introduced a policy of not merely subjugating the Herreros, but of eliminating them.[20]

'The handling of the Herreros', wrote Rathenau, 'involved the greatest atrocity brought about by German military policy.'

The Kaiser ennobled seven Jews during his reign, but never Rathenau. In addition to these seven, there were a number of converted Jews among these men of commerce and industry who accounted for a growing proportion of those given a 'von'.[21]

Rehabilitated by necessity by 1914 as an influential member of the international capitalist structure, Rathenau was a visiting friend of both the Kaiser and Chancellor Bethmann, who lived close by.

Rathenau wrote, 'Three hundred men, all acquainted with each other, control the economic destiny of the Continent.'[22]

---

18    Volkov, *Rathenau*, p. 9.
19    Volkov, *Rathenau*, pp. 67-71.
20    Heal, *The War of The Raven.*
21    Clarke, *Kaiser Wilhelm*, pp. 351-2.
22    Rosenberg, *Imperial Germany*, p. 39. Friedrich, *Before the Deluge*, pp. 99-100.

Rathenau played a key role in convincing the War Ministry to set up the War Materials Department (KRA) of which he was put in charge in August 1914. KRA focussed on raw materials threatened by the British blockade as well as supplies from occupied Belgium and France. It set prices and regulated the distribution to vital war industries and this success of Rathenau's work went a long way to extending Germany's ability to stay in the war.

After the war, Rathenau's wife, Edith, entertained lavishly in their elegant villa, holding open house on Sunday afternoons, where the entire economic and cultural elite of the capital, gathered for food, but more especially for lively and brilliant conversation.[23]

It was here, in Königsallee, as well as at his own 'at-homes', that Salomon Marx, and Erith and Eva Gerth, mixed freely.

Rathenau continued to be affected by the insults 'hurled at him by the radical parliamentary right wing party, the *Deutschnationale*, led in the Reichstag by Rathenau's old war-time rival, Karl Helfferich'.[24] By the end of 1921, 'expressions of hostility became ever more threatening'.

*Day by day speeches in the Reichstag and the various Diets [by the Nationalists led by the former Imperial Vice-Chancellor, Karl Helfferich], leading articles, vast popular meetings, pilloried him as the Jew responsible for the depths of shame to which Germany had been brought and for the ruin of the German middle classes. In the imagination of millions of impoverished and famished Germans, Rathenau became a sort of arch-traitor, in league with the Jews, the Bolsheviks, and the Entente to give the death-blow to Germany. An Upper Silesian semi-military organisation, Selbstschutz, used to tramp the roads singing, 'God damn Walther Rathenau. Shoot him down, the dirty Jew.'[25]*

Two months after signing the Treaty of Rapallo, which renounced German territorial claims against Russia from World War I, Rathenau was assassinated. During his last motor trip, he was passed by a Mercedes touring car with Ernst Werner Techow behind the wheel and Leutnant Erwin Kern and Hermann Fischer on the backseats. Kern opened fire with the sub-machinegun at close range, Fischer threw the hand grenade. Also in the plot were Techow's younger

---

23   Volkov, *Rathenau*, p. 57.
24   Volkov, *Rathenau*, pp. 197-98.
25   Kessler, *Rathenau*, p. 365. Volkov, *Rathenau*, p. 197, 'uniformed youth adorned with large swastikas'.

brother, Hans Gerd Techow, future writer Ernst von Salomon, and Willi Günther, aided and abetted by seven others, some of them schoolboys.[26] A memorial stone in the Königsallee in Grunewald marks the scene of the crime.

The murder was soon cleared up. Günther bragged in public about his participation. After his arrest on 26 June, he confessed fully to the crime. Hans Gerd Techow was arrested the following day, Ernst Werner Techow, who was visiting his uncle, three days later. Fischer and Kern remained on the loose. After a daring flight, which kept Germany in suspense for more than two weeks, they were finally spotted at the castle of Saaleck in Thuringia, whose owner was a secret member of 'Operation Consul'. On 17 July, the pair were confronted by two police detectives. While waiting for reinforcements during the stand-off, one of the detectives fired at a window, unknowingly killing Kern by a bullet to the head. Fischer then took his own life.

When they seized power in 1933, the Nazis wiped out public commemoration of Rathenau by destroying monuments to him, closing the Walther-Rathenau-Museum in his former mansion and renaming streets and schools dedicated to him. Instead, a memorial plaque to Kern and Fischer was solemnly unveiled at Saaleck Castle in July 1933 and in October 1933 a monument was erected on the assassins' grave.[27]

Once more, Canaris entered the scene because of suspected links to Rathenau's murder through his involvement with Ehrhardt and 'Operation Consul'.

Canaris was identified as the chief activist at the Baltic Naval Station where he supported the radical right-wing putsch movement with financial and material help.[28] The money distributed by Canaris helped set up the Ehrhardt terror organisation to assist the rise of Hitler's SA and his putsch of November 1923. Canaris maintained secret hoards of weapons and misappropriated military equipment for 'Operation Consul' under the noses of the Allies, and the German Naval Command knew and tolerated it. The *Gauleiter* for 'Organisation Consul' in Holstein, Mecklenburg and Pomerania was Kapitänleutnant Kurt Wende whose adjutant, Erwin Kern, was later killed while on the run after the murder of Rathenau.

---

26    Friedrich, *Before the Deluge*, pp. 99, 106-7.
27    Rathenau is acknowledged to be, in part, the basis for the German nobleman and industrialist Paul Arnheim, a character in Robert Musil's novel, *The Man Without Qualities*.
28    Mueller, Canaris, pp. 57, 77, 79.

Canaris was now firmly identified by the republicans in the Reichstag and in the Press as a supporter of terror. His past was put under the microscope: his contacts with 'Operation Consul', links to the Hitler Putsch, allegations about the Rathenau murder, his military connections to Spain with secret funding, involvement in the Lohmann Affair, the escape of Otto Runge convicted in the murder of Liebknecht, and the funding of pro-Fatherland groups, including the *Wikingbund*, the renamed 'Operation Consul'. An investigation by members of the Reichstag into many of these matters refused to have Canaris as a witness because of his public taint.

Diarist Kessler claimed, and many thought it proven, that the death of Rathenau gave the French confidence to invade the Ruhr and to seek to set up the area as an independent state, the Rhenish Republic. Kessler had a lengthy argument by letter with French Prime Minister Raymond Poincaré.

> *At the very moment that Poincaré was prepared to strike a death-blow at German unity his more serious obstacle was suddenly removed; that is to say, the measure of confidence and trust which Rathenau as director of Germany's foreign policy had won for himself and his country. One blow cleared the way for a renewal of the prejudices which had made possible the Treaty of Versailles. Poincaré had to thank those responsible for the assassination of Rathenau when he found himself at liberty to occupy the Ruhr without encountering any serious opposition from French or British opinion.*[29]

At the beginning of 1923, French and Belgian troops had marched in to the Ruhr to enforce payment of arrears of war reparations. About 130 German civilians died in a number of skirmishes. The government of Gustav Stresemann called a general strike throughout Germany.

> *Poincaré did not anticipate passive resistance. Though aware he was playing France's last trump in a decisive contest and critically short of troops and coal, he never considered barring food shipments to force the Ruhr miners back to work. Despite the recent precedent of Germany's refusal to feed civilians in territories it conquered in the war, he was neither so foolish nor so brutal.*[30]

---

29    Kessler, *Rathenau*, pp. 380-81.
30    Marks, '1918 and After', p. 39.

In one view, to finance this resistance, the Germans printed money and 'there resulted the notorious period when the value of the Reichsmark fell by the day and by the hour until trunkfuls of paper were needed for the smallest purchase'.

In another, from historian Sally Marks, the French made a profit after costs of nearly 900 million gold Reichsmark from their Rhineland adventure; German hyper-inflation was due to other causes.[31]

> *[Inflation] was a disastrous ploy, sweeping away the savings of the middle classes, bankrupting thousands, reintroducing hunger to the streets of the cities, further loosening the ties of society and unleashing a bitterness and restlessness that were harnessed by revolutionaries and nationalists for their own ends ... While the middle classes were ruined and workers thrown on the streets, the Army high command received one hundred million in gold at the height of the crisis for the purpose of rearmament outside Versailles limits; a portion of this was passed on to the Navy and incorporated in two secret rearmament funds.*[32]
>
> *By the middle of 1923, the whole of Germany had become delirious. Whoever had a job got paid every day, usually at noon, and then ran to the nearest store, with a sack full of banknotes, to buy anything he could get, at any price. In their frenzy, people paid millions and even billions of marks for cuckoo clocks, shoes that didn't fit, anything that could be traded for something else.*[33]

French occupation forces facilitated the minority Ruhr Separatists in many ways including providing considerable sums of money, permitted the carrying of arms and the carrying out of military manoeuvres 'both of which were, of course, forbidden to the loyal section of the population under threat of the severest penalties'.[34] In the chief towns of the Ruhr, from Dusseldorf to Trier, where Georg Gerth was now working, everything was done by the French civil and military occupation authorities to ensure the success of putsches designed to bring about the 'Rhenish Republic' including disarming the police before the main putsch took place and protecting the Separatists.

---

31    Marks, '1918 and After', p. 30.
32    Padfield, *Dönitz*, p. 104.
33    Friedrich, *Before the Deluge*, p. 124.
34    Kessler, *Rathenau*, pp. 383-88.

The French withdrew in June 1930. They also abandoned 'one by one the cherished possessions of the Reparations Commission', the right of sanctions, economic occupation and military operations.[35]

Diarist Kessler in his biography of Rathenau said that, 'Political murder had at that time become one of the commonplaces of German public life to a degree hardly credible'.[36] Most of the victims were on the left wing of the political spectrum and 'only a few were prominent political figures'.[37]

Kessler cites a pamphlet by Emil Gumbel, a statistical lecturer at the University of Heidelberg, '*Four Years of Political Murder*, 1922, which names 354 assassinations by right-wing groups and twenty-two by left-wing groups during the four years after the war, all quite separate from those killed in civil war or street fighting.[38]

Friedrich takes the analysis further.[39] For the twenty-two murders by the left, seventeen brought heavy sentences, including ten executions; for the right, 326 went unpunished. The average prison sentence for murder was fifteen years for left-wingers and four months for right-wingers. 'Organisation Consul' was making a 'concerted effort to undermine the republic by well-chosen political assassinations' and was seemingly supported by the judiciary.[40]

The years 1922 and 1923 were also the time when Hitler and the *Nationalsozialistische Deutsche Arbeiterpartei*, the NSDAP, 'National Socialist German Workers' Party', formed the first incarnations of their two most influential party organisations, the *Jungsturm Adolf Hitler* and the *Jugendbund der NSDAP*, which would become the Hitler Youth, and the *Stabswache*, 'Staff Guard', quickly renamed the *Stoßtrupp-Hitler*, 'Shock Troop-Hitler', which became the infamous *Schutzstaffel*, the SS. The first coup in May took over a barracks and weapons, but 'the order to march never came'.

In November, in the famous 'Beer Hall Putsch', sixteen NSDAP members and four police officers were killed in the attempted *coup d'état*. Hitler was arrested and put on trial for high treason in 1924.[41] Sentenced to five years imprisonment at Landsberg, Hitler was pardoned by the Bavarian Supreme

---

35    Marks, 'Myths of Reparations', pp. 246-52.
36    Kessler, *Rathenau*, p. 362.
37    Volkov, *Rathenau*, pp. 196-97.
38    Gumbel, *Vier Jahre politischer Mord* (Verlag der Neuen Gesellschaft, Berlin-Fichtenau), 1922.
39    Friedrich, *Before the Deluge*, pp. 117-18.
40    Volkov, *Rathenau*, p. 197.
41    Padfield, *Dönitz*, p. 107.

Court on Christmas Eve that year, but not before he had dictated the first volume of *Mein Kampf*, principally to his deputy Rudolf Hess.[42]

The putsch attempt of the *Freikorps* in 1920 failed as did the two coup attempts by Hitler in 1923. By the end of 1924, there were signs that all of this activity was taking on a coherent political form. The most viable patriotic associations that emerged from among the scattered remnants of the *Freikorps* and Home Guards were the *Stahlhelm*, 'Steel Helmets', and the *Jungdeutscher Orden*, 'Young German Order', became 'major political forces'.[43] The *Freikorps* 'sank mostly into oblivion'.[44] It was only early in 1933 and Hitler's arrival in power that they were 'widely recognised as fascist *avant la lettre* and publicly commemorated as political heroes which is why most of the great histories of the *Freikorps* movement and memoirs of its veterans appeared after 1933. The *Freikorps* were in the vanguard of Nazism mainly because the Nazis declared them so.'

The first round of Germany's first-ever democratic presidential election in 1925 saw the stalking horse candidate of the German right, Karl Jarres, take almost forty per cent of the vote, but still well short of the clear majority that was needed in this round. The SDP candidate, Otto Braun, and Wilhelm Marx of the Catholic Centre Party, were some distance off. Ludendorff with the fringe German Völkisch Freedom Party was in seventh place and this marked the demise of his last chance of becoming a serious politician.

In the second round, Jarres withdrew in favour of a late entry, Paul von Hindenburg, who stood, supposedly reluctantly, as an independent. The democratic SDP and the Centre parties combined under Wilhelm Marx to ensure Hindenburg's defeat. Hindenburg won with 48 per cent of the vote, 900,000 more than Marx and took the presidency, which he held until his death in 1934. Hitler stood against Hindenburg for the Presidency in 1932 and lost, but gained thirty-seven per cent of the popular vote.

No party obtained a Reichstag majority so Hindenburg ruled through presidential decree with an appointed chancellor, Franz von Papen. The Hitler and Nazi Party bandwagon steadily gained votes in several elections to 1932 through a mixture of Hitler's undoubted oratory as he criss-crossed the country

---

42    *Mein Kampf*, 'My Struggle', was originally entitled 'Four and a Half Years of Struggle against Lies, Stupidity, and Cowardice'.

43    Fritzsche, *Germans into Nazis*, p. 134.

44    Fritzsche, *Germans into Nazis*, pp. 122-24.

by air, sweeping terror tactics and conventional campaigning. Papen left office and Hindenburg reluctantly appointed Hitler as chancellor, even though he was without an absolute Reichstag majority.

> *Marchers cutting their boots against asphalt streets, growing louder, cheers swallowing up the winter stillness, torchlights and searchlights advancing on the darkness … the New York Times later reported a 'gigantic demonstration that has not been witnessed' in Berlin, at least not since that November afternoon some fourteen years earlier, in 1918, when 'Fritz Ebert reviewed the masses'. The day was Monday 30 January 1933; Adolf Hitler had just been named Chancellor of Germany and stood overlooking Wilhelmstraße, reviewing a newer, larger, more threatening version of Germany's masses … Newspaper trucks parked up and down the street, their cables and spotlights furbishing the big moment with electric excitement. By early evening, members of the SA, Sturmabteilung or stormtroops, and the SS Schutzstaffel, the party's smaller security guard, as well as the nationalist Stahlhelm, assembled in the Tiergarten for a full-dress parade through the Brandenburg Gate, down Wilhelmstraße, and into the old city of Berlin. What was not anticipated was the sheer number of civilian well-wishers who also gathered. In this ostensibly 'red' city, thousands of Berliners stood and cheered Hitler and Hindenburg, the President of the Republic. The old songs were dusted off including Deutschland über Alles, The Watch on the Rhine and the Nazi anthem, the Horst Wessel Song.[45]*

Some argue that Hugenberg's major achievement by 1930 was to assist the growth of the Nazis to become the major political force on the right. 'The squat bespectacled Hugenberg did not have Hitler's personal magnetism and failed to exploit the economic and political crises which he had foretold'.[46] Hitler used his position to unleash a campaign of violence against all of the Nazi's left-wing parliamentary opposition during the 1933 election. Hitler took forty-four per cent of the vote.

On 7 March 1933, a supposedly communist-laid arson attack partially burned down the Reichstag. The Reichstag Fire Decree, signed the next day by Hindenburg, suspended most civil liberties in Germany, including habeas corpus, freedom of expression, freedom of the press, the right of free association

---

45    Fritzsche, *Germans into Nazis*, pp. 139-40.
46    Walker, 'Nationalist People's Party', p. 642.

and public assembly, the secrecy of the post and telephone and transferred state powers to the Reich government. The decree was quickly followed by the *Gesetz zur Behebung der Not von Volk und Reich*, an 'Enabling Act' to remedy the distress of the people. The amendment gave the German Cabinet, in effect Hitler as the new chancellor, plenary power to enact laws without the involvement of the Reichstag. It was approved by the Reichstag and Hindenburg on the same day, 24 March. With the support of all the non-socialist parties, Hitler assumed dictatorial power.

*Hitler won such decisive elections in 1932 and 1933 because the Nazis departed from established political traditions in that they were identified at once with a distinctly popular form of ethnic nationalism and with the basic social reforms most Germans counted on to ensure national well-being.*[47]

Hugenberg was a part of Hitler's first government which set up the Enabling Act. He held the posts of Reich and Prussian ministers of the economy and of food and agriculture in what the *Berliner Lokal-Anzeiger* claimed was the best position in the cabinet.[48] Hugenberg as an extreme nationalist was seen by Mussolini, and also by the French ambassador and the Polish government, as more dangerous and a greater threat to the *status quo* than even Hitler and the NSDAP. He immediately facilitated Ufa's use by Goebbels as a propaganda machine. On 29 March 1933, Ufa management fired several Jewish employees. In the summer, the Nazis created the Film Chamber of the Reich which excluded Jewish filmmakers from all German studios.

Hindenburg chose Hugenberg as a balance to the NSDAP members in the government. The plan was for Hugenberg to manipulate Hitler and 'restrain the radicalism of the Nazi movement'.[49]

*Conservatives, convinced that society should be subject to the state and the regime could control the state, thought that they had outwitted the Nazis. In their hubris, Hugenberg and his associates could not imagine a revolution from below. Ensconced in his ministry, Hugenberg believed he could remodel Germany. Within five months, he*

---

47    Fritzsche, *Germans into Nazis*, pp. 8-9.
48    Leopold, *Hugenberg*, p. 137, citing *Berliner Lokal-Anzeiger*, 30/1/1933.
49    Jones, 'Greatest Stupidity', p. 76.

*was forced to admit that he had totally misjudged the political scene. The manipulators had become the manipulated. German nationalism and its leader were obsolete.*[50]

At Hitler's first cabinet, Hugenberg fought unsuccessfully to have the Communist party proscribed. Quickly, all of his other plans for power went astray. By June, Hugenberg admitted complete defeat and resigned. His life-long plans for the organisation of Germany were shattered.[51] Hugenberg was later reputed to have remarked, 'I've just committed the greatest stupidity of my life; I have allied myself with the greatest demagogue in world history.'[52] He made a despondent comment:

> *I am indeed of the opinion that we all have cause to go home and to crawl into our closets or go into the woods. In the last days and weeks it has been my chief goal to remain respectable in every way and not to allow my good name to be marred. I would hope that in a difficult situation I have succeeded in this and would find for that reason a great peace and relief. You don't know what you ought to say in days like these, but one thought has gone through my mind in these hours and I would still like to add it: if anyone should hear that I have committed suicide, do not believe it at all. I would not do it and I do not believe in suicide.*

Hitler's power became absolute when Hindenburg died next year and took with him the last hint of restraint. The Nazis did not persecute Hugenberg, but they 'circumcised his power'. 'Germany's new rulers treated him gently as a superfluous elder statesman.'

Was this deduction by Hugenburg's biographer, Leopold, completely accurate? The Nazis may not have wished to publicly humiliate him and alienate his powerful industrial supporters or his ultra-right-wing political followers. Yet, they did need to neuter his power base and, therefore, his ability to cause further trouble. The Nazi state swallowed up Hugenberg's and Salomon Marx's Ufa as a coveted and persuasive tool and gave it to Joseph Goebbels, the Reich Minister of Propaganda.

---

50    Leopold, *Hugenberg*, p. 139.
51    Leopold, *Hugenberg*, pp. 163-65.
52    Jones, 'Greatest Stupidity', p. 63.

Hugenberg and his allies, including Salomon Marx, were forced to sell their shares. Marx was no longer needed and, perhaps knew too much. Anyway, Marx was a born Jew and, therefore, official prey.

Maria de la Paz de Bourbon, Spanish infanta, daughter of Queen Isabella II, who recommended Erich for a position at the German Foreign Ministry in 1922.

Konstantin von Neurath, whose diplomatic sensibilities were upset by Erich and Eva in Rome in 1924; later Protector of Bohemia and, finally, a convicted war criminal.

Wilhelm Marx, leader of the central catholic party, twice German Chancellor in the 1920s, covered up German naval rearmament; his father was cousin to Salomon Marx.

Erich in raincoat and felt hat about to board an early Lufthansa flight. *Family archive*

Heinrich Brüning, Christian Democrat Chancellor, devout Roman Catholic and co-organiser with Erich Gerth of masses for peace in the 1930s; fled Germany in 1934.

Maximilian Harden, Jewish intellectual, publisher, journalist, actor and critic; friend and business supporter of Salomon Marx; eventual fierce critic of the Kaiser.

Alfred Hugenberg, leader of Krupp, the steel and armament firm; bought Ufa, Germany's largest film studio while working with Salomon Marx; failed to outwit Adolf Hitler and was humiliated in 1936.

Adolf Hitler and Joseph Goebbels visit Ufa in 1935. Not long afterwards, the film studios became a part of Goebbels's propaganda empire.

Erich's gravestone in the private garden of the German cemetery inside the Vatican, Campo Santo Teutonico. *Emanuele Ojetti*

Eva and her four children, probably in the United States in the 1950s. *Family archive*

# 14

# GERTH: THE FOREIGN OFFICE

*In Germany, they came first for the Communists,*
*And I didn't speak up because I wasn't a Communist;*
*And then they came for the trade unionists,*
*And I didn't speak up because I wasn't a trade unionist;*
*And then they came for the Jews,*
*And I didn't speak up because I wasn't a Jew;*
*And then . . . they came for me . . .*
*And by that time there was no one left to speak.*[1]

Erich Gerth's application to the Foreign Office, much trailed in these pages, was made on 30 December 1922 after he had completed a year of developmental employment in two of Salomon Marx's companies. During this time, and at least until 1925, Erich and Eva lived in Berlin at Schwäbischestraße 8 in the south-west of the city near Barbarossaplatz.[2]

After his acceptance on 1 March 1923, Gerth prepared for the examinations needed for diplomatic-consular duties. These he passed on 20 December 1924 with a Grade 2, 'good'. The exam consisted of three essays which received a mixed reception from the head of the examination committee, Gustav Stresemann. Stresemann, who had a distinguished Foreign Office career, was

---

1    Martin Niemöller, who brought *UC 67* home to Kiel in the dash from Pola in 1918, wrote this famous and widely quoted poem about the persecutions by the Nazis. The poem exists in many versions, often modified to reflect a specific persecuted group. In a 1971 interview, Niemöller said that this was his preferred version.
2    *Berlin Telephone Directory*, 1923 (ancestry.com). Erich's number was Lutzow 89 67.

known to Salomon Marx as a brother-in-law of Kurt von Kleefeld, a frequent visitor to Marx's dinner parties.

Erich wrote his first paper of 108 pages on the 'German-English alliance negotiations between 1898 and 1901 against the background of the English imperial policy between 1895 and 1902 and the German naval policy since 1897/98', for which he received a Grade 2 as 'he worked more intelligently and independently than his colleagues'.[3] This essay might have come easily to Gerth as he could rely on his training and experience as a naval cadet and junior officer.

However, his legal paper on the 'Jurisdiction of Foreign States' was considered only a Grade 4, 'Sufficient', as it 'did not refer to foreign law sources and lacked depth'.

A third paper on the 'Dissolution of the Danube Monarchy', the Catholic Austro-Hungarian Empire, with ninety-two pages, was Graded 1, 'Very good', perhaps benefitting from input from Eva's many contacts in the senior echelons of the Bavarian Catholic community.

A much greater influence on his acceptance than these essay results came from the group of twelve stellar individuals who, as the application form requested, were 'able to give reference about you due to personal acquaintance'. For the first time, Canaris is not mentioned or needed, but one senses he is close at hand. Nor did the list include father-in-law Salomon Marx, but he was discreetly mentioned in answer to other questions. Nothing demonstrates better than these proffered referees Gerth's whirlwind rise into the world of prestige and influence following his marriage to Eva Marx.

The list had just one family member. Somewhat surprisingly, it was Frau Gräfin Franziska von Ahlefeldt-Eschelsmark in Schlesien, Eva's ex-mother-in-law. Eva's first husband was killed in 1916. Not only did Eva keep a close connection with her previous noble family, but was able to introduce her second husband amid sufficient good humour and respect for the Gräfin to provide a reference six years later.

Erich's previous boss, Admiral Adolf von Trotha, until 1920 chief of the *Obersten Marineleitung*, was an obvious, but serious, addition to the list for a lowly ex-u-boat commander.

---

3     *Auswärtiges Amt*, Politisches Archiv, Gz: 117-251.09.

Then came four of Salmon Marx's business and political contacts, all, presumably, meeting Gerth at social events at Brückenallee, and at which he evidently impressed: Minister of State Friedrich von Loebell, President of the *Reichsbürgerrats Berlin*, founded by Salomon Marx in January 1919. Leobell was also soon to become chairman of the supervisory board of Marx's *Internationale Handelsbank* where Gerth spent part of his commercial training year before entry into the diplomatic corps; Foreign Minister Gottlieb von Jagow, who had retired in 1916, 'a quiet, unassuming and scholarly man, perhaps the worst speaker in the Reichstag'; Gustaf Schlieper, owner of the Berlin finance business, *Diskonto-Gesellschaft*, a leading German banking organisation and closely associated with Rothschild and Krupp until its 1929 merger into *Deutsche Bank*; and, finally, Ottmar Strauss, co-founder of the iron wholesaler Otto Wolff, one of the largest businesses in pre-war Germany. Strauss was a Jewish business contact of Salomon Marx from when they both lived and worked in Cologne.

The remaining six referees all came from the upper-reaches of the Catholic community in Germany.

Salomon Marx would have introduced Erich to the son of his cousin, Senate President Wilhelm Marx, Chairman of the Catholic *Zentrum* Party of the Reichstag, already discussed in several places, and to become Chancellor for the first time next year.

Erich's Foreign Office application was signed in Munich, suggesting he and Eva were living there in 1922 with ready social access to the remaining referees.

Pre-eminent among Eva Marx's contribution, acting as one referee, were their Royal Highnesses, Prince Ludwig Ferdinand von Bayern and his wife, his maternal first cousin, Princess Maria de la Paz de Bourbon, Infantin von Spanien whom he married in 1883. Maria de la Paz was the second-youngest daughter of King Francis and Queen Regnant Isabella II of Spain. Prince Ludwig, a Hapsburg, was a member of the Bavarian Royal House of Wittelsbach with royal links to Catholic Bavaria and Spain. As a gynaecologist, he was one of only a few European princes doing an ordinary job outside government or the military and, during World War I, worked as head of the surgery department of the Munich Military Hospital. The family were close to their distant relative, Kaiser Wilhelm, and frequently corresponded.[4] Princess Maria lived in the Bavarian Republic at Schloss Nymphenburg, near Munich.

Next, Freiherr Karl von Papius was Legation Councillor of the Bavarian Embassy in Berlin and was Erich's godfather. He had strong links to Würzburg, the home town of the Leineckers who married into the Gerth family. Papius studied law at the universities of Munich and Heidelberg and passed the examination for public service in 1864 in Würzburg where he also received his doctorate two years later.

Then came their Excellencies Pablo Soler and Diego von Bergen, ambassadors of His Majesty the King of Spain in Berlin.

Finally, Monsignore Eugenio Pacelli, was the Vatican's papal envoy in Germany, based for much of his time in Munich, and who was to become Pope Pius XII in 1939.

It is possible that all these leading Catholics, joined by Eva and Erich, met at the Eucharist Congress in Rome in May in 1922 and which Princess Maria recorded as 'an important contribution to the cause of international goodwill'.[5] And, surely, Pacelli would have arranged, and been present at, a personal meeting between the Princess, his friend from Munich, and his pope. As she noted in her diary,

> *Pope Pius XI gave us a private audience. Again after many years I passed through those halls that I had crossed first as a child, and then as a young mother. Much has changed in the world, but the principles for which the Vatican stands remain eternal. In the same room where I had met Pius IX, I now met Pius XI ... For the first time in my life I spoke German to a pope. That gave me special pleasure.*

There is a note on Erich's Foreign Office file for April 1924 which suggests that Erich's new career in Berlin was not without question marks.

'It is advisable to transfer Gerth later as his first foreign post not to a diplomatic mission, but a busy general consulate, like St Petersburg or Poznań, and only to send him to an embassy after he has proven himself at a general consulate.'[6]

---

4    Princess Ludwig, *Through Four Revolutions*, p. xiii and following.
5    Princess Ludwig, *Through Four Revolutions*, pp. 334-35.
6    File note, 27/4/1924, unsigned (Obituary, Matthias Lohr).

It is worth recalling that Erich was from a staunch Lutheran family and Eva's first marriage was as a Jew, the religion of her father, although her mother was Catholic. Eva converted to Catholicism in 1918 and Erich followed, possibly, in 1919, but certainly by 1922. Erich's early career in the Foreign Office, especially during holidays to Rome and his postings to Copenhagen and Paris, saw him identify with leading Catholics and the Catholic faith. Eva spent the winters in Rome if she could and Erich visited her there, at least in 1921 and again in 1924, when he needed to ask for leave to do so.

During this latter visit, Erich and Eva, seriously displeased the Ambassador, Konstantin Hermann Karl Freiherr von Neurath. Neurath took up his ambassadorship early in 1922 and found a 'totally disorganised embassy, a staff of well-paid but incompetent agents, and an Augean stable of legal cases concerning confiscated German property including even the old embassy building'.[7]

In his personal relationships, Neurath adhered to a strict moral code, believing that decency and honesty were necessary forms for daily life. His favourite poem, which he often quoted and which was read at his funeral, 'caught this sense of a private man struggling to endure the stresses of a public world':

*Think and be quiet*
*Feel more than you show*
*Bow down before God*
*And you stay your own master.*

Neurath was a well trained diplomat with insights into world problems, formidable linguistic skills, and determined political and economic views. 'Above all, he mastered two difficult virtues: he could mask his feelings and private opinions from even the most astute observer, and he could remain calm in the most distressing circumstances.' He despised artificial solutions, which he claimed were concocted by intellectual scheming and marred by emotional involvement. Politicians and intellectuals, he implied, could enjoy such parties; a civil servant, especially in the foreign service, had to live by another code:

---

7    Heineman, *Neurath*, pp. 3-4, 24.

recognition that personal desires and fantasies must be submerged in serving the nation's broader realities.

Neurath 'did not like society and he despised politics'. On more than one occasion, he complained that the most difficult part of his life was the social whirl accompanying international diplomacy. All of these skills combined to help him develop a personal relationship with the preening Benito Mussolini which lasted for years and was of great benefit to Germany's foreign relations.

Neurath wrote in 1924 to the headquarters of the Foreign Office at Wilhelmstraße:[8]

> *For several months, a Herr Gerth, Attaché in the Foreign Office, has been staying here with his wife. The couple, the female part of which dresses and acts quite flamboyantly, almost exclusively keeps company with Vatican circles. It has been reported repeatedly to me by Germans that among themselves, even if they are together with Germans, they use the French language, although Herr Gerth as far as I know, was formerly a German naval officer and Frau Gerth is a daughter of the well-known Consul Marx in Berlin. The bad taste of this conduct, for which, by the way, the Romans have a very fine sense, seems to me topped by the fact that a few days ago Herr Gerth submitted the attached business card to me. I leave it to you to form your own opinion about this hopeful young colleague in the Foreign Service but considered it my duty to inform you about the Roman activities of the 'Attaché'.*

The card had the French text: 'E Gerth, Attaché au Ministère des Affaires Etrangères, Berlin'.

The French affectation, the access to money well above the salary of a junior diplomat, the winning ways within the Vatican, and the career precociousness did not sit well with the Neurath style. There is nothing in Neurath's character that suggests that he harboured long-term dislike, according to his biographer Heinemann, but Neurath thought Erich needed disciplining and to be taken down a peg. No 'Neurath effect' was immediately apparent, but his reappearance in Erich Gerth's story in 1933 did have serious impact.

Gerth was meant to report to the Embassy in Bucharest in March 1925 because of a 'terribly complicated personnel situation' and to prepare the

---

8    Letter, Neurath to von Kühlmann, 4/10/1924 (Berlin Foreign Office personnel file, with thanks to Matthias Löhr and Martina Nibbeling-Wriessnig).

Romanian White Book.[9] This, however, did not happen due to Gerth's ailing wife. Then, Erich went sick with a streptococcal infection and left with Eva for two weeks at the *Pensione Lucchesi* in Florence to recover.

On 1 August 1925, Erich Gerth started his service at the embassy in Copenhagen and on 22 May 1926 was promoted to Legation Secretary. There is a testimonial of his work in Copenhagen.[10]

> *His personality is extraordinarily amiable and pleasing, demonstrating in his social interaction and in his relationships with the German colony as well as the local authorities, his gift to act as a balancing force and avoid conflict. He is also truly kind hearted. This is illustrated in particular in his relationship to the small Catholic-German community in Copenhagen. Before their departure the couple has undertook with great skill and success to socially unite the younger members of the diplomatic corps at their house.*

Erich held a minor position, dealing with consular matters, but it was noted that his potential was higher. His language skills in English and French were described as just 'satisfactory'; he preferred Spanish.

The testimonial continues. 'Once his wife's health has been restored, I would like to recommend for Gerth and his wife for reasons of the physical and moral climate, the Catholic South [of Europe] as employment area.' Somebody placed a question mark under the wording 'moral climate'. A Foreign Office source thought this last sentence 'very unusual'. While it is common to finish a performance testimonial with a recommendation for the next post, the 'repeated highlighting of the Catholic theme is a hidden comment that this young diplomat was one-sided and preferred to follow his specific personal interests'.

Eva's health did not improve and she stayed for long periods at the spa resort of Arosa, Switzerland. Erich tried to get a post in Geneva to be near her. At his urgent request, he was moved from 24 September 1926 to become Vice Consul in Genoa.

On 3 July 1928, Gerth was transferred to the Paris Embassy. Erich Gerth's surviving personnel files in the Foreign Office concentrate on three topics:

---

9    Foreign Office cables Nos. 31,42 (IH 1098), 5,31/3/1925.
10   Report 22 IB, 20/4/1926, signed by 'Mutius'.

health issues, continuing contacts with the upper echelon of Catholic society, and promotion, or perhaps more accurately, the need for more income which is surprising given Eva's father's fortune which allowed her, for instance, to convalesce in Switzerland and Italy.

Gerth was proud of his health. He told the Foreign Office that he was 'completely healthy and fit to serve in the tropics. I have been examined several times for this and always found to be fit.'[11] This was called into question the following year when a doctor diagnosed a 'raised diaphragm and several nervous phenomena'. The Foreign Office was concerned when seen together with his wife's frailty, and they insisted on medical confirmation, which was received, that he was ready for service.

In September 1929, a doctor in Nassau in the Rhineland wrote that Gerth was suffering from a 'neurosis of the sympathetic nerve as a reaction to untreated inner secretoric [sic] exhaustion symptoms'. The heart had moved upwards, pushing the diaphragm, and 'leading to an unstable circulation and disturbances in the digestive organs'. The doctor felt that the condition was temporary, could be cured, and urged that treatment should not be interrupted. This last plea smacks a little of Erich fearing for his employment. He had an operation on his tonsils in Berlin and returned to his post in Paris in November 1929. When visiting Berlin, the couple always stayed with Salomon Marx at Brückenallee.

Erich was not lacking for 'career' friends in high places. Twice-chancellor Wilhelm Marx wrote from the Reichstag on 15 April 1930 to Foreign Minister Julius Curtius, saying that he had already spoken to State Secretary Baron Ago von Maltzan about Erich 'and found full comprehension' for the desire to either promote him or to adjust his service age to better recognise his military service. This was so that he would earn more.

Curtius replied on 28 April 1930 regretting that all the posts in Paris that carried a promotion were taken, but that a recheck of Erich's service age level had been ordered. A further letter explained that Erich had already been treated in a privileged way and that no more could be done.

Erich wrote asking 'not for a financial privilege vis-à-vis his fellows', but because at age 44, he would 'never be able to finance his family'.

---

11    30/12/1922.

In August the following year, 1931, Salomon Marx, writing from his *Handelsbank* in Berlin, was on the financial case, this time emphasising to Dr Köpke at the ministry Erich's roles as u-boat officer and as a Catholic intermediary.[12]

'In the conversation which you kindly granted me yesterday, I also took the liberty to bring up the issue of my son-in-law's career. You kindly told me that the ambassador, Herr von Hoesch, would give him a good qualification and that my son-in-law was of great value in Paris, especially as a connection officer between the embassy and the high clergy and further Catholic-interest circles.'

Marx asked that Erich be kept in Paris and promoted, citing Erich's 'long years in which he successfully served as a submarine commander'. As Köpke then left on holiday, his deputy, Ernest Freiherr von Grünau, Head of Personnel, dealt with the request, but turned it down initially with some sympathy. 'I am fully aware of the fact that the impossibility to grant you a financially better position by taking into account your many years of service as an officer comprises a certain severity.'

It may be that the determination of Erich and his father-in-law to increase Erich's earnings was because, unexpectedly, Eva was carrying a child. Son Marco was born on 10 January 1932 and, later that year, pressure told when Erich was promoted to First Secretary of the Paris legation.[13]

Daughter Marie-Diana was born early next year. Eva went on to have four children while she was between thirty-seven and forty-two years, remarkable given that there were no children in the first thirteen years of marriage. Perhaps her earlier frailties, had been related to difficult pregnancies.

Erich wrote to Grünau expressing his 'deep gratitude'.[14] Grünau, incidentally, an ex-member of the Kaiser's personal staff, had fought strongly against the introduction in 1917 of unrestricted submarine warfare.[15]

There is a confidential letter of 12 June 1931 with an obscured sender, possibly 'Brümmermann', from the address of the Foreign Office at Wilhelmstraße, and

---

12    Letter, Salomon Marx to Dr Köpke, 'Min. Dir., Berlin', 7/8/1931. Reply 19/8/1931. Further
       letters 1,12/9/1932.
13    Marco Gerth born 10/1/1932, Marie-Diane 19/2/1933, Isabella 7/8/1935 and Roger
       30/11/1937.
14    Letter 9/8/1933.
15    Matthias Lohr email.

no addressee, except for the salutation *Lieber Freund, persönlich und vertraulich*, 'Dear friend, personal and confidential'. The letter says,

> *Frau Gräfin Dolly de Castellane, widowed Princess Fürstenberg, the wife of the current 'President' of the city of Paris, whose great social influence in Paris is known to you, gave me at my last journey through Paris the attached card and asked me to tell the German Chancellor, Dr Heinrich Brüning [a devout Roman Catholic] that Botschaftssekretär, 'Embassy Secretary', Gerth had undertaken to form close links with all organised Catholic powers in France. This relationship was in her opinion extraordinarily important not only for the work in Paris itself, but also for the whole nature of German-French relations. De Castellane therefore demands that Gerth should not be removed from Paris.*[16]

Dorothée, 'Dolly', de Talleyrand-Périgord, daughter of Napoléon-Louis de Talleyrand-Périgord, Duke of Talleyrand, Valençay and Sagan, and Pauline de Castellane, was a great *salonière* and society lady. She married Jean de Castellane after the death of her first husband, Prince Karl Egon IV of Fürstenberg. At the beginning of the twentieth century, the Fürstenbergs, were leaders and role models for the aristocratic *jeunesse d'orée*, 'gilded youth', and presided over the group in a luxurious foreign lifestyle at their Berlin mansion at Wilhelmstraße 23.[17] Kaiser Wilhelm I often dropped in unexpectedly for tea.

After her second marriage, Dolly was a rival in high society circles in Paris to her cousin and aunt, Marie Radziwill: Radziwill represented the *grandes dames* of the eighteenth and nineteenth centuries; Dolly was the more Bohemian salon lady of the early twentieth century as portrayed by Marcel Proust and

---

16    Comte Jean de Castellane was a French cavalry officer who left the army in 1902 to stand successfully in legislative elections. He was disqualified for bribery and beaten in the subsequent by-election. He became a municipal counsellor in Paris from 1919 to 1944 and was vice-president of the municipal council in 1928 and then from 1930 to 1931. Chancellor Brüning established presidential government in the final days of the Weimar Republic, but was forced out when President Paul von Hindenburg refused to sign further decrees. He was author of a plan to reinstate the Hohenzollern monarchy in a British-style constitution. Hindenburg refused his support unless the Kaiser was called back from the Netherlands. When Brüning explained this would not be possible, Hindenburg dismissed him. Fearing arrest by the Nazis, Brüning fled Germany in 1934, settling in Switzerland, then the United Kingdom and, finally, the United States. Brüning warned the American public about Hitler's plans for war and, later, about Soviet aggression and expansion (wikipedia).

17    Erbe, *Das vornehme Berlin*, p. 25.

fulfilling Balzac's ideal of the modern, elegant and correct woman, the *femme comme il faut*.[18] 'Their family went to great lengths to avoid a meeting of these two powerful women at the family's summer palace Rochecotte.'

> *Dolly was less exclusive in her choice of guests invited to her salon – she embraced zeitgeist changes and received actresses and artists, and by doing so established a link between the aristocracy and the demi-monde.*[19]

Dolly was described as a *valkyrie* with majestic beauty, looking as if she had just returned from a visit at *Wotan*'s; other contemporaries saw her as 'clever, a typical *grande dame*, but natural, free of any affectation.[20] Not conventionally beautiful, her lively eyes and full red lips gave her an air of joy of life.'[21] Her portrait was painted by Philip Alexius de László. Dolly was fluent in German and French, the latter was spoken the world over in 'sophisticated circles' and this may have encouraged Erich and Eva Gerth's performance in Rome that so upset Ambassador Neurath.

Dolly's proficiency in German meant that when she lived in France she was able to act as an intermediary between both countries and cultures. She became one of the most influential figures of her time: her city palace was a meeting place for politicians, diplomats, scholars and artists as well as high-ranking foreign visitors including good personal contacts with Kaiser Wilhelm II whom, until the beginning of the war, she always met during her annual visit to Berlin.[22]

After the war, Dolly's 'overriding political endeavour was to achieve a rapprochement between Germany and France', which explains her

---

18   Honoré de Balzac, *La Femme comme il faut*. Erbe, *Das vornehme Berlin*, p. 154.
19   *Demi-monde*, people on the edge of respectable society. *Zeitgeist*, the defining spirit or mood of a particular period of history as shown by the ideas and beliefs of the time.
20   Grenaud and Marcailhou, *Boni de Castellane*, Book 1, p. 207. Richard Wagner's opera cycle, *Der Ring des Nibelungen*. In Norse mythology, a *Valkyrie* is one of a host of females who choose those who will live and die in battle, bringing their chosen to the after-life hall of the slain, *Valhalla*, ruled over by the god *Odin*. *Wotan* is a character based on the god.
21   Erbe, *Das vornehme Berlin*, pp. 204-8.
22   There was some criticism of Dolly's lack of national [French] feeling during the war, but this turned into resentment when her cosmopolitanism was reflected in a questionable attitude towards the Third Reich (Erbe, *Das vornehme Berlin*), fn. 690. Price Jean-Louis Faucigny-Lucinge, *Un gentilhomme cosmopolite*, p. 64, fn. states that Jean and Dolly de Castellane were collaborating with the German occupying power.

determination to keep Erich and Eva in Paris. Radziwill's biographer, Erbe, gives no information about Dolly's Catholicism, but does describe Marie Radziwill's holy communions in 1851 and 1854 and a visit to Rome to attend the ceremonies, also in 1854, for the 'Proclamation of the Dogma of Mary's Immaculate Conception' by Pope Pius IX.[23] One can only assume the same level of devotion from her cousin. If so, Dolly de Castellane may well have joined Erich Gerth, Pacelli, Princess Maria and the rest at the Eucharist Congress in Rome in 1922.

Where in all this high society hobnobbing, with its swirl of parties and crystal glass chatter, is the thread? Were Erich and Eva just the consummate Catholic hosts and guests? Assessments of the Gerth brothers suggest this could be so. Georg, the serious ex-sailor and thinker, a preferred recluse, was chalk and cheese to Erich, the extrovert party goer.[24] And, yet, any consideration of Erich's career, withstanding the rigours of the naval cadet programme, the intricacies and danger of South American spying, the determination to see action in a u-boat, the selection by Trotha as one of his 'chosen men', the continued close association with Salomon Marx and Wilhelm Canaris, suggest another side to Erich comprising commitment and determination.

Was there more behind Dolly de Castellane's sponsorship of a couple who she thought useful to her political purpose?

Family evidence comes down firmly on the side of Erich as a consummate peacemaker.[25] Erich came to the embassy in Paris in 1928 against the background of the 1925 Locarno Treaties of Reconciliation for which Aristide Briand and Gustav Stresemann, the respective Foreign Ministers of France and Germany, received the Nobel Peace Prize in 1926. This was the same Stresemann who made marked Erich's diplomatic essays in 1922.

*Henceforth the spirit of Locarno would reign, substituting conciliation for enforcement as the basis for peace. Yet for some peace remained a desperate hope rather than an actuality. A few men knew that the spirit of Locarno was a fragile foundation on which to build a lasting peace.*[26]

---

23    Erbe, *Das vornehme Berlin*, p. 37, fn.
24    Interview with Christa-Maria Gerth, 15/11/2016.
25    Email, Roger Gerth, 22/1/2018.
26    Marks, *Illusion of Peace*, p. 89.

# 15

# GERTH: RUPTURE IN CHRISTIAN UNITY

Erich Gerth's son, Roger, explains that, against the background of Locarno, Erich 'viewed the mutual hostility and distrust between the two countries [as] the result of a rupture of Christian unity, fundamentally a spiritual problem requiring a spiritual approach to a solution'.

After cultivating the key Catholic influencers in Paris and Germany, Erich organised a series of peace and reconciliation masses at Notre Dame des Victoires, the designated Catholic church for diplomats in Paris. At one of these masses in 1931, the German side was represented by Christian Democrat Chancellor Heinrich Brüning [mentioned by Dolly de Castellane] and on the French side by Auguste Champetier de Ribes, a jurist and junior minister in several governments, and later a French prosecutor at the Nuremberg Trials.

*As a government delegate assisting Chancellor Brüning and convinced of the necessity for a Franco-German reconciliation, [Gerth] attended a mass for peace held on 19 July 1931 at Notre-Dame des Victoires church. Contacts were established between French and German democrats, but they were interrupted by the advent of Hitler and wrecked all hope of reconciliation. In the face of the insatiable demands of the Chancellor of the Reich, Brüning advocated a policy of firmness, the only way, according to him, of safeguarding peace. He was appalled at the concessions granted to Germany at Munich which, six months later, resulted in the occupation of Czechoslovakia.*[1]

*This was the calibre of the people attracted to Erich's reconciliation work. Erich also used the figure of St Albert the Great, a leading philosopher and theologian of the thirteenth century, as a bridging figure between Germany and France.*[2] *... It was at a great feast in 1933 for Albert the Great in a large public venue which Eva recalled often and described as looking like it had snowed because, in addition to many others, there was a large number of Dominican [nuns] attending in their white habits. It was celebrated as an important event of reconciliation.*[3]

Erich's very public espousal of the Catholic interest in the cause of reconciliation while in Copenhagen and Paris was a most risky undertaking for a young delegate in the foreign service of his country. The trail of distrust that clung to Catholic relations with the German and French states remained 'poisonous' well beyond Gerth's time as a junior diplomat.[4] Open embracing of the German Catholic community in Paris to aid post-war reconciliation was a dangerous strategy for Erich's political career. Support given to his initiatives by well-placed Catholic friends would be seen as a mixed blessing among his Prussian superiors at Wilhelmstraße.

There are some scattered places to look for further answers, in the turbulent recent history of the Vatican's relationships with France and Germany, and in the papers and biographies of Erich's referee, Eugenio Pacelli. Pacelli was not yet an anointed successor to Pope Pius XI, but he was recognised as a 'coming man' with his enormous self-confidence and evident intellect.[5]

---

1    Extracted by Roger Gerth from a French National Assembly document about Auguste Champetier de Ribes. See also, Guieu, 'Le rapprochement franco-allemand', *Les Cahiers Sirice*, 2016/1 ; Delori, 'La genèse de la coopération franco-allemande', *Revue française de science politique*, 2006/3.

2    Albert was a German Dominican friar, and later bishop, who became a highly acclaimed and successful professor at the University of Paris. To this day, there is a Rue Maître Albert in Paris, not far from the University.

3    Email, Roger Gerth, 22/1/2018.

4    Ulrich, *Bismarck*, p. 91.

5    Pacelli's papers while nuncio in Munich and Berlin, and his correspondence with German bishops while he served as secretary of state at the Vatican, were among the 30,000 files of the pontificate of Pope Pius XI opened to researchers in 2006. These were followed in 2007 by Pacelli's war-time diaries (Coppa, *Pius XXI*), p. xxi.

The bitter struggle in the 1870s on the part of Bismarck to subject the Catholic church to state controls led to the term *Kulturkampf*, 'culture struggle'. Bismarck was looking for a common enemy to which he could divert dissatisfaction with the newly-created German reunification. He lighted on the concern that Catholics could not be fully loyal to Germany if their affairs were also ruled by the Vatican. Catholics could never be 'good' Germans.

At the time of reunification the new German Empire included over twenty-five million Protestants, 62 per cent, and fifteen million Catholics, 36 per cent; these populations were geographically concentrated, particularly in the Polish east and in the Bavarian south.

Education was separate, usually in the hands of the churches. There was little mutual tolerance or intermarriage. The ideological struggle was sparked by three promulgations from Rome: in 1854, the proclamation of Mary's immaculate conception; in 1864, an encyclical which condemned as false eighty philosophical and political statements, many of which countered the arguments for the foundation of the nation state, and forbade a large number of books; and, in 1870, the dogma of papal infallibility.[6]

If the pope was always right, where did Germany stand? 'As far as the [German] liberal elites were concerned, Catholics were subjects of the Pope … a foreign power within the state.'[7]

Bismarck responded from 1871 with twenty-two laws, starting with threatening two years in prison for any clergyman who addressed political matters from the pulpit, the *Kanzelparagraf*. The next year, 'hated' Jesuits were expelled across the empire, not returning until 1917; all religious schools were to have government inspections; all religious teachers were moved from government schools; and, in December, diplomatic relations with the Vatican ended. In a move, which had repercussions for Erich Gerth, Catholics were banned from representing Germany abroad. 'Bismarck sought to lame Catholicism as a political force'.[8]

---

6    In 1864, the *Quanta cura* and *Syllabus of Errors*. In 1870, the infallibility dogma was declared at the First Vatican Council. Gross, *War Against Catholicism*. Bunson, 'German Catholics under the Iron Fist'.

7    Gross, *War Against Catholicism*, p. 248.

8    Ulrich, *Bismarck*, p. 91.

'The hatred of the Catholics can only be called fanatical', but the extent of the Catholic backlash took Bismarck by surprise.[9] Increasingly severe tit-for-tat measures followed between all parties including government attempts to control the appointment of bishops, marriage being deemed a civil ceremony, the banning of religious orders, confiscation of church property and the arrest of over 200 priests and 130 newspaper editors.

'With each new piece of legislation and every new outrage and arrest, the levels of Catholic anger grew, but Catholics did not riot in the streets or plot violent revolution.'[10] However, there was an assassination attempt on Bismarck in 1874. The year before, Pope Pius IX issued an encyclical,

*No wonder, then, that the former religious tranquillity has been gravely disturbed in that Empire by this kind of law and other plans and actions of the Prussian government most hostile to the Church. But who would wish to falsely cast blame of the disturbance on the Catholics of the German Empire!*[11]

Over seven years, Bismarck's failing strategy brought considerable and lasting damage to relations between Rome and Berlin and within the German people. Bismarck capitulated to overtures from a new pope, Leo XIII, and most of the laws were rescinded by 1887, but the *Kanzelparagraf* lasted until 1953.

In the elections on 1873, the Catholic Centre Party, founded to defend the position of the church in the new empire, doubled its membership in the Landtag and the next year secured ninety-one members in the Reichstag. Bismarck turned his attention to the socialists and this eventually brought his downfall.

Similar determination for state control over church occurred in many European countries at this time, principally Italy, France and Spain.

During Pacelli's career, Church-State affairs in France saw 'rampant anti-clericalism'.[12] The French government was antagonistic towards the Catholic hierarchy and clergy because of their perceived royalist tendencies. The government forbade religious orders from teaching and boasted that 13,904 Catholic schools had been closed. 'Elected at the height of the French anti-

---

9    Gross, *War Against Catholicism*, p. 90.
10   Bunson, 'German Catholics under the Iron Fist', p. 25.
11   Encyclical *Etsi Multa*, EM 15, 21/11/1873.
12   Cornwell, *Hitler's Pope*, pp. 45-46.

clerical persecution', Pius X had made it clear that he wanted no 'appeasement of the French republic' which responded by cutting off diplomatic relations with the Vatican, then passed an act separating Church and State in France.

Pacelli was despatched to Bavaria in 1917 as nuncio and appointed as a 'political' archbishop of Sardi, entrusted with the 'delicate and difficult task of gaining German support for the papal peace effort. The new pope, Benedict, felt 'tormented by the spectacle of Christians waging war against Christians, Catholics against Catholics'. On election, Benedict published a protest to the world condemning the 'horrible butchery'.[13] Pacelli was upset by the ever-changing German attitude on peace, lamenting that 'when things went well militarily ... the Germans abandoned themselves to the most lunatic of illusions'.[14]

*Pacelli set off in remarkable style from Rome for Munich. Not only had Pacelli commandeered his own private compartment, but an additional sealed carriage had been added to the train to transport sixty cases of groceries to ensure that his troublesome stomach would not be affected by the food of wartime Germany.*[15]

Pacelli was seen as a 'surprising, indeed extraordinary appointment'.[16] His previous international experience was limited and often unsuccessful: ceremonial rather than substantive visits to London in 1905, a criticised concordat with Serbia in 1914, and a brief visit to Vienna the following year. Yet, he was a renowned Germanophile, applauded for tireless work to ameliorate the condition of Allied and German prisoners-of-war, sympathetic to German interests and fitted easily as the epicentre of Bavarian Catholic society. In June 1920, Pacelli was accredited as apostolic nuncio to the Weimar Republic.

*Soon after becoming Pope [in 1939], Pacelli told a group of pilgrims from Germany: 'We have always loved Germany where We were able to spend many years of Our*

---

13    Cornwell, *Hitler's Pope*, p. 60.
14    Herber, 'Pacelli's Mission', p. 48.
15    Cornwell, *Hitler's Pope*, p. 62.
16    Coppa, *Pius XII*, pp. 74-75. Pacelli was appointed archbishop of Sardi on 13 May 1917 on the sudden death of his predecessor. Sardi, or Sardes, was not an actual diocese with a cure of souls, but one of the seven hundred dioceses of Eastern Christendom destroyed by the Muslim invasion (Cornwell, *Hitler's Pope*), p. 61.

*life, and We love Germany even more today. We rejoice in Germany's greatness, rise, and well-being, and it would be false to assert that We do not desire a flourishing, great, and strong Germany.' German foreign minister von Ribbentrop, following a meeting, said: The Pope has always his heart in Germany and a great and lasting desire to reach a firm and lasting understanding with Hitler.*[17]

What were the public and private Catholic objectives of the time?

Pacelli branded the Versailles Treaty an 'international absurdity', deplored the Spartacists, Liebknecht and Luxemburg, and was delighted with the fall of the 'Bolshevik' government in Bavaria with its Jewish leaders. He also declined to reprove the French for its invasion of the Ruhr on the grounds that it was not his place and, on the grounds of impartiality, the Vatican had not criticised the German invasion of Belgium.[18]

Parallel with the schemes for the French takeover of the Ruhr Valley ran the French encouragement of Bavarian separatism, with the idea of forming a great German Catholic block against Prussia, to include perhaps Austria.[19] In pursuit of this aim, 'France was at one time even prepared to contemplate the Wittelsbach Monarchy being restored' of which Prince Ludwig Ferdinand von Bayern and Princess Maria de la Paz de Bourbon would have been close beneficiaries.

From the Vatican's point of view, the state of Bavaria with its large Catholic population and historic links with the Church of Rome, was an 'obvious starting point for the first state concordat'.[20] Between 1920 and March 1924, Pacelli concluded delicate negotiations with Bavaria which granted the Vatican broad power over the educational system and ensured the continuation of religious instruction in schools and universities.[21] It was passed by the Bavarian parliament by seventy-three votes to fifty-two.

With the move to Lutheran Berlin in 1925, Pacelli had a less favourable climate in which to negotiate. He was given three major papal tasks. Two were public: to negotiate concordats with Prussia and with the central German government seeking religious liberty, but also concessions on Catholic control

17    Coppa, *Pius XII*, p. 74.
18    Coppa, *Pius XII*, p. 87.
19    Gedye, *Revolver Republic*, p. 39.
20    Cornwell, *Hitler's Pope*, p. 87.
21    Coppa, *Pius XII*, pp. 91-100.

on education. A third was secret: to resolve differences between the Soviet Union and the Vatican through the Soviet ambassador in Berlin.

Pacelli found that the lay Catholic political leadership of Germany saw the nation's new situation as a striking opportunity. 'Having shown unquestioning loyalty through the war, German Catholics trusted that their days of inferiority, their days of having been regarded as Reichsfeinde, 'enemies of the Fatherland', had at last ended.'[22]

Pacelli settled into a splendid residence in the Tiergarten quarter. 'Tall, elegant, in his purple silk cloak, he became a familiar figure in the capital, arriving in his limousine at the Reich and Prussian ministries, or sweeping into receptions at embassies.'[23] He threw parties for the diplomatic and official elite; Paul von Hindenburg, Foreign Minister Gustav Stresemann and other cabinet members were regulars.

This is not where Erich Gerth made first acquaintance as Pacelli had already agreed three years before to become a referee. Canaris was, of course, never far away and knew Pacelli well when he was nuncio in Berlin.[24] In 1939, Joseph Muller, a Catholic lawyer, was sent after discussions with Canaris to the Vatican to re-establish connections with Pacelli, now Pope Pius XII. The object was to use the Vatican to make contact with the British Government to obtain their support for a coup attempt against Hitler and Himmler. On 12 January 1940, Pacelli spoke on the matter with the British Envoy Extraordinary and Minister Plenipotentiary to the Vatican, Sir Francis d'Arcy Godolphin Osborne, and again on 7 February, and received an assurance from the British Government transmitted by Pacelli to Berlin in which 'the will for a just peace' was guaranteed provided that Hitler was toppled.[25]

When word reached Berlin of the success, and the German embassy involvement through Erich Gerth in the Mass of Reconciliation in Paris in 1933, Erich was recalled and 'told in no uncertain terms that reconciliation was considered defeatist thinking and, further, that henceforth the Bismarck

---

22   Cornwell, *Hitler's Pope*, p. 80.
23   Cornwell, *Hitler's Pope*, p. 101.
24   Mueller, *Canaris*, pp. 180-82.
25   Osborne played a key part, as did Pacelli, in the plot in 1940 to overthrow Hitler. Osborne ran with others an escape line for up to 4,000 Allied soldiers on the run in Italy, almost all of whom survived the war (Chadwick, *Britain and the Vatican During the Second World War*), p. 86 and following. See the 1983 film *The Scarlet and the Black*, starring Gregory Peck.

attitude that no Catholic should ever represent Germany abroad was now re-instated'.[26]

The final threat hurled at him was, 'By the time we get through with you, you will be lucky if you can sell newspapers on the corner.'

26    Email, Roger Gerth, 22/1/2018.

# 16

# GERTH: THE BEGINNING OF THE END

And then the wider world fell in – for Erich Gerth, for Salomon Marx and his family, for German Jews, and for the nation.

Gerth was recalled from Paris to Berlin on 12 May 1933, but was briefly delayed because of work. On 30 September, he was placed in temporary retirement.

'For official reasons the dismissal of the legation secretary at the embassy in Paris, Erich Gerth, is urgently required. As there is currently no other position available his transfer into provisional retirement could not be avoided.'

The certificate was prepared by Grünau, recent supporter from Personnel, signed personally by President Paul von Hindenburg and countersigned by the latest Foreign Minister, Konstantin von Neurath, who Gerth managed to upset nine years before in Rome. On 19 March 1934, Gerth was placed without review into final retirement. This was a bevy of powerful men to move one First Secretary. Overnight, Gerth's salary fell from a base of 6,000 Reichsmark plus a further 7,000 as a Paris allowance to a pension of 420.50.[1]

After banning all other political parties on 7 April 1933, two months after coming to power, the Nazis introduced the 'Civil Service Restoration Act' which claimed to re-establish a 'national' and 'professional' civil service. Racially or

---

1    IG 336 5/10, 9/10/1933.

politically unwanted civil servants were to be fired or forced into retirement, Clause 3(1). In the first instance, the 'unwanted' were either members of the Communist party or were those who had just one Jewish grandparent, whatever their current religion. The stricture applied to anyone in government employ or needing a government licence to work: teachers, professors, judges, diplomats, lawyers, doctors, tax consultants, musicians and notaries.

Hindenburg objected to the bill until three classes of civil servants were excluded: veterans who had served at the front, those who had been in the civil service since August 1914, and those who had lost a father or son in combat, Clause 3(2).

Under Clause 6, civil servants could be forced into retirement without cause and this was Gerth's fate. When Hindenburg died in 1934, his exclusions were swept away. It was the first time since German Jews had been emancipated in 1871 that an anti-Semitic law had been passed in Germany.

Albert Einstein resigned from the Prussian Academy of Sciences and emigrated to the United States before he could be expelled.[2] Erich's fellow u-boat commander from Pola, Martin Niemöller, now a pastor, spoke against Jews, but protected them in his church. In 1933, he co-founded the *Pfarrernotbund*, 'Emergency Covenant of Pastors', to combat the discrimination against Christians of Jewish background and particularly the discriminatory 'Aryan Paragraph' anchored in the 'Law for the Restoration of the Professional Civil Service'.[3]

Until the revelations about Erich Gerth's Catholic activities, disclosed in this book, the reason for the action against him was seemingly evident. Eva Gerth, though thoroughly Catholic, was half-Jewish by birth and her father, Salomon, was already under attack by the Nazis perhaps because he was Jewish, perhaps because he was cheek by jowl with Hugenberg, but also perhaps because the film company Ufa was coveted?

No mention of any 'reason' was ever included in Gerth's file. Erich was to suffer by association. A simple route would be to use the Civil Service Act to force Erich and Eva back to Germany. The act's provisions were broad and could not be appealed. Gerth was not Jewish and had fought on the front line. A note in the files dated 8 September 1933 states that 'Gerth was a combatant

---

2    wikipedia.
3    Niemöller, *From U-boat to Pulpit.*

according to the attached war service certificate by the Command of the Navy Station, Baltic Sea. He took part in the operations of the submarine flotilla in the Mediterranean, based in Pola and Cattaro'.[4]

The certificate itself was returned to Gerth so that this defence was not available to those at the Foreign Office.

Was Neurath taking some sort of delayed retribution? It looks doubtful as a primary reason as he was as much caught up in events as Gerth. After his term at the Foreign Office, Neurath frustrated Hitler once too often and was sent away as Protector of Bohemia and Moravia when the area was taken over in 1939. Here, Neurath had, hopelessly, to deal with his deputy, Reinhard Heydrich, joint main architect of the holocaust and known as the 'Butcher of Prague'. Neurath ended his life as a 'war criminal', convicted after the second world war at Nuremberg as a foreign minister who led his country and his people into 'wars of aggression and crimes against humanity'. It was a prosecution, says his biographer, in which 'had he been given access to his documents, a defence lawyer who understood the court proceedings, and a court seeking historical truth rather than legal technicalities, he would have been acquitted'.[5]

*Neurath, a virtuous and decent gentleman, had allowed his talents and capabilities to serve forces which he only imperfectly understood and frequently rejected personally. Perhaps in another time, good intentions and private virtues would have sufficed. In Hitler's Germany they proved disastrous to a baron born for another century. Neurath's story is one of a man trying to tame a whirlwind. His fate reflects that of a generation of well-meaning Germans and speaks to one of the great questions of modern history: how could decent and honourable men serve the evil that was National Socialism.*[6]

Once you start these things, blind policies, there are often unintended consequences. Tirpitz's wife, Marie Lipke, was a baptised Protestant, born in West Prussia in 1860. Her father, Gustav Lipke, was born in 1820 in Berlin to a wealthy assimilated Jewish banking and business family and who, at eighteen,

---

4   Personnel file, Berlin, 120-29 B 4/8, Kiel, 4/7/1933.
5   Heineman, *Neurath*, pp. 2, 226.
6   Heineman, *Neurath*, p. 246.

converted to Protestantism.[7] He was a lawyer who served in the Prussian Diet and in the Imperial Reichstag. Tirpitz, as with Erich Gerth, was married to a Jewess. Tirpitz's salary on retirement was 45,000 Reichsmark, plus another 15,000 for office expenses. At his death in 1930, his pension was half his salary. Had Tirpitz lived until 1933 and the introduction of the Civil Service Restoration Act, he might have seen his pension cut to just ten per cent, 4,500 Reichsmark.[8]

There is now another, compelling, option for the termination of Erich Gerth's diplomatic career. His determined cultivation of the most senior Catholics in Paris and his attempts at Franco-German reconciliation was of serious concern to the Nazi direction of travel. The Catholic Centre Party was a prominent voice in the Weimar Republic, holding the chancellorship eight times, including under Wilhelm Marx, Eva Marx's relation. However, in the face of Nazi hostility, even this party dissolved itself in 1933 before Hitler could disband it.

'The clash of *Kulturkampf* in the German Empire laid the groundwork for the repression of Catholics in Germany and Europe under Adolf Hitler.'[9] It was the Nazi view, as with Bismarck, that to be a good German meant being a good Protestant. Protestant Christianity was positioned within the concept of Nazi anti-Semitism by removing the Old Testament and presenting Jesus as the original anti-Semite.

*National Socialism was antithetical to Catholicism. Nazi leaders and members who had come from a Catholic background were apostates and often bitterly opposed to Catholicism. By the time that the Nazis were in power, it was clear to them that institutional Catholicism was opposed to National Socialism and that being a loyal Catholic meant being loyal to a power that was not German.*[10]

In power, the Nazis were intent on destroying Catholic influence in Germany. A rapprochement with the French was the opposite of official policy; the long-term plan was the continuation of the first world war. Erich Gerth in Paris could not be more out of step with his new masters if he had tried.

---

7    Kelly, *Tirpitz and the Imperial German Navy*, pp. 69-70.
8    Kelly, *Tirpitz*, pp. 410, 443-45.
9    Bunson, 'German Catholics under the Iron Fist', p. 27.
10   Steigmann-Gall, *Holy Reich*. Hastings, *Catholicism and the Roots of Nazism*.

On 8 April 1934, Gerth wrote a painful letter from Villa Patroncinio, Malaga, in Spain, to Grünau. 'For health reasons I am unable to travel ... I can't believe otherwise than the approach of the Foreign Office against me is based on insufficient information and erroneous considerations. It only remains for me to hope that one day this will turn out right and that an opportunity will be found to make up for the injustice committed to me and my family.'

A stream of further pleadings flowed from Gerth.

'My financial situation has deteriorated significantly during the night' ... 'news of my transfer to permanent retirement throws me completely off track and brings my family into the trouble which hit me at Easter' ... 'Heaven knows how I will get my feet back on solid ground'.[11] 'Difficulties of looking for a new livelihood as my health is very shaken by recent events and I can do little for the time being'... 'Whether we will come back after my recovery to Paris or somewhere else to take our place of residence, I don't know today ... in particular, where may I manage to find a new livelihood ... will my foreign pension be paid in time ... I'm dependent entirely on my pension which is only 300 Reichsmark per month'.

Erich did regain his health and strength brought about by Spanish sun and by Eva cooking a vegetarian diet with fresh vegetables and fruits. Local orange growers advised that the diet should include the white pulp from inside the orange peels which contained many valuable nutrients, usually overlooked. On the couple's return to Germany in 1935, people who knew Erich before and after Spain said that he looked ten years younger.

---

11    Letter from Erich Gerth to Herr Freudenberg, Personnel Department, Foreign Ministry, 9/4/1934.

# 17

# MARX: THE HUMILIATION

The Nazis also moved in 1935 to finish with Salomon Marx and others in his family.

Marx was classed a *Volljude*, a full blooded Jew, as both his parents were Jewish and, therefore, his private bank was classified as a Jewish business. His share in Haus Vaterland was lost during an aggressive takeover by a company called *Kempinski*. The Nazis made him sell his shares in Ufa after the downfall of Alfred Hugenberg. In 1935, Salomon Marx's last positions on supervisory boards, once forty, were reduced from thirteen to four, causing a considerable reduction in his income. Marx tried to keep ownership of his *Internationale Handelsbank*, but he was forced into liquidation with a loss of several hundred thousand Reichsmark. Salomon then had to sell all his real estate.

*After the decree of the Nuremberg Laws, Salomon lost his right of citizenship of the German Reich.[1] He suffered constant harassment of his business, the arrest and*

---

1    wikipedia: The *Nürnberger Gesetze*, Nuremberg Laws, were introduced on 15/9/1935 at a special meeting convened at the Nazi Party's annual Nuremberg Rally. The two laws were for the 'Protection of German Blood and German Honour', which forbade marriages and extramarital intercourse between Jews and Germans and the employment of German females under forty-five in Jewish households; and the 'Reich Citizenship Law', which declared that only those of German or related blood were eligible to be Reich citizens; the remainder were classed as state subjects, without citizenship rights. A supplementary decree outlining the definition of who was Jewish was passed on 14/11/1935 when the 'Reich Citizenship Law' came into force. The laws were expanded on 26/11/1935 to include Romani and black people. This supplementary decree defined Gypsies as 'enemies of the race-based state', the same category as Jews. Because of

*imprisonment of his banking partner Alexander Elfer [who later escaped to New York], termination of credits and loss of his honorary and supervisory positions. His home was regarded as a Jewish home and this meant that no domestic servants were allowed to be kept. His estimated income fell steadily: 1930, 80,000 Reichsmark; 1931: 50,000; 1932, 40,000.*[2]

George Martos confirmed that he knew Salomon Marx well, both socially and as his doctor from 1925 until his death in 1936. Marx underwent a 'psychological and physical change' as a consequence of his loss of professional and social status.[3] Martos said Marx had an active mind, was full of vitality and energy, and enjoyed the highest respect in industry, art and literature. In 1933, when he first lost his honorary positions and later had to surrender the management of the bank 'for reasons of political persecution', he completely changed and due to an increasing paranoia suffered from bouts of *angina pectoris* which became increasingly frequent and severe.

'It is unquestionable that the persecution caused his early demise.'

Marx's son, Eduard, who as a doctor treated his father for the last five years of his life, confirmed the diagnosis.[4] Eduard claimed that Marx's angina was cured completely in the spa resort of Bad Nassau and he was fully able to work until 1931. He undertook a 4,500 kilometre car journey throughout Western Europe without any problems or medical issues. The first severe relapses occurred at the beginning of 1933.

'My father was worried about the increasing strength of the national socialists. As a leading businessman, he was also aware of the consequences that a seizure of power by the Nazis would have for him. My father was deeply affected by the deprivation of rights as a result of the Nuremberg Laws which he saw as a terrible injustice.'

---

concern for the Olympics to be held in 1936 in Berlin, prosecutions under the two laws did not start until after the games finished.

2    *LABO*, Documents Marx Family 1951-58, file Salomon Marx/304.641, 'Declaration for the Entschädigungsamt by Dr Eduard Marx, 29/5/1956, p. A5.

3    *LABO*, Documents Marx Family 1951-58, file Salomon Marx/304.641, 'Certificate of Dr George Martos', 23/5/1956, p. A3.

4    *LABO*, Documents Marx Family 1951-58, file Salomon Marx/304.641, 'Declaration for the Entschädigungsamt' Dr Eduard Marx, 29/5/1956, p. A5.

From 1935, Salomon Marx's health deteriorated rapidly, each act of harassment by the Nazis triggered new attacks and bouts of depression.

*The loss of his supervisory positions in leading companies such as Ufa, Lindström and Engelhardt not only damaged him economically, but had a detrimental effect on his existing angina pectoris which up to then had caused him little discomfort. The feeling of suddenly being dubbed an undesirable and inferior human being by a government that acted unlawfully, the prohibition to keep domestic servants, to work in an executive position and all further restrictions and humiliations accelerated the course of his existing illness.*

Salomon's wife, Charlotte, described how the loss of economic and social status, financial worries and growing isolation led to his heart attacks and depression. In his last days, Salomon rarely left his flat. He died on 24 October 1936 of heart failure.[5] Charlotte received one quarter of his much reduced inheritance and his two children from his first marriage, Eduard Marx and Eva Gerth, three-eights each.

Could there be another reason for this early and concerted attack by the Nazis on a prominent and wealthy businessman who happened to be a Jew? Was Marx to be impoverished because of his importance to Hugenberg who had dared to try to manipulate Hitler? Hugenberg might be allowed the façade of freedom, but his ability to respond to Nazi aggression had to be eliminated and Marx was a part of his potential toolbox.

Action against Hugenberg and Marx would also deliver the Ufa film studios, a most useful propaganda tool, into Himmler's hands.

Nazi steps against Salomon Marx extended to his family. In 1933, his younger brother, Karl Marx, who fought in the trenches in the first world war, lost his positions as a government councillor and building officer in the construction industry because of his Jewish heritage. He 'fell in 1945 as a member of a Jewish labour squad defending the city of Breslau'. Salomon's oldest brother, Otto Marx of Una in Westphalia, died aged eighty-three in the Theresienstadt, now Terezín, walled ghetto, near Prague. The ghetto was used as a transit centre for western Jews on their way to Auschwitz and other extermination

---

5    *LABO*, Documents Marx Family 1951-58, file Salomon Marx/304.641, 'Letter by solicitor Dr Georg Lancelle, Berlin 4/10/1957, pp. M19-20.

camps.[6] No date has been found for Otto's death, but it is probable that he died while Konstantin Neurath was Protector of Bohemia.

---

6     The 7,000 Czechs that lived in the town before the Nazis took over were expelled during June of 1942, making way for some 50,000 Jews. About 155,000 Jews were brought to Theresienstadt during the war. Approximately 87,000 were deported to concentration camps farther east, while about 34,000 died in the ghetto. Of the more than 10,500 children who lived in the ghetto before being deported east, only 245 survived the war.

# 18

# GERTH: ON THE RUN

In May 1935, the Gerth family moved from Spain back to Germany, probably motivated by the approaching Spanish Civil War. They moved into Ahornallee 6 in Berlin; Eva gave birth to Isabella in August.

Erich was hired on 15 June by *Fritz Werner Maschinenfabrik* in Marienfelde, a 3,000 employee engineering factory. Erich explained to the Foreign Office that he was a junior employee in the machinery section and earned a low salary of 400 Reichsmark. Fritz Werner made machine tools, but in 1938 became a small armaments plant with a contract from the Portuguese government. With war the next year, Werner's produced arms for the German army using forced labour from a camp at the Daimler-Benz street corner in Berlin. The slaves were housed in underground cells under Daimler Street. Eva was, therefore, in Berlin when her father died in October 1936.

At the same time as he took the position at the Werner company, Gerth applied for work to the Air District Command VI in Kiel. The Command asked for background to his forced retirement from the Foreign Office. The request and reply were classified secret. The Foreign Office said that Gerth had 'proven himself during his career in the foreign service as a diligent and reliable official', but nothing came of the opportunity in the air force. The real reason for his retirement was not mentioned.

Three years later, the opportunity returned and, perhaps, Gerth reapplied. By this time, the Nazi party had the final say in matters to do with Gerth so the Foreign Ministry wrote to Rudolf Hess, Deputy Fuhrer to Hitler, on

23 June 1938. Hess's department simply confirmed that in 1935 a favourable assessment had been sent to the air district command.

In 1937, Eva was expecting a fourth child and, well aware of the actions against her family, used the excuse of attending the Paris Exposition so that the birth did not happen in Nazi Germany.[1] The couple stayed in a rented top floor corner apartment in the Eighth Arrondissement from which Eva could see the basilica of the Sacré-Coeur from one window and the Eiffel Tower from the other.

Eva was visited by Gestapo attached to the embassy, Erich's old place of work. Even though Erich was no longer employed, a watch was kept on those on the 'list'. At her bedside, Eva was asked why the wife of a former delegate had a Jewish doctor, Levi Solal, for the birth. Eva replied that Solal was the best obstetrician in Paris which the Gestapo duly noted and left. Roger, who was born prematurely, was baptized Roger Andre Marie Rüdiger, plus six other names as was the custom.

Gerth's health issues flared up again. That summer, doctors found far too late *ulcerous granuloma* at the roots of several teeth which were extracted three at a time. The last doctor's declaration of that year confirmed that Erich had *angina pectoris*, chronic gout and kidney disease. However, the Foreign Office official doctor turned down a recommendation to send their disgraced pensioner Gerth to a sanatorium in Switzerland. In January 1938, Erich wrote that he had suffered for 'quite some time' from angina, cramps of the coronary blood vessels, circulatory disturbance, gout and renal colic.

Both Salomon's sons, Eduard and Dr Eberhard Marx, who lived at Gritznerstrasse 45 in Steglitz in the south-west of Berlin, were considered a *Mischling*, a mongrel, with first-degree mixed-blood, having one Aryan parent.[2] Because of this, Eduard was unable to marry his chosen Ilse Geue, seven years his junior, also a *Mischling*. In 1937, they travelled quietly to Glasgow, in Scotland, to marry 'illegally', violating the Nuremberg laws.[3]

---

1    The 1937 Exposition Internationale des Arts et Techniques dans la Vie Moderne, 'International Exposition of Art and Technology in Modern Life', in Paris was the city's sixth International Exposition after fairs held in 1855, 1867, 1878, 1889, and 1900. It took place between 25/5-25/11, centred upon the Trocadéro, just across the Seine from the Eiffel Tower.

2    *Mischling* was used before the Nazi era as describing mongrel dogs.

3    Married in Blythswood, Glasgow, 9 or 17/5/1937. Ilse's parents lived at Kirchstraße 13 in Berlin. Her father Paul Geue was a foreman in an optical company; her mother was Elise Schultz.

An employee at the Glasgow registry office tipped off the London Press about this 'very unusual foreign marriage'.

*Our names and photos were on the title page of the Daily Express with the comment that we had flouted Nazi laws by getting married. The mentioned newspaper was also sold in Berlin. Lack of money forced us to return to Berlin where we were in constant danger of being arrested. The Schwarze Corps, 'Black Corps', launched a spiteful personal attack against me.*

Eduard stated that he never knew how he and Ilse managed to escape arrest.

In 1938, Erich Gerth received a message from his long-term friend, Canaris, that a so-called *Aktion M* was being prepared which aimed at the extermination of all mixed-race persons. The lives of Eduard Marx and his sister Eva Gerth and her four children were now in immediate danger.

'We were urgently advised by Canaris to obtain Aryan certificates in order to escape this action' and an introduction was made to a 'professional genealogist', previous-Kapitänleutnant Walter Firnhaber. While working for the Fritz Werner company, Erich Gerth met Firnhaber in the Gerths' flat in Berlin in the autumn to discuss research designed to establish the ancestry of the paternal family of Erich's wife.[4] At this stage, the provision of fake documents was not mentioned. About two weeks later, Firnhaber returned to the flat and confirmed that it would be difficult, unsurprisingly, to obtain suitable documents for the paternal line of Gerth's wife, Salomon Marx's Jewish family.

Matters turned illegal when Firnhaber explained that he would be able to provide a forged, faultless, pure Aryan ancestor pass for Gerth and his family. At the same time, Firnhaber explained that he would have to increase his fee from 300 to 3,000 Reichsmark.

Firnhaber was no fly-by-night. Production of the officially certified *Ahnenpass*, the Nazi's genealogical passport, was a major business as people scrambled to secure protection from the extermination camps.

'The Ahnenpass spawned its own cottage industry', competing with the state-licensed kinship researcher, *Berufssippenforscher*.[5] There were many 'how-

---

4    *LABO*, Documents Marx Family 1951-58, file Salomon Marx/304.641, 'Duplicate of prosecution papers against Walter Firnhaber and Dr Eduard Marx, Berlin 28/7/1942, pp. C4-6.

5    Ehrenreich, *Nazi Ancestral Proof*, pp. 69-75.

to' guides, smart, printed documents for personal completion with the 'proofs', research services and arranged official scrutiny and approvals. One company, *RNK Papier- und Schreibwaren* in Berlin produced a product called 'Firnhaber's Little Ahnenpass', named after its designer, Walter Firnhaber. This was a passport-sized document which unfolded into a full genealogical table that could be viewed all at once.

RNK sent an example to Martin Bormann, convicted murderer and Hitler's private secretary, who sent back his personal approval. RNK used Bormann's endorsement in a four-page advertisement and, as a result, got into a serious spat with the civil registrars' publishing house who saw RNK as gaining unfair advantage over all competition. Eventually, Bormann ordered Firnhaber to 'stop the advertisement and to remove all such items from commerce'.

'The producers of these products designed to prove racial purity fought for market share' with steely determination. Firnhaber's business was much damaged and there was more than a hint that Canaris, now leader of the Abwehr, and Germany's pre-eminent spy service, saw a useful and discreet service provider for his operation and was happy to recommend Firnhaber to Gerth, an old friend in need.

The story is taken up in prosecution papers prepared for an eventual trial of Walter Firnhaber and Eduard Marx.[6] Erich Gerth considered 3,000 Reichsmark too much and decided to talk to Marx. He asked Firnhaber to return in a few days. Eduard Marx agreed to buy an ancestor pass for himself and to contribute to the fee. In the next few days, Marx and Erich and Eva Gerth met Firnhaber at the Gerths' flat and he was asked for seven ancestor passports for the Gerths, their four children, and Marx, but, interestingly, not for his wife, Ilse. Firnhaber initially demanded a fee of 5,000 Reichsmark which he dropped to 4,500 Reichsmark after negotiation.

Marx and his sister, Eva, went to the 79th Depositenkasse of the *Dresdner Bank* and withdrew their share of the money and gave it all to Firnhaber in the street without a receipt.

Firnhaber then set about forging baptism and marriage certificates for Eduard and Eva's grandparents, Eduard and Bertha, née Hecht, Marx, the parents of Salomon Marx. On 21 September 1938, Firnhaber went to the

---

6    This information was confirmed by Walter Firnhaber, now a district counsellor, in Wiesbaden, 23/10/1952 (*LABO*, Documents Marx Family 1951-58, file Salomon Marx/304.641), p. E41.

Catholic parish office in Schwerte, Salomon's birthplace, where he asked for the baptism and marriage documents of randomly selected persons in the church register. He had copies made of these entries, written out in ink, and signed and stamped by the local priest. The same day in his hotel room, he removed the personal details on the copies with 'ink killer' and replaced them later in Berlin with the names and dates of Eduard and Bertha Marx.

Satisfied with these forgeries, Firnhaber destroyed them and returned to Schwerte, this time with his own blank copies of baptism and marriage forms. When the parish assistant left the room, Firnhaber stamped the blanks with the original church seal. He later entered all the personal details of Eduard and Bertha Marx and copied the signature of the priest, had the documents certified by a notary, and burned the background evidence. In December, Firnhaber met with Marx and the Gerths and handed over their seven ancestor passports with certified duplicate copies of six supporting documents.

Firnhaber advised that, if possible, it was better not to use the ancestor passports in Germany. Gerth did not use the passports, intending them for travel abroad or in case he or his family encountered difficulties in getting foreign visas or in securing education for his children, especially his son, Marco, in his planned career, surprisingly, as an army officer.

Eduard Marx, however, went to his medical association in Berlin, showed his documents, and declared that he could now prove he was of pure German blood and that all the previous statements that he was a first-degree *Mischling* were wrong. Only Aryan doctors were eligible to join the 'Union of German Doctors' and display their sign at the door of their surgery and this was Marx's goal.[7]

When Marx later registered his doctor's car, he submitted his forged documents again. During these repeated ancestry checks, some irregularity was spotted and the matter was referred to the *Rasse- und Siedlungshauptamt*, the SS office for Race and Settlement. Canaris intervened personally with the investigation, but advised Marx that matters could only be delayed until late 1943. However, Firnhaber was implicated. After long and persistent denial, Firnhaber made a comprehensive confession which led to legal charges in July

---

7    There were covert identification marks in the official list for doctors: a comma for non-Aryans, a semicolon for Jews.

1942 in which he, Eduard Marx and Erich and Eva Gerth were all named and accused.

Fear of the German government had becomes serious by 1939 when Erich and Eva tried to flee Germany for South America. They travelled to Portugal to get a Clipper flight but, when they arrived, found that the last flying boat had left.[8] Imagine the desperation at the airport and the bitter sweet consequences.

Erich and Eva returned to Berlin. At least, that is the story and it comes only from family memory.[9]

The first question is why, flight missed, they did not stay in neutral Portugal? The answer, one expects, was a need to return to their children.

Second, why during their trip to Portugal did Erich and Eva leave their four children in Berlin with Eduard Marx, Eva's brother, and two nannies?[10] This was surely not an abandonment of their loved children on the brink of war. From many perspectives, Eduard was in as much danger as Eva. The thought is that only one of them was travelling onwards. Erich or Eva always intended an immediate return to Germany to resume care of the children and to make plans to follow when the other was settled.

The remaining question is, then, who would help with refuge and a new life in South America? The suggestion is that it was the von Ahlefeldts, the family of Eva's first husband, Graf Karl-Christian, who was killed in 1916. It may be remembered that Frau Gräfin Franziska von Ahlefeldt-Eschelsmark, Eva's ex-mother-in-law, was in 1922 prepared to support Erich's application to the Foreign Office showing that a close relationship continued. Also, Graf Friedrich Karl, leader of the only surviving branch of Karl-Christian's family, emigrated in 1890 from Denmark to the Argentine, and his descendants lived near Buenos Aires.

There is one further hint. Just before Christmas, 1922, Eva 'von Mark', a photographer in her twenties, Catholic, left Hamburg in first class aboard the steamer *Carias* for Santos, the port for São Paulo.[11] Was this Eva Gerth visiting

---

8    The Boeing 314 Clipper was a long-range flying boat produced between 1938 and 1941. One of the largest aircraft of the time, it had a massive wing to achieve the range necessary for flights across the Atlantic and Pacific Oceans (wikipedia).

9    Telephone conversation, Marc Gerth, 15/1/2018; email, Roger Gerth, 19/1/2018.

10   After the second world war, on one of his trips to Germany, Marc Gerth, met again with one of his nannies.

11   Hamburg passenger lists, 20/12/1922 (ancestry.com).

the relatives of her dead first husband and cementing a contact that would later become valuable?

Weeks afterwards, the Gerth family left Berlin for good. At the end of 1939, Erich, Eva and the children took a train from Berlin for Rome. They rented an apartment at Via Zara 13, which was owned by an Italian Senator. The building was near where the street runs into Via Nomentana, across from Mussolini's Villa Torlonia residence. Georg Gerth's son, Ernst, visited at this time.

Mussolini's wife, Donna Rachele, the daughter of a peasant family, did her own shopping in a nearby open air market.

'The people seemed to really like her. It was said in the neighbourhood that she was doing her own shopping because she did not think that her husband's 'dictator thing' would last and she did not want to get out of practice.'[12]

When Mussolini was dismissed by King Victor Emmanuel III in 1943, the Germans occupied Rome and began rounding up Jews and others on their lists. The senator returned to re-occupy his apartment forcing the Gerth family to find another apartment, which they did adjacent to the nearby Parco Paganini. One early morning, German troops surrounded the building and an officer knocked on the door looking for the previous occupiers, a Communist underground newspaper. When Erich answered the door, they realized they were too late and departed without incident.

Court papers, even after his death, gave Erich's occupation in Rome as a representative of *Fritz Werner*, the Berlin firm he had joined in 1935. He now worked in security, screening visitors and protecting the firm's war secrets. He flew to Germany from Italy several times on business. Erich continued ill and took nitro-glycerine tablets for his angina.

Erich had every incentive to seek some small sanctuary, at the least some safer distance, among the powerful Catholic community in Rome.

'It was prudent to escape the attention of the German government'.[13]

Erich was caught up in a formidable mixture of threats and, today, it is difficult to know which, or which combination, was the most dangerous. Most immediately, the investigation into Eduard Marx and the confession of Walter Firnhaber were available to the Nazis and Erich and Eva were to be charged

---

12    Email, Roger Gerth, 20/1/2018.
13    Telephone conversation, Marc Gerth, 15/1/2018.

with offences concerning their false passports. Their co-conspirator, Eduard, had travelled illegally to Glasgow to get married and had been lauded in British newspapers for breaking the Nuremburg laws. Erich and Eva had run away to Portugal in an attempt to get one of them to South America, and this may have been known to the German authorities; they certainly knew they were now in Rome. There was unfinished business from 1933: first, Eva was a *Mischling* and her freedom and, eventually, that of her quarter-blood children would come to an end; second, Erich and Eva's public work in Paris among the French and German Catholic communities calling for reconciliation, and which had attracted so much official attention, had angered the Nazis. Eva's father, Salomon Marx, had been the right-hand man of Alfred Hugenberg, whom the Nazis had 'circumcised' for daring to try to manipulate Hitler. The Nazis had stolen Salomon's property, reduced him to a mental wreck, and probably sent him to an early grave.

Some combination of these 'threats' might explain why the highest Nazis, Hindenburg, Neurath and Hess, all signed parts of the papers forcing Erich from the Foreign Office and ignored his pleas for reinstatement. Perhaps Neurath also harboured some dark personal memory.

Finally, there was the awkwardness of knowing Wilhelm Canaris, Erich's friend and protector, and who knows how far their links really went. Canaris's time was running out, even in 1939. Heinrich Himmler, Reichsführer of the SS and acquirer of Ufa, was working to bring him down.

Sooner or later, someone in the Nazi hierarchy might place all this damning information about Erich together and decide to take executive action.

Erich Gerth did not survive the war. He died in Rome on 12 December 1943, age fifty-seven, of *Herzschwäche*, 'heart disease'.[14] He was travelling in a car to the train station at Settebagni on his way to Germany; his eleven-year-old son, Marco, with him to wave goodbye, was sitting in the front seat. On the way they passed the airport where there were many destroyed *Luftwaffe* planes.

Erich was sitting in the back between two men whom Marco had never seen before and never saw again. Erich did not speak, went red in the face, and died quickly.

Eva was always convinced, although Marco, late in life, was not, that Erich had been assassinated.

---

14    Freiburg, MSG2/18635, p. xiii.

There was no autopsy. Unusually, there is only one photograph of Erich in his personal file in the Berlin Foreign Office. It is stuck firmly onto the bottom of his application of 1922, except that the top half, the half showing his face, has been torn off in a manner that would be a most unlikely accident. Staff searching the archive as research for this book thought that the picture had been deliberately defaced.

Perhaps it is wrong to read too much into these things?

Erich was buried in the private garden of the German cemetery inside the Vatican, *Campo Santo Teutonico*, today inaccessible behind high walls to the crowds of tourists.

The Vatican secretariat confirms that burial here required previous strict attendance to religious rules of a Catholic confraternity. There were only three other German internments during the war years: Theobald Heintzel, born the same year as Erich, a Prussian who served in a Munich infantry regiment in WW1, and an elderly couple, the Gieffers, Wilhelm and Filippine, who both died in their eighties.

Eva wrote in January 1944, care of the German Embassy at the Holy See, to the Foreign Office asking for 1,000 Reichsmark quickly for the costs of Erich's doctor and the funeral. She was told she would receive 509 Reichsmark and she asked for the money and her widow's income to be sent to Erich's brother, Georg, who was living in Würzburg.

# 19

# GERTH: LIFE AFTER DEATH

When Erich died, murdered Eva believed, she decided it was time to go into hiding.

Marco, who previous to the American bombing of Frascati in September 1943, had been at the Mondragone Jesuit boarding school, now went into sanctuary with the Jesuits in Rome. The two daughters, Diana and Isabella, were already safe at their French boarding school, the Sacré-Coeur, atop the Spanish Steps. Eva found a place for herself and Roger in a convent of French nuns near the Trevi Fountain.

The nuns had responded to the urging of Pope Pius XII, who had signed Erich's job application over twenty-five years before, for the convents of Rome to open their doors to people who were at risk of persecution, Jews and Christians alike. While hiding in the convent, Roger fell ill and required medication. Eva went to a pharmacy near Via Rasella just as Italian partisans attacked a column of German SS Police. Eva heard the explosion and shots. She knew what would happen next: nearby streets would be blocked and everyone rounded up as retaliation. Eva took a long detour and returned safely to the convent.

It was from the convent windows on the evening of 4 June 1944, after waiting all day for it to happen, that Roger caught sight of the first Allied troops.

*They came sauntering across the Piazza della Pilotta. They looked so casual, compared to the spit-and-polish German soldiers who had just departed, that I wondered how they could be the ones winning the war. And yet it was such a joyous occasion. For all practical purposes, the war for the Gerth family was now over. We finally felt safe. None of us thought about what awaited us when we would return to a devastated Germany.*[1]

When Eduard Marx received his bill of indictment for falsification of documents and submission of forged Aryan certificates in 1942, he suffered his first severe heart attack and was unable to work for a long period.

Matters got steadily worse.

Eduard's brother-in-law, Erich Gerth, died at the end of the next year.

At the same time, Canaris had been defeated in his power battle against Himmler and was unable to help further. Canaris was executed in 1945 in Flossenbürg concentration camp for his part in an assassination attempt on Adolf Hitler.

Eduard's home, his father's last house at Lessingstraße 31 in Berlin, was destroyed by bombing at the end of 1943. Marx tried to establish a doctor's practice in Moabit, however he was ordered by the Commissioner for Jews in the Berlin Medical Association, SS-doctor Arno Hermann, to a post outside of Berlin as a locum. Hermann also told Marx in a telephone conversation that criminal proceedings for fraud had been filed against him and that 'he would soon discover the consequences'.

Marx worked in Eichwalde where a local doctor, Machowicz, a staunch Nazi and close friend of Hermann, filed charges against Eduard for sabotage for writing too many sick notes for women working in arms factories, for wasting petrol, and also for his connection with Canaris. It was alleged that Eduard had lists of partisans in Eichwalde which should have been destroyed in case the plot against Hitler of 20 July 1944 did not succeed. In the evening of 22 November 1944, Eduard suffered 'several severe heart attacks' and left Eichwalde to escape arrest and to join his family in the remote village of Klein-Köris. He lived illegally until the end of the war without food ration cards and relied for help on a local shop owner, a friend of his wife.

In February 1944, Eduard was sentenced to twelve months in prison for possession of false identification papers, but he appealed in November. There were no further proceedings before the end of the war.

---

1    Email, Roger Gerth, 20/1/2018.

'The ancestor passports were returned to me and are my property. I also have the grey ID card for the politically and racially persecuted.'[2]

The criminal charges against Erich and Eva Gerth fell away. In 1945, Firnhaber was also given a jail sentence, but the case was deemed 'political' and the criminal proceedings were suspended at war end.

After the liberation of Rome, the Gerth family moved to the Pensione Villa Mater Dei on the Viale delle Mura Aurelie, overlooking St Peter's basilica. This time was 'mostly a very happy memory for the Gerth children as there were also other families with children'. The villa was managed by an order of German nuns from Mainz and is now a residence for German bishops visiting Rome. Eva received a long letter from Georg, her brother-in-law, inviting the family to his home in Würzburg.

A further question arises, that of money.

With Salomon Marx's death after the loss of his fortune, followed closely by the serious drop in Erich's income from the Foreign Office and his many protestations of poverty, one might assume that the family were in dire straits. This was not the case. They lived for many months up to 1937 at a villa in Malaga and then felt comfortable enough to move to Paris to have their fourth child where they occupied a prestige apartment and enjoyed the services of the 'best obstetrician'. Back in Berlin, 4,500 Reichsmark were spent on forged passports and papers. Erich and Eva then dashed to Portugal intending, at least, for one of them to fly to South America. After a return to Berlin, they took the train to Italy where, until Erich was 'murdered' in 1943 and Eva and the children went into hiding, they lived in apartments in the city centre. Marc and his two sisters were at boarding schools. After the Americans arrived in 1944, the family stayed in Rome for more than two years.

It would seem that savings, added to by inheritance and a continuing small income from Salomon's estate, and a limited salary from the firm of *Fritz Werner*, was more than enough to get by.

The twice-widowed Eva Gerth with her four children left Rome by train at 2020 on 4 November 1946 for Germany where they moved to Würzburg, the home of Georg Gerth's family. A loan made pre-war by Erich to Georg's Leinecker coffee firm was repaid and used for immediate living expenses.

---

2    *LABO*, Documents Marx Family 1951-58, file Salomon Marx/304.641, 'Affidavit by Dr Eduard Marx', Berlin-Schöneberg, 6/11/1957, p. A12.

Eva and the children then stayed for a short time in Baden Baden on the edge of the Black Forest near the border with France. Eva and her eldest daughter also returned briefly to Italy.

The family was given the choice by the National Catholic Welfare Conference of a paid-for emigration to either France or the United States. Eva shared the decision with her children and they chose America.

They left Bremerhaven in Germany for Boston, USA, in 1949 on an assisted passage aboard the USAT *General M L Hersey*, 12,420 tons, a passenger ship built during 1944 for use as an American Navy transport.[3] At the time of Eva's voyage, the ship was one of five which had been transferred to the US Army for the carriage of displaced persons and refugees from Europe to the USA and Australia in support of the International Refugee Organisation (IRO).[4] The IRO was an intergovernmental organisation founded on 20 April 1946 to deal with the massive refugee problem created by the war.[5] The *Hersey*'s manifest shows that the Gerth party had eight trunks and seven valises.[6] This was a sizable collection of luggage. They were not coming back.

Roger Gerth explains,

*Unfortunately, we could not bring any money with us. We were told that US government regulations prohibited immigrants from bringing any hard currency out of Europe. I think that the US was investing significant amounts of money in the reconstruction of Europe and did not want the large number of departing immigrants to take money out, since this would be counter-productive to the money being pumped in. Therefore, we had to spend all of the money we had in Germany and had no money when we arrived in the USA. But we did have tailor-made clothes and other items bought with the money we otherwise could have brought with us. As luck would have it, my new clothes included a suit that had short pants and another one was in the knickerbocker style, neither of which were in fashion for boys in America.[7]*

3    Shipindex.org, ID 6903228, accessed 2/2017.

4    *The New York Times*, 'Shipping News and Notes', 29/1/1950.

5    In 1952, the IRO was replaced by the Office of the United Nations High Commissioner for Refugees (UNHCR).

6    Passenger Lists of Vessels arriving at Boston, NAI No. 2668739 (Massachusetts Passenger and Crew Lists, ancestry.com).

7    Email, Roger Gerth, 21/1/2018.

Eva was fifty-four-years-old, fifty-three by the manifest; Marco, seventeen; Maria (Marie-Diana), sixteen; another Marie (Isabella), thirteen; and Roger, eleven. The family's destination was 53e Edgemere Drive South East, Grand Rapids, Michigan. They did not have a dollar to their name. Only Eva spoke any English.

Well-clothed, maybe, but it was going to be a tough beginning.

Why did the widow, former diplomatic wife and short-term countess, Eva Gerth, and her four children emigrate to America?

Her family believe that sometime during WWII, Erich told her, 'After the war, take the first ship to America.' Both he and Eva's father had been to the USA several times and were enthusiastic about what they saw. To that guidance can be added the general destruction and confusion in Germany that they found after returning there from Rome. And there was also the educational and economic opportunities for her children.[8]

After arrival in Boston Harbour, the family was met by their primary sponsor, a distant relative of a Redemptorist priest friend in Rome. The sponsoring couple then drove them to Grand Rapids, Michigan, where they were initially split up, the children all going to different farm families and Eva to a well-to-do dentist's family, where she was to help with the cooking.

After a short time of seeing her limited cooking ability, she was let go with the observation, 'This is not a cook, this is a countess!'

Eva then found a place to stay and work as a kitchen assistant at a Catholic boarding school for girls in Grand Rapids. After a month or so, Marc, Diana and Roger left the farms for other homes. The family was able to hold a reunion at Eva's girls school at Christmas. It was at that reunion that they received a phone call from a Jesuit priest friend who the whole family knew from Marc's years at the Jesuit boarding school at Mondragone. He invited them to come to Buffalo, New York, where he was now serving in a parish.

In 1950, Eva moved ahead of the children from Grand Rapids to Buffalo. There she worked as a translator for Remington Rand and later taught foreign languages at a girls school. The children gradually joined her.

A little later in the year the whole family was able to establish themselves independently in an apartment. At that time Marc and Diana started working while Isabel and Roger were still in school. Eva moved to Florida in 1955 with

Isabel. She bought a four-bedroom house in Fort Lauderdale, part of which, in her enterprising way, could be rented out to winter tourists or could be used to welcome visiting family members and friends.

Eva returned to Europe several times. Her niece, Christa-Maria Gerth, remembers meeting her once in Germany although the visit is not dated. Eva's long-time preference for the sun won through, leading her, finally, to California where she moved initially to perform grandmother baby-sitting duties for Marc's family. After that she lived in Ventura, California and several other cities in southern California.

She was living in Orange County when she died on 23 July 1994, a month before her ninety-ninth birthday. Eva was buried at Pacific View Memorial Park in Corona del Mar, California, over 6,000 miles from her beloved Erich at the Vatican. She was survived by her four children and thirteen grandchildren.

# 20

# GERTH: THE LONG ARM OF THE WAR

Dr Eduard Marx claimed assistance for financial reimbursement and a pension from the *Entschädigungsamt*, the Berlin Compensation Office, in the year it was established in 1951, for damage done to the family during the Nazi era. He applied on his own behalf, that of his step mother, Charlotte Marx, and, in 1955, that of his sister, Eva Gerth, now living in Buffalo, New York.[1]

Eduard described his own physical damage caused by his persecution as a half-Jew as 'cardiac insufficiency' following a heart attack from 1941 brought about by 'permanent persecution by the Gestapo, permanent threat of arrest and imprisonment in a concentration camp, ordered and carried out by the Berlin Chamber of Doctors and the Racial Political Office of the SS through Dr Arno Hermann, dismissal from positions of trust, and living illegally in inhuman conditions similar to imprisonment in Klein-Köris'.

---

1   *LABO*, Documents Marx Family 1951-58, file Salomon Marx/304.641, 'Claim form for Class B 'Damage to body and health', p. B1, and 'Claim for Class C Damage to liberty', p. C1, Dr Eduard Marx, Berlin-Schöneberg, 25/4/1951, both submitted 10/7/1951: 'Affidavit', p. C2, Eduard Marx, Berlin-Wilmersdorf, 17/1/1952; 'Power of Attorney' drafted, Eva Gerth, Buffalo, USA, certified by the German consulate, New York, 27/09/1955, p. M30; 'Application', Charlotte Marx, Berlin-Schöneberg, 9/9/1956, p. M1; 'Form claiming damage to career progress', pp. E1-E2, Charlotte Marx, 2/12/1956; 'Letter by solicitor, Dr Georg Lancelle', Berlin, 12/3/1957, p. M13.

Eduard attached medical attestations by doctors Biedermann and Rosenhagen and other evidence and claimed for capital compensation of 10,000 Deutschmark.

From Salomon Marx's death, his wife Charlotte Marx lived in a flat at the house in Lessingstraße from which she also received a small rental income. When the house was bombed in 1943, she lost almost all of her possessions except for a few pieces of furniture that had been stored elsewhere. A few salvaged valuables were sold. Charlotte applied for emergency aid.

As late as 1956, aged seventy, Charlotte was without a pension and had to rely on financial support from her step son, Eduard, and from a son from her first marriage named Gert Mayer-Schalburg, each giving her 150 Deutschmark per month. By this time, Eduard Marx had married again. His new wife was Jutta Therese Marie Luise Mayer-Schalburg, the daughter of his step mother, now also his mother-in-law.

Charlotte's claim for compensation rested on 'damage to life', a pension or financial compensation as Salomon Marx was 'killed by the violent actions inflicted by the Nazis or as a result of such measures', severe damage to property and possessions, damage to career and economic progress by restricting self-employment and by her dismissal from private employment. Her lawyer asked for accelerated processing of the compensation case as a *Katastrophenfall*, a catastrophic emergency, arguing that Charlotte, who registered her claim years ago, had been ill advised. Charlotte would have received a 'regular and considerable income' from the bank owned by her husband if he had died normally. Due to the liquidation of the bank enforced by the Nazis, valuable assets were lost. Her claim for compensation was also 10,000 Deutschmark covering both a pension and a lump sum.

There was much delay. In expert opinion in 1958, a Dr Kreis stated,

*It cannot be accepted as likely that the death of [Marx] at the age of seventy in 1936 in Berlin was the result of damages caused by persecution as the existing coronary sclerosis which finally led to his death had not been affected by the influences of the persecution between 1933 and 1935 to such an extent that we would be justified to assume that there had been a causal connection between these influences and [his] death at the age of seventy.*

Today, the papers relating to the inheritance court proceedings are not included in the file and are seemingly lost.

What sum was finally paid by the authorities is unknown although there is a blank form from April 1958 that suggests a payment was made to someone. Also, in 1959, the Berlin *Kammergericht*, 'Superior Court of Justice' suggested a settlement without the amount identified to the 'Marx petitioners' on the basis of their original inheritance. Widow Charlotte received a quarter of this and children Eduard Marx and Eva Gerth, three eighths each.

In 1952, Eva Marx wrote to an acquaintance, a German parliamentarian, about her financial position. After investigation, the German government reinstated Erich's career as if he had not been forcible retired by the Nazis, adding expected promotions until his death in 1943. Eva's pension was adjusted upwards to the 'should-have-been' salary and her immediate money problems were relieved.

Erich Gerth was not able through his work in Paris in the 1930s to bring about a reconciliation that might have prevented WWII.

In 1962, his Catholic masses at Notre Dame des Victoires were mirrored in a similar ceremony.[2] President Charles de Gaulle and Federal Chancellor Konrad Adenauer 'understood the spiritual dimension of reconciliation' when they attended a Mass of Reconciliation at Rheims Cathedral, celebrated by Monseigneur François Marty, the archbishop, later cardinal and Archbishop of Paris. They had previously watched a parade of French and German troops at Mourmelon military camp.

An Élysée Palace political event was not sufficient for the occasion. The choice of Rheims was meaningful on a number of levels. The Merovingian King, Clovis I, was baptised and Ludwig 1, the son Charlemagne, were crowned there. For centuries, the coronation of every French king was held in the cathedral. The city was occupied during the Franco-Prussian war, became a 'martyred' city in the first world war, and was where the German army surrendered to the Allies on 7 May 1945.

---

2    Email, Roger Gerth, 22/1/2018.

# ABBREVIATIONS & COMMON GERMAN WORDS

| | |
|---|---|
| Abitur | A set of examinations taken in the final year of secondary school |
| ASDIC | Allied Submarine Detection Investigation Committee |
| BIR | Board of Investigation and Research, Royal Navy |
| BRT | Gross registered tonnage |
| CID | Committee for Imperial Defence |
| DRASSM | Le Département des Recherches Archéologiques Subaquatiques et Sous-Marines, Department of Underwater Archaeological Research |
| Ecpad | Etablissement de Communication et de Production Audiovisuelle de la Défense |
| Fähnrich | Midshipman |
| Freicorps | Post-World War 1 German para-military unit |
| Great War | World War 1, 1914-1918 |
| GPS | Global positioning system |
| HVB | Handelsverkehrsbuch |
| HMS | His Majesty's Ship |
| ICRC | International Committee of the Red Cross |
| Kaiser | Kaiser Wilhelm II, 1890-1919 |
| Kaiserliche Marine | The Imperial German Navy, 1871-1919 |
| Kriegsmarine | Navy of Nazi Germany, 1935-1945 |
| KTB | Kriegstagebuch, War Diary |

| | |
|---|---|
| KRA | German War Materials Department |
| MA-BA | Bundesarchiv-Militär Archiv, Federal Military Archives, Freiburg, Germany |
| NARA | National Archives and Records Administration, Washington, DC |
| NID | Naval Intelligence Division, Royal Navy |
| NMM | National Maritime Museum, Greenwich, London |
| OHL | Oberste Heeresleitung, Supreme Army Command, Germany |
| PGL | Pan-German League |
| Reichsmark | German currency before the Deutschmark |
| Seeoffiziere | Naval executive officer |
| SHD | Service historique de la Défense, Historical Defence Service, headquarters Vincennes, France |
| SHOM | Service d'Hydrologie et d'Océanographie de la Marine – the French Navy Hydrology and Oceanography Service |
| SKN | Signalbuch der Kaiserliche Marine, German navy signal book |
| SMS | Seiner Majestät Schiff, His Majesty's Ship ` |
| SPD | Sozialdemokratische Partei Deutschlands, Social Democratic Party |
| TNA | The National Archives, Kew, London |
| VB code | Verkehrsbuch Weimar German Republic, 1919-1933 |
| Weltpolitik | German expansionist overseas foreign policy, 1890-1919 |
| ZAN | Zone des Armées du Nord |
| Zur See | Naval executive officer |

# Bibliography

Abel, Theodore, *Why Hitler Came into Power* (1938, reprint Harvard University Press, 1966)

Adler, Selig, 'The War-Guilt Question and American Disillusionment, 1918-1928', *The Journal of Modern History*, Vol. 23, No. 1, 1951, pp. 1-28

Afflerbach, Holger, Falkenhayn: Politisches Denken Und Handeln Im Kaiserreich, Beitrage Zur Militargeschichte (Oldenbourg Wissensch, 1994)

Albertini, Luigi, trans. Masset, Isabella *The Origins of the War of 1914* (1952; Enigma Books, New York 2005), 3 Vols.

Anonymous

*La Guerre Navale Racontée Par Nos Amiraux* (Librairie Schwartz, Paris, undated)

*The Starving of Germany*, Papers read at Extraordinary Meeting of United Medical Societies held at headquarters of Berlin Medical Society, Berlin, 18 December 1918 (Berlin, 1919)

Arnold-Forster, W, *The Blockade 1914-1919, Before the Armistice – and After* (Oxford Pamphlets on World Affairs, No 17, Clarendon Press 1939)

Ascherson, Neal, *The King Incorporated, Leopold II in the Age of Trusts* (Allen & Unwin, London 1963)

Aspinall-Oglander, Cecil, *Roger Keyes, Being the Biography of Admiral of the Fleet Lord Keyes of Zeebrugge and Dover* (Hogarth Press, London 1951)

Asprey, Robert B, *The German High Command at War, Hindenburg and Ludendorff and the First World War* (William Morrow, New York 1991)

Bacon, Admiral Sir Reginald H

*The Dover Patrol, 1915-1917*, Vols. 1&2 (Hutchinson, London 1919)

*The Concise Story of the Dover Patrol* (Hutchinson, London 1932)

Baecken, Charles, *L'Historique du 5th Régiment de Lanciers* (Maréchal de Logis, undated)

Bane, Suda Lorena, and Lutz, Ralph Haswell, *The Blockade of Germany After the Armistice, 1918-1919; Selected Documents of the Supreme Economic Council, Superior Blockade Council, American Relief Administration, and Other Wartime Organizations* (Stanford University Press, 1942; Howard Fertig, New York 1972)

Banks, Arthur, *A Military Atlas of the First World War* (Leo Cooper, Barnsley 1997)

Barnett, L Margaret, *British Food Policy During The First World War* (Allen & Unwin, Winchester, Mass., 1985)

Barrett, Michael B, *Operation Albion, The German Conquest of the Baltic Islands* (Indiana University Press, 2009)

Bauer, Hermann, *Als Führer der U-Boote im Weltkriege* (Koehler & Amelang, Leipzig 1941)

Beesley, Patrick, *Room 40: British Naval Intelligence 1914-1918* (Hamish Hamilton, London 1992)

Becker, Annette, *Oubliés de la Grande Guerre, Humanitaire et culture de guerre 1914-1918, Populations occupées, déportés civils, prisonniers de guerre* (Pluriel 2012)

Bell, A C, *A History of the Blockade of Germany and of the countries associated with her in the Great War: Austria-Hungary, Bulgaria, and Turkey 1914-1918* (HMSO, London 1937)

Bell, Christopher M

  'Sir John Fisher's Naval Revolution Reconsidered: Winston Churchill at the Admiralty, 1911-1914', *War in History*, 18(3), 2011, pp. 333-56

  'On Standards and Scholarship: A Response to Nicholas Lambert', *War in History*, 20(3), 2013, pp. 381-409

  *Churchill and Sea Power* (Oxford University Press, 2013)

Bendert, Harald

  *Die UB-Boote der Kaiserlichen Marine 1914 – 1918. Einsätze, Erfolge, Schicksal* (E S Mittler, Hamburg 2000)

  *Die UC-Boote der Kaiserlichen Marine 1914-1918, Minenkreig mit U-Booten* (E S Mittler, Hamburg 2001)

Birnbaum, Karl E, *Peace Moves and U-Boat Warfare: A Study of Imperial Germany's Policy towards the United States April 18, 1916 – January 9, 1917* (Almqvist & Wiksell, Stockholm 1958)

Blahut, Fred, 'The Allied Attempt to Starve Germany in 1919', *The Barnes Review*, April 1996, pp. 11-14

Blanton, Smiley, *Mental and Nervous Changes in the Children of the Volksschulen of Trier, Germany, Caused by Malnutrition* (The National Committee for Mental Hygiene, New York 1919); reprint from *Mental Hygiene*, July 1919, No. 3, pp. 343-386

Bloch, Ivan Stanislavovich, *Is War Now Impossible?: Being an Abridgment of 'The War of the Future in Its Technical, Economic & Political Relations'* (Grant Richards, London 1899; eprint War College Series 2017)

Blond, Georges, *The Marne, The Battle that Saved Paris and Changed the Course of the First World War* (Prion, London 2002)

Blücher, von Wahlstatt, Evelyn M, *An English Wife in Berlin: A Private Memoir of Events, Politics and Daily Life in Germany Throughout the War and the Social Revolution of 1918* (Constable, London 1920)

Blum, Matthias, 'Government Decisions Before and During the First World War and the Living Standards in Germany During a Drastic Natural Experiment', *Explorations in Economic History*, Vol. 48, Issue 4, Dec 2011

Boemeke, Manfred F; Feldman, Gerald D; and Glaser, Elisabeth, eds., *The Treaty of Versailles, A Reassessment after 75 Years* (The German Historical Institute, Washington, DC; Cambridge University Press 1998)

Bouton, S Miles, *And The Kaiser Abdicates, The German Revolution November 1918-August 1919* (Yale University Press 1920; reprint Wildside Press 2016)

Bowles, Thomas Gibson, *The Declaration of Paris of 1856: being an account of the maritime rights of Great Britain; a consideration of their importance; a history of their surrender by the signature of the Declaration of Paris; and an argument for their resumption by the denunciation and repudiation of that declaration* (Low, Marston, London 1900; Relnk Books, Delhi, India 2017)

Bown, Stephen R, *A Most Damnable Invention, Dynamite, Nitrates, and the Making of the Modern World* (Thomas Dunne, New York 2005)

Boyle, David, *Before Enigma, The Room 40 codebreakers of the First World War* (Real Press, 2016)

Brandt, Karl, *Management of Agriculture and Food in the German-Occupied and Other Areas of Fortress Europe, A Study in Military Government*; Germany's Agricultural and Food Policies in *World War II*, Vol. 2 (Stanford University Press, Bridgland, Tony, *Outrage at Sea, Naval Atrocities in the First World War* (Leo Cooper, Barnsley 2002)

Bridgman, Jon M, *The Revolt of the Hereros, Perspectives on Southern Africa* (California University Press, 1992)

Bruntz, George G, *Allied Propaganda and the Collapse of the German Empire in 1918* (Stanford University Press 1938; SN Books reprint, India 2017)

Canini, Gerard, 'L'utilisation des prisonniers de guerre comme main-d'oeuvre 1914-1916, *Les Fronts invisible, nourrier, fournir, soigner'* (Pressue universitaire de Nancy, 1984), pp. 247-262

Carter, Geoffrey, *The Royal Navy at Portland Since 1845* (Maritime Books, Liskeard 1987)

Carpenter, Captain Alfred F B, *The Blocking of Zeebrugge* (Herbert Jenkins, London 1922)

Chambers, Frank P, *The War Behind The War 1914-1918, A History of the Political and Civilian Fronts* (Faber and Faber, London 1939)

Chatelle, A, and Le Bon, E, *Boulogne et sa marine pendant la guerre 1914-1918* (Imprimeries réunies, Boulogne-sur-Mer 1921)

Chatelle, Albert, and Tison, G, *Calais Pendant La Guerre 1914-1918* (Librairie Aristide Quillet, Paris 1927)

Chatelle, Albert, *La Base Navale du Havre et La Guerre Sous-Marine Secrète en Manche 1914-1918* (Les Éditions Médicis, Paris 1949)

Chatterton, E Keble
    *Q-ships and their story* (Sidgwick and Jackson, London 1922; facsimile reprint 2016)
    *The Big Blockade* (Hurst & Blackett, London 1932)

Chickering, Roger
    *We Men Who Feel Most German, A Cultural Study of the Pan-German League, 1886-1914* (George Allen & Unwin, Boston, USA 1984)
    *The Great War and Urban Life in Germany, Freiburg, 1914-1918* (Cambridge University Press, 2007)

Churchill, Winston S
    *The World Crisis 1911-1918* (1930, reprint Four Square, London 1964);
    *The World Crisis 1915* (Thornton Butterworth, London 1923)

Clark, Christopher
    *Iron Kingdom* (Penguin, London 2006)
    *Kaiser Wilhelm II* (Penguin, London 2009)
    *The Sleepwalkers, How Europe went to War in 1914* (Penguin, London 2013)

Clausewitz, von Carl, trans. Graham, J J, *On War* (Wordsworth Classics, Ware 1997)

Cobb, Stephen, *Preparing for Blockade 1885-1914, Naval Contingency for Economic Warfare* (Ashgate, Farnham 2013)

Coles, Alan, *Slaughter at Sea, The Truth Behind a Naval War Crime* (Robert Hale, London 1986)

Compton-Hall, Richard, *Submarines at War 1914-1918* (1991, reprint Periscope Publishing, Penzance 2004)

Connolly, James B, & Schenk, Karl von, *U-Boat War 1914-1918: Two Contrasting Accounts from Both Sides of the Conflict at Sea During the Great War: The U-Boat Hunters; The Diary of a U-Boat Commander* (Leonaur, 2008)

Consett, Rear Admiral M W W P, *The Triumph of Unarmed Forces (1914-1918): An account of the transactions by which Germany during the Great War was able to obtain supplies prior to her collapse under the pressure of economic forces* (Williams and Norgate, London 1923; electronic reprint 2016)

Coogan, John W, *The End of Neutrality, The United States, Britain, and Maritime Rights 1899-1915* (Cornell University Press, 1981)

Cooper, Caroline Ethel (the Letters of), *Behind the Lines, One Woman's War 1914-18*, ed. Denholm, Decie (Norman & Hobhouse, London 1982)

Corbett, Sir Julian, *Some Principles of Maritime Strategy* (1911; Conway, London 1972)

Corbett, Sir Julian S, and Newbolt, Henry, *History of the Great War, Naval Operations*, (Longmans Green, London 1920-31), 5 Vols

Cox, Frederick J, 'The French Peace Plans, 1918-1919: The Germ of the Conflict Between Ferdinand Foch and Georges Clemenceau' in Cox et al, eds., *Studies in Modern European History in Honor of Franklin Charles Palm* (Bookman, New York, USA, 1956), pp. 81-104

Cravioto, Joaquin, 'Application of New Knowledge of Nutrition on Physical and Mental Growth and Development', *American Journal of Public Health*, No. 53, 1963, pp. 1803-9

Cron, Hermann, trans. Colton, C F, *Imperial German Army 1914-18: Organisation, Structure, Orders of Battle* (*Geshichte des Deutschen Heeres im Weltkreig 1914-1918*, Berlin 1937; reprint Helion, Solihull 2002)

Cruttwell, C R M F, *A History of the Great War 1914-1918* (Granada, St Albans 1936)

David, Patrick and Serge, *14-18 La Guerre Maritime en Manche et en mer du Nord* (Du Bout du Monde, undated)

Davis, Belinda J, *Food Politics, and Everyday Life in World War I Berlin: Home Fires Burning* (University of North Carolina Press, 2000)

de Chair, Admiral Sir Dudley, *The Sea is Strong* (Harrap, London 1961)

Delanoy, Gilbert, *Guerre 1914-18, Citations à L'Ordre de L'Armée des Formations and des Bâtiments de la Marine Française*

Delpal, Bernard, 'Prisonniers de guerre en France, 1914-1920', pp. 145-159, in Gueslin, André; Kalifa, Dominique; *Les Exclus en Europe, 1830-1930* (Ouvrières, L'Atelier, Paris 1999)

Devlin, Patrick, *Too Proud to Fight, Woodrow Wilson's neutrality* (Oxford University Press, 1971)

Ditte, Général, *Calais (1914-1918)* (Militaire Universelle, Fournier, Paris, undated)

Docherty, Gerry, and Macgregor, Jim, *Hidden History: The Secret Origins of the First World War* (Mainstream Publishing, Edinburgh 2013)

Doenitz, Grand Admiral Karl, *Memoirs: Ten Years and Twenty Days* (1958; Frontline Books, Barnsley 2015)

Dorling, Taprell (Taffrail), *Swept Channels being an Account of the Work of the Minesweepers in the Great War* (Hodder and Stoughton, London 1935)

Dorpalen, Andreas, *Heinrich von Treitschke* (Kennikat, New York 1973)

Doty, Madelaine Zabriskie, *Short Rations: An American Woman in Germany 1915-1916* (Century, New York 1917)

Doyle, Arthur Conan, 'Danger! Being the Log of Captain John Sirius', pp. 7-31, also 'Preface', pp. 5-6, in *Danger! and Other Stories* (1912; Serenity, Rockville, Maryland 2011)

Dufeil, Yves, *Kaiserliche Marine U-Boote 1914-1918, Dictionnaire Biographique des Commandants de la Marine Imperiale Allemande* (Histomar, 2016)

Dufossé, Franck
  *Histoire de Wissant, des origines aux années 1930* (Éditions AMA, Paris 2002)
  *Wissant 1914-1918* (Art et Histoire de Wissant, Mairie de Wissant 2014)

Dufour, Pierre, 'Les prisonniers du guerre allemands', *14-18: Le magazine de la Grande Guerre*, August/September/October 2016, pp. 8-23

Dyson, Will, *Kultur Cartoons* (Stanley Paul, London 1915)

Edmonds, James E, *Military operations: France and Belgium, 1914*, Vol. 1: 'Mons, the Retreat to the Seine, the Marne and the Aisne, August-October 1914' (Official History: Imperial War Museum, London 1992)

*Ehrenrangliste Der Deutschen Marine 1914-1918*, CD (Deutsches Wehrkundearchiv, Helion)

Eley, Geoff, 'Reshaping the Right: Radical Nationalism and the German Navy League, 1898-1908', *The Historical Journal*, Vol. 21, No. 2, June 1978, pp. 327-354

Emmerson, Charles, 1913, *The World Before the Great War* (Vintage, London 2013)

Erbe, Günter, Das Vornehme Berlin, Fürstin Marie Radziwill und die grossen Damen der Gesellschaft 1871-1918 (Böhlau Verlag, Köln 2015)

Essen, Léon van der, *The Invasion & The War in Belgium from Liège to the Yser with a Sketch of the Diplomatic Negotiations Preceding the Conflict* (Fisher Unwin, London 1917)

Ewart, John S, *The Roots and Causes of the Wars (1914-1918)*, Vols. 1&2 (George Doran, New York 1925)

Fayle, C Ernest, *Official History of the Great War: Seaborne Trade*, Vol. 2, 'Submarine Campaign', Vol. 3, 'The Period of Unrestricted Submarine Warfare' (1920-4; Imperial War Museum, London 1997)

Feldman, Gerald D

  *Army, Industry and Labor in Germany 1914-1918* (Berg, Providence, Rhode Island 1966)

  *The Great Disorder: Politics, Economics, and Society in the German Inflation, 1914-1924* (Oxford University Press, 1997)

  *Die Deutsche Inflation / The German Inflation Reconsidered: Eine Zwischenbilanz / A Preliminary Balance* (Gruyter online, 2011)

Ferguson, Niall

  *The Pity of War* (Penguin, London 1999)

  *The House of Rothschild, The World's Banker 1849-1999* (Penguin, New York 2000)

Fischer, Fritz, *Germany's Aims in the First World War* (Chatto & Windus, London 1977)

Flemming, Jens, *Landwirtschaftliche Interessen und Demokratie, Ländliche Gesellschaft, Agrarverbände und Staat 1890–1925* (Verlag Neue Gesellschaft, Bonn 1978)

Fletcher, R A, *In the Days of the Tall Ships* (Brentano's, London 1928)

Forstnerr, Georg-Gunther von, König, Paul, Peckelsheim, Baron Spiegel von Und Zu, *U-Boat War 1914-1918:* Vol. 2 - *Three accounts of German submarines during the Great War: The Journal of Submarine Commander von Forstner, The Voyage of the "Deutschland" & The Adventures of the U-202* (Leonaur, 2010)

Forstner, Georg-Gunther von, *The Journal of Submarine Commander von Forstner (1916, abridged; USA 2016)*

Frey, Marc, 'Bullying the Neutrals, The case of the Netherlands', in Chickering, Roger, Förster, Stig, eds., *Great War, Total War: Combat and Mobilization of the Western Front, 1914-1918* (German Historical Institute and Cambridge University Press, 2000), pp. 227-244

Friedman, Norman, introduction, *German Warships of World War I: The Royal Navy's Official Guide to the Capital Ships, Cruisers, Destroyers, Submarines and Small Craft, 1914-1918* (1918, reprint Greenhill Books, London, 1992)

Friedrich, Otto, *Blood and Iron, From Bismarck to Hitler the von Moltke's Family's Impact on German History* (Harper Collins, New York 1995)

Fuehr, Alexander, *The Neutrality of Belgium* (Funk and Wagnall, London 1915)

Fürbringer, Werner, *FIPS: Legendary U-boat Commander 1915-1918*, trans. & ed., Brooks, Geoffrey (1933; Leo Cooper, Barnsley 1999)

Gayer, Captain Albert, *General Survey of the History of the Submarine Warfare in all Theatres of War, 1914-18* (Stencilled and printed, Naval War College, Newport RI, 1930)

Geyer, Michael, 'Insurrectionary Warfare: The German Debate about Levée en Masse in October 1918', *Journal of Modern History*, Vol. 73, No. 3, 2001, pp. 459-527

Gibson, Hugh, *A Journal from Our Legation in Belgium* (Doubleday, Page, New York 1918)

Gibson, R H, and Prendergast, Maurice, *The German Submarine War 1914-1918* (John Constable, London 1931; reprint Periscope Publishing, Penzance 2002)

Glaeser, Ernst, *Class 1902* (1928; University of South Carolina, 2008)

Goffic, Charles le, trans. Simmonds, Florence, *Dixmude: The Epic of the French Marines (October 7-November 10 1914)* (1916; CreateSpace, USA 2014)

Grainger, John D, ed., *The Maritime Blockade of Germany in the Great War: The Northern Patrol, 1914-1918* (Ashgate, Navy Records Society 2003)

Graham, G G, 'Growth during Recovery from Infantile Malnutrition', *Journal of the American Medical Women's Association*, No. 21, 1966, pp. 740 onwards

Grant, Robert M

   *U-Boats Destroyed: The Effect of Anti-Submarine Warfare 1914-18* (1964, Periscope
   Publishing, Penzance 2002)
   *U-Boat Intelligence, Admiralty Intelligence Division and the Defeat of the U-boats
   1914-1918* (1969, Periscope Publishing, Penzance 2002)
   *U-Boat Hunters: Code Breakers, Divers and the Defeat of the U-Boats, 1914-1918*
   (Written unpublished 1971; Periscope Publishing, Penzance 2003)

Gray, Edwyn A

   *The Killing Time: The German U-boats 1914-18* (Seeley, Service 1972)
   *British Submarines at War 1914 – 1918* (reprint Pen & Sword Maritime,
   Barnsley 2016), first published as *A Damned Un-English Weapon* (Charles
   Scribner's Sons, 1973)

Grelling, Richard, *('A German'), translated Gray, Alexander, J'Accuse (Hodder and
   Stoughton, London 1915)*

Greenhill, Basil

   The Mariner's Mirror, 'The Rise and Fall of the British Coastal Steamer',
   Vol. 27, Issue 3, 1941, pp 243-259
   The Merchant Schooners, Vol. II (David & Charles, Newton Abbot 1968)

Grimes, Shawn T, *Strategy and War Planning in the British Navy, 1887-1918 (Boydell
   Press, Woodbridge 2012)*

Gröner, Erich, *German Warships 1815-1945*

   Vol. 1: Major Surface Vessels (1983; Conway, London 1990)
   Vol. 2: U-Boats and Mine Warfare Vessels (1968; revised and expanded by
   Jung, Dieter, and Maass, Martin, 1983; translated by Thomas, Keith, and
   Magowan, Rachel, Conway Maritime Press, London 1991)

Guichard, Louis

   *Au Large* (1914-1918) (La Renaissance du Livre, Paris 1919)
   *Bleu Marine* (Société d'éditions géographiques, maritimes et coloniales, 1927)
   *Les Guerres des Enseignes* (La Renaissance du Livre, Paris 1929)
   *The Naval Blockade 1914-1918*, trans. & ed. Turner, Christopher R, (Phillip
   Allen, London 1930)

Fouqueray, Charles, *La Guerre Navale Racontée par Nos Amiraux* (Librairie Schwarz,
   Paris 1920)

Hadley, Michael L, *Count Not the Dead, The Popular Image of the German Submarine
   (Mc-Gill-Queen's University Press, Montreal 1995)*

Hankey, Lord, *The Supreme Command 1914-1918, Vols. 1&2 (George Allen & Unwin, London 1961)*

Hashagen, Ernst, *The Log of a U-boat Commander or U-boats Westward - 1914-1918 (Unwin, London 1931)*

Hampshire, A Cecil, *The* Blockaders (William Kimber, London 1980)

Haws, Duncan, *Merchant Fleets – Britain's Railway Steamers – Eastern and North-Western Companies + Zeeland and Stena* (TCL Publications, Hereford 1993)

Heal, Chris

  *Sound of Hunger* (Unicorn, London 2018)

  *The War of The Raven* (Chattaway and Spottiswood, Hampshire, UK 2023)

Heal, Chris, and Lesoin, Henri, *La dernière patrouille de l'UC 61* (Art et Histoire de Wissant, 2023)

Heimburg, Heino von, *U-Boot gegen U-Boot* (Scherl, Berlin 1917)

Herwig, Holger H

  'Admirals versus Generals: The War Aims of the Imperial German Navy, 1914-1918', *Central European History*, Vol. 5, No. 3 (September 1972), pp. 208-233

  *The German Naval Officer Corps, A Social and Political History, 1890-1918* (Clarendon Press, Oxford 1973)

  *The First World War: Germany and Austria-Hungary 1914-1918* (Arnold, London 1997)

  'The Dynamics of Uncertainty: German Military Policy during The First World War' in Millett, Allan R, and Murray, Williamson, eds., *Military Effectiveness*, Vol. 1, *The First World War* (Allen & Unwin, Winchester, Mass., USA 1988), pp. 80-115

  'Total Rhetoric, Limited War: Germany's U-Boat Campaign 1917-1918', *Journal of Military and Strategic Studies*, Vol. 1, issue 1, May 1998, and in Chickering, Roger, Förster, Stig, eds., *Great War, Total War: Combat and Mobilization of the Western Front, 1914-1918* (German Historical Institute and Cambridge University Press, 2000), pp. 169-188

  *The Marne, 1914, The Opening of World War 1 and the Battle That Changed the World* (Random House, New York, 2011)

  *'Luxury' Fleet: The Imperial German Navy 1888-1918* (George Allen & Unwin, London 1980; reprint Routledge, Abingdon 2014)

Herzog, Bodo, *Deutsche U-Boote 1906-1966* (Pawlak, Koblenz 1990)

Hezlet, Vice Admiral Sir Arthur

*The Submarine and Sea Power* (Peter Davis, London 1967)

*Electronics and Sea Power* (Stein and Day, New York 1975)

Hinchcliffe, John & Vicki, *Dive Dorset: A Diver Guide* (Underwater World Publications, Teddington 1999)

Hobhouse, Emily

'*Report* to the Committee of the Distress Fund for South African Women and Children of *a Visit to the Camps of Women and Children in the Cape and Orange River Colonies*' (Friars, London 1901)

*The Brunt Of The War And Where It Fell* (1902; reprint Read Books, 2013)

Hobson, Rolf, *Imperialism at Sea, Naval Strategic Thought, the Ideology of Sea Power and the Tirpitz Plan, 1875-1914* (Brill, Boston 2002)

Hochschild, Adam, *King Leopold's Ghost, A Story of Greed, Terror and Heroism in Colonial Africa* (Pan, London 2006)

Hollweg, Konteradmiral Karl, *Unser Recht Auf Den U-Bootskrieg* (1917; Nabu reprint, USA 2016)

Hollweg, Theobald von Bethmann, trans. Young, George, *Reflections on the World War, Vol. 1* (Butterworth, London 1920; digital reprint Forgotten Books, 2015)

Horn, Daniel, *Mutiny on the High Seas, The Imperial German Naval Mutinies of World War One* (Leslie Freewin, London 1973)

Horne, John and Kramer, Alan, 'War Between Soldiers and Enemy Civilians, 1914-1915', in Chickering, Roger, Förster, Stig, eds., *Great War, Total War: Combat and Mobilization of the Western Front, 1914-1918* (German Historical Institute and Cambridge University Press, 2000), pp. 153-168

Howard, Keble (Bell, J Keble), *The Zeebrugge Affair* (George H Doran, New York, 1918)

Howard, N P

'Men against Fire: Expectations of War in 1914', *International Security*, Vol. 9, No. 1 (Summer, 1984), pp. 41-57

'The Social and Political Consequences of the Allied Food Blockade of Germany, 1918–19', *German History*, Vol. 11, No. 2 (June 1993), pp. 161-188

Hull, Isabel V

*The Entourage of Kaiser Wilhelm II, 1988-1918* (Cambridge University Press 1982)

*Absolute Destruction, Military Culture and the Practices of War in Imperial Germany* (Cornell University Press 2005)

*A Scrap of Paper, Breaking and Making International Law during the Great War* (Cornell University Press 2014)

Humphreys, Roy, *The Dover Patrol 1914-18* (Sutton Publishing, Stroud 1988)

James, Admiral Sir William, *The Code Breakers of Room Forty* (St Martin's Press, New York 1956; reprint Literary Licensing, 2016)

Jamieson, Alan G, 'Martyr or Pirate? The Case of Captain Fryatt in the Great War', *The Mariner's Mirror*, Vol. 85, No. 2, 1999, pp. 196-202

*Jane's Fighting Ships of World War I* (1919; reprint Studio Editions, London 1990)

Janicki, D A, 'The British Blockade During World War 1: The Weapon of Deprivation', *Student Pulse*, 6(06), 2014

Jasper, Willi, trans. Spencer, Stewart, *Lusitania: The Cultural History of a Catastrophe* (Yale University Press 2016)

Jellicoe, Admiral of the Fleet, The Right Hon. The Earl, *The Submarine Peril: The Admiralty Policy in 1917* (Cassell, London 1934)

Johnson, Niall, and Müller, Jürgen, 'Updating the Accounts', *Bulletin of the History of Medicine*, 2002, pp. 105-15.

Joll, James, *1914: The Unspoken Assumptions* (Weidenfeld and Nicholson, London School of Economics and Political Science 1968)

Joll, James, and Martel, Gordon, *The Origins of the First World War* (Pearson, Harlow 2007)

Jones, Heather,
    *Violence against Prisoners of War in the First World War: Britain, France and Germany, 1914-1920* (Cambridge University Press, 2011)
    'The Enemy Disarmed: Prisoners of War and the Violence of Wartime: Britain, France and Germany 1914-1918', PhD dissertation (Trinity College, University of Dublin, December 2005)

Jung, Hans, 'The New Berlin Horse Railway Company', *Traffic History Sheets*, Berlin, Issue 4, 1960, pp. 17-18

Karau, Mark D, *The Naval Flank of the Western Front, The German MarineKorps Flandern 1914-1918* (Seaforth Publishing, Barnsley 2003)

Keyser, Carl de, and Reybrouck, David van, *The First World War, Unseen Glass Plate Photographs of the Western Front* (University of Chicago 2015)

Kelly, Patrick J, *Tirpitz and the Imperial German Navy* (Indiana University Press, 2011)

Kemp, Paul, *U-Boats Destroyed, German Submarine Losses in the World Wars* (Arms & Armour, London 1997)

Kennedy, Greg
'Intelligence and the Blockade, 1914-1917: A Study in Administration, Friction and Command', *Intelligence and National Security*, No 5, October 2007
'The North Atlantic Triangle and the blockade, 1914–1915', *Journal of Transatlantic Studies*, Vol. 6, No 1, 2008

Kennedy, Paul
*The War Plans of the Great Powers 1880-1914*, edited (Allen &Unwin, London 1979)
'Britain in the First World War', in Millett, Allan R, and Murray, Williamson, eds., *Military Effectiveness*, Vol. 1, *The First World War* (Allen & Unwin, Winchester, Mass., USA 1988), pp. 31-79

Keyes, Sir Roger, *The Naval Memoires of Admiral of the Fleet, Scapa Flow to the Dover Straits 1916-1918* (Thornton Butterworth, London 1935)

Keynes, J M, *Two Memoirs, Dr Melchior: A Defeated Enemy and My Early Beliefs* (Hart-Davis, London 1949)

King, M S, Woodrow *Wilson: Warmonger, A Brief Analysis of How America was Deceived Into World War I* (Author, USA 2016)

King-Hall, Sir William Stephen Richard, *The Diary of a U-boat Commander* (Amazon reprint)

Kitchen, Martin, *The Silent Dictatorship, The politics of the German High Command under Hindenburg and Ludendorff, 1916-1918* (Croom Helm, London 1976)

Kloot, William van der, 'Ernest Starling's Analysis of the Energy Balance of the German People During the Blockade 1914-1919', *Notes and Records of the Royal Society of London*, Vol 57, No 2, May 2003

Koebner, Richard, and Schmidt, Helmut Dan, *Imperialism, The Story and Significance of a Political World, 1840-1960* (Cambridge University Press, 1965)

Koerver, Hans Joachim
*German Submarine Warfare 1914-1918 in the Eyes of British Intelligence* (LIS Reinisch, Steinbach 2012)
*War of Numbers 1914-1916, The Kaiser's Navy Gone Rogue* (LIS Reinisch, Steinbach 2016)

Kramer, Alan R, 'Prisoners in the First World War', Chap. 4, in Scheipers, Sibylle, ed, *Prisoners in War* (Oxford University Press, 2010)

Kühnis, Beni, 'Deutsche Kriegsinternierte in Davos während des 1. Weltkrieges' (Extended A-level Project Essay, 2014)

Kutz, Martin, 'Kriegserfahrung und Kriegsvorbereitung. Die agrarwirtschaftliche Vorbereitung des Zweiten Weltkrieges in Deutscheland vor dem Hintergrund de Weltkrieg I – Erfahtung', *Zeitschrift für Agrargeschichte und Agrarsoziologie*, No. 32, 1984, pp. 59-82, 135-163

Langmaid, Captain Kenneth, *The Approaches are Mined!* (Jarrolds, London 1965)

Lambert, Nicholas A

*Sir John Fisher's Naval Revolution* (University of South Carolina Press 1999)

'On Standards: A Reply to Christopher Bell', *War in History*, 2012, 19(2), pp. 217-240

*Planning Armageddon: British Economic Warfare and the First World War* (Harvard University Press, London 2012)

Langsdorff, von Werner, *U-Boote am Feind, 45 deutsche U-Boot-Führer erzählen* (Bertelsmann, Gütersloh 1937)

Larn, Richard & Bridget, *Shipwreck Index of the British Isles: Isles of Scilly, Cornwall, Devon, Dorset* (Lloyd's Register of Shipping, London 1995)

Laurens, Alphonse

Le Blocus et la Guerre sous-marine, 1914-1918 (Libraire Armand Colin, Paris 1924)

Histoire de la Guerre Sous-Marine Allemande, 1914-1918 (Société d'Éditions, Paris 1930)

Leith, Captain Lockhart, *The History of British Minefields 1914-1918* (Admiralty private use, 1920, charts added 1932, Library of the Royal Naval Museums, Portsmouth)

Liddell Hart, B H, *History of the First World War* (1930; Cassell, London 1973)

Lindsay, Samuel McCune, Swiss Commission in the United States, edited, *Bulletin of Social Legislation on the Henry Bergh Foundation for the Promotion of Humane Education, No. 5, Swiss Internment of Prisoners of War, An Experiment in International Humane Legislation and Administration* (Columbia University Press, New York 1917)

Lipkes, Jeff, *Rehearsals: The German Army in Belgium, August 1914* (Leuven University Press 2007)

Low, Professor A M, *Mine and Countermine* (Hutchinson, London 1940)

Lowenthal, David, *The Past is a Foreign Country* (Cambridge University Press, 1986)

Lubbock, Basil, *Last of the Windjammers*, Vol. 1 (Brown, Son & Ferguson, Glasgow 1927)

Ludendorff, Erich von

*Ludendorff's Own Story: August 1914-November 1918*, Vol. I (1919, Harper; reprint Kessinger Legacy, USA 2016)

*My War Memories, 1914-1918*, Vol. II (Hutchinson, London 1919)

Lutz, Ralph Haswell, *The Causes of the German Collapse in 1918: Sections of the officially authorized report of the Commission of the German Constituent Assembly and of the German Reichstag, 1919-1928, the selection and the translation officially approved by the commission* (1934; Archon, USA 1969)

McCartney, Innes

*Lost Patrols: Submarine Wrecks of the English Channel* (Periscope Publishing, Penzance 2003)

*British Submarines of Word War I* (Osprey, Oxford 2008)

*The Maritime Archaeology of a Modern Conflict: Comparing the Archaeology of German Submarine Wrecks to the Historical Text* (Routledge, Abingdon 2015)

'The *Tin Openers* Myth and Reality: Intelligence from U-boat Wrecks During WW1', *Proceedings of the Twenty-Fourth Annual Historical Diving Conference*, Poole, November 2014, www.researchgate.net/publication/275957885

'The Historical Archaeology of World War I U-boats and the Compilation of Admiralty History: The Case of (UC79)', *UNESCO Conference, Bruges*, 26 June 2014, chapter July 2015, researchgate.net/publication/280925727

'Paying the Prize for the German Submarine War: U-boats destroyed and the Admiralty Prize Fund, 1919-1932', *The Mariner's Mirror*, Vol. 104:1, February 2018, pp. 40-57

McDermott, John, 'Trading with the Enemy: British Business and the Law During the First World War', *Canadian Journal of History / Annales Canadiennes d'Histoire*, XXXII, No 2, Aug 1997

McDowell, Duncan, *Steel at the Sault* (University of Toronto Press, 1988)

Macintyre, Captain Donald, *Jutland* (Evans Brothers, London 1957)

Mahan, Captain Alfred Thayer

*The Influence of Sea Power upon History* 1660-1805 (1890, Bison, London 1980)

*The Influence of Sea Power upon the French Revolution and Empire 1793-1812*, Vol. II (Sampson, Low, Marston, London 1896)

Manning, T D, *The British Destroyer* (Putnam, London 1961)

March, Edgar J, *British Destroyers, A History of Development 1892-1953* (Seeley Service, London 1966)

Marder, Arthur J

  *Portrait of an Admiral; the life and papers of Sir Herbert Richmond* (Harvard University Press, 1952)

  From the Dreadnought to Scapa Flow, The Royal Navy in the Fisher Era 1904 – 1919,

  Vol. I: *The Road to War: 1904-1914* (Oxford University Press, London 1961)

  Vol. II: *The War Years: To the Eve of Jutland 1914-1916* (1965; Seaforth Publishing, Barnsley 2013)

  Vol. IV: *1917: Year of Crisis* (1969; Seaforth Publishing, Barnsley 2014)

  Vol. V: *Victory and Aftermath January 1918-June 1919* (Oxford University Press 1970)

Marreo, Javier Ponce, 'Logistics for Commerce War in the Atlantic during the First World War: The German *Etappe* System in Action', *The Mariner's Mirror*, Vol. 92, No. 4, November 2006, pp. 455-64

Martel, Gordon, *The Origins of the First World War* (1987; Longman, London 1996)

Massie, Robert K

  *Dreadnought: Britain, Germany, and the Coming of the Great War* (1991; Vintage, London 2007)

  *Castles of Steel: Britain, Germany and the Winning of the Great War at Sea* (Vintage, London 2007)

Mayer, Arno J, *The Persistence of the Old Regime, Europe to the Great War* (Croom Helm, London 1981)

Mead, Margaret, 'The Changing Significance of Food', *American Scientist*, No. 58, 1970, pp. 176 onwards

Messimer, Dwight R

  *The Merchant U-boat: Adventures of the 'Deutschland', 1916-18* (Naval Institute Press, Maryland, USA 1988)

  *Find and Destroy: Antisubmarine Warfare in World War I* (Naval Institute Press, Maryland, USA 2001)

  *Verschollen: World War I U-Boat Losses* (Naval Institute Press, Maryland, USA 2002)

Messinger, Gary S, *British Propaganda and the State in the First World War* (Manchester University Press 1992)

Molodowsky, N, 'German Foreign Trade in 1899-1913', *The Quarterly Journal of Economics*, Vol. 41, No 4, Aug 1927

Mommsen, Wolfgang J, 'The Debate of German War Aims', *Journal of Contemporary History*, Vol. 1, No. 3, July 1966, pp. 47-72

Morel, Edmund D

   *The Congo Slave State, A Protest against the new African Slavery; and an Appeal to the Public of Great Britain, of the United States, and of the Continent of Europe* (Richardson, Liverpool 1903)

   *The Fruits of Victory. Have our Statesmen Won the Peace our Soldiers Fought For?* (Union of Democratic Control, London 1919)

   *Military Preparation for the Great War, Fact versus Fiction* (Labour Publishing, London 1922)

   *The Secret History of a Great Betrayal* (Owen, Washington 1924)

Mueller, Michael, trans. Brooks, Geoffrey, *Canaris, The Life and Death of Hitler's Spymaster* (Greenhill, Barnsley 2017)

Munro, Dana C, Sellery, George C & Krey, August C, *German Treatment of Conquered Territory being Part II of 'German War Practices'* (The Committee of Public Information, Washington DC, USA, 1918; reprint Kessinger Publishing, 2016)

Mulligan, Timothy P, *Neither Sharks Nor Wolves* (Chatham, London 1999)

Murray, H Robertson, *Krupp's and the International Armaments Ring, The Scandal of Modern Civilisation* (Holden & Hardingham, London 1915)

Murray, Stewart Lygon, *The Reality of War, a Companion to 'Clausewitz'* (Hodder and Stoughton, London 1914)

Neureuther, Karl, and Bergen, Claus, eds., *U-Boat Stories. Narratives of German U-boat sailors* (*Wir leben noch!*, 1931; reprint The Naval & Military Press, Uckfield 2005)

Newbold, J T Walton

   *The War Trust Exposed* (National Labour Trust, Manchester 1913)

   *How Asquith Helped the Armaments Ring* (National Labour Trust, undated pamphlet)

   *How Europe Armed for War 1871-1914* (1916; reprint Isha, New Delhi 2013)

Newbolt, Henry

   *A Note of the History of the Submarine War* (George Doran, New York 1917)

   *Submarine and Anti-Submarine, The Allied Under-Sea Conflict During the First World War* (Leonaur, 2013 reprint)

*A Naval History of the War, 1914-1918* (Hodder and Stoughton, London 1919-20)

Niemöller, Martin, *From U-boat to Concentration Camp: The Autobiography of Martin Niemöller* (William Hodge, London 1939)

O'Brien, Patrick, 'The Economic Effects of the Great War,' *History Today*, Vol. 44, Issue 12, Dec 1994

Offer, Avner

'The Working Classes, British Naval Plans and the Coming of the Great War', *Past and Present*, no. 107 (May 1985), pp. 204-226

'Morality and Admiralty: 'Jacky Fisher', Economic Warfare and the Laws of War', *Journal of Contemporary History*, Vol. 23 (Jan 1988), pp. 99-118

*The First World War: An Agrarian Interpretation* (Clarendon Press, Oxford 1989)

'Bounded Rationality in Action: The German submarine campaign, 1915-18' in Gerrard, Bill, ed., *The Economics of Rationality* (Routledge, London 1993), pp. 179-202

'The Blockade of Germany and the Strategy of Starvation, 1914-1918', in Chickering, Roger, Förster, Stig, eds., *Great War, Total War: Combat and Mobilization of the Western Front, 1914-1918* (German Historical Institute and Cambridge University Press, 2000), pp. 169-188

Ogden, C K, *Sailing Directions of the North Coast of France*, Part 1 (Imray, Norie & Wilson, London 1908)

Olusoga, David, and Erichsen, Casper W, *The Kaiser's Holocaust, Germany's Forgotten Genocide and the Colonial Roots of Nazism* (Faber and Faber, London 2010)

Osborne, Eric W, *Britain's Economic Blockade of Germany 1914-1919* (Routledge, Abingdon 2013)

Pakenham, Thomas

*The Boer War* (Abacus, London 1991)

*The Scramble for Africa 1876-1912* (Weidenfeld and Nicolson, London 1997)

Paddock, Troy R E, ed., *A Call to Arms: Propaganda, Public Opinion, and Newspapers in the Great War* (Praeger, Westport, CT, 2004)

Parmelee, Maurice, *Blockade and Sea Power: The Blockade, 1914-1919, and its Significance for a World State* (Hutchinson, London 1924)

Patterson, A Temple, *Jellicoe: A Biography* (Macmillan, London 1969)

Patterson, David, & Pyle, Gerald, 'Geography and Mortality', *Bulletin of the History of Medicine*, 1991, pp. 4-21.

Peterson, H C, *Propaganda for War: The Campaign Against American Neutrality, 1914-17* (University of Oklahoma Press, 1939)

Pitt, Barrie, *Zeebrugge* (Ballantine Books, New York 1959)

Phillips, Ethel, 'American Participation in Belligerent Commercial Controls 1914-1917', *The American Journal of International Law*, Vol. 27, No 4, Oct 1933

Poolman, Kenneth, *Armed Merchant Cruisers* (Leo Cooper, London 1985)

Porch, Douglas, 'The French Army in the First World War' in Millett, Allan R, and Murray, Williamson, eds., *Military Effectiveness*, Vol. 1, *The First World War* (Allen & Unwin, Winchester, Mass., USA 1988), pp. 190-228

Quigley, Carroll, *Tragedy and Hope, A History of the World in Our Time* (Macmillan, New York, 1966)

Raico, Ralph
    Review, Vincent, *Politics of Hunger, Review of Austrian Economics*, Vol. 3, No. 1, 12/1989
    *Great Wars and Great Leaders, A libertarian Rebuttal* (Ludwig von Mises Institute, Auburn, Alabama 2010)

Ramsay, David, *'Blinker' Hall: Spymaster, The Man who Brought America into World War 1* (Spellmount, Stroud 2009)

Ranft, Bryan McL, ed
    'The protection of British seaborne trade and the development of systematic planning for war, 1860-1906' in *Technical Change and British Naval Policy 1860-1939* (Hodder and Stoughton, Sevenoaks 1977)
    *The Beatty Papers 1902-1918*, Vol. 1 (Scholar Press, Navy Records Society Aldershot 1989)

Read, James Morgan, *Atrocity Propaganda 1914-1919* (Yale University Press 1941)

Reader, W J, *'At Duty's Call', A Study in Obsolete Patriotism* (Manchester University Press 1988)

Reichs-Marine-Amt
    *Vorschriften für die Ergänzung des Seeoffizierkorps nebst Ausführungsbestimmungen* (Reichs-Marine-Amt, Berlin 1909)
    *Vorschriften für die Ausbildung der Seekadetten auf den Schulschiffen* (Reichs-Marine-Amt Berlin, 1910)

*Reports of British Officers on the Economic Conditions Prevailing in German, December 1918 – March 1919*; Cmd-52, Army (HMSO, London 1919)

Richard, Alain, and Coulon, Jef, 'La guerre sous-marin en 1914-1918 dans le Détroit du Pas-de-Calais: armes utilisées par les sous-marins allemands et lutte anti-sous-marins des alliés', *Sucellus: Dossiers archéologiques, historiques et cultural du Nord-Pas de-Calais*, No. 56, 2005, pp. 41-58

Richard, Alain, Coulon, Jef, and Lowrey, Michael, 'L'odyssée de 5 sous marins allemands, mouilleurs de mines, coules en 1917-19 dans le Detroit du Pas-de-Calais UC26 – UC46 – UC61 – UC64 – UC79', *Sucellus:* No. 57, 2006, pp. 61-85

Richardson, Matthew, *The Hunger War, Food, Rations and Rationing 1914-1918* (Pen & Sword, Barnsley 2015)

Richter, Lina Speiss, *Family life in Germany under the blockade*, preface Shaw, Bernard (National Labour Press, London, 1919)

Ritter, Gerhard, *The Schlieffen Plan* (Oswald Wolff, London 1958)

Ronarc'h, Admiral Pierre-Alexis, Souvenirs De La Guerre, Vol. 1 (Payot, Paris 1921)

Rose, Gerhard, *Krieg nach dem Kriege. Der Kampf des deutschen Volkes um die Heimkehr seiner Kriegsgefangenen* (Dem Rockbound zum Schultze der deutschen Krieges- und Zivilgefangenen, Berlin 1920)

Rössler, Eberhard, trans. Erenberg, Harold, *The U-boat, The evolution and technical history of German submarines* (Arms & Armour Press, London 1981)

Roth, Joseph
    *What I saw, Reports from Berlin 1920-33* (Granta, London 2013)
    *Job, The Story of a Simple Man* (1930; Granta, London 2013)

Rüger, Jan, *The Great Naval Game, Britain and Germany in the Age of Empire* (Cambridge University Press, New York 2007)

Russell, Bertrand, *Justice in War Time* (Spokesman, Nottingham 1917)

Ryheul, John, *Marinekorps Flandern 1914-1918* (E S Mittler, Hamburg 1997)

Saville, Allison Winthrop, 'The Development of the German U-boat Arm, 1919-1935' (PhD dissertation, University of Washington, USA, 1963)

Scheer, Reinhard, Admiral, *Germany's High Sea Fleet in the World War* (1919; Shilka Publishing, Truro 2013)

Schierbrand, Wolf von, *Kaiser's Speeches Forming A Character Portrait of Kaiser Wilhelm II* (Harper Brothers, New York 1903)

Schneider, William, Operations Research Applications for Intelligence, Surveillance and Reconnaissance: Report of the Defense Science Board Advisory Group on Defense Intelligence (Diane Publishing, Darby, PA, 2009)

Schoenermarck, A, ed., *Helden-Gedenkmappe des deutschen Adels* (Petri, Stuttgart 1921)

Schreiner, George Abel, *The Iron Ration: The Economic and Social Effects of the Allied Blockade on Germany and the German People* (John Murray, London 1918)

Schröder, Joachim, *Die U-Boote des Kaisers: Die Geschichte des deutschen U-Boot-Krieges Gegen Großbritannien im Ersten Weltkrieg* (Bernard & Graefe Verlag, Bonn 2003)

Sedrati, Mouncef, Anthony, Edward J, 'Confronting coastal morphodynamics with countererosion engineering: the emblematic case of Wissant Bay, Dover Strait', *Journal of Coastal Conservation*, Springer Verlag, 2014, 18 (5), pp. 483-494

Seligmann, Matthew, *Spies in Uniform, British Military and Naval Intelligence on the Eve of the First World War* (Oxford University Press 2006)

Seligmann, Matthew S, Nägler, Frank, and Epkenhans, Michael, eds., *The Naval Route to the Abyss, The Anglo-German Naval Race 1895-1914* (Ashgate, Naval History Society, Farnham 2015)

Sims, William Sowden, *The Victory at Sea, The Allied Campaign Against U-Boats During the First World War 1917-18* (1920, reprint USA, 2016)

Siney, Marion C, *The Allied Blockade of Germany 1914-1916* (University of Michigan Press 1957)

Spies, S B, *Methods of Barbarism? Roberts and Kitchener and Civilians in the Boer Republics, January 1900-May 1902* (Human and Rousseau, Cape Town 1977)

Spiess, Johannes, *Six Ans de Croisières en Sous-marin* (Payot, Paris 1927)

Spiegel, Edgar, Baron von und zu Pecklesheim, *The Adventures of the U-202, An Actual Narrative* (1917; Project Guttenberg EBook 2010)

Spindler, Arno

> *Der Krieg zur See 1914-1918: Der Handelskrieg mit U-Booten*, Band 3, Oktober 1915 bis Januar 1917 (E S Mittler, Berlin, 1934)

> *Der Krieg zur See 1914-1918: Der Handelskrieg mit U-Booten*, Band 4, Februar bis Dezember 1917 (E S Mittler, Berlin 1941; reprint 1964)

Starling, E H, 'The food supply of Germany during the war', *Journal of the Royal Statistical Society*, No. 83, pp. 225-254, 1920

Strachan, Hew, *The First World War* (Pocket Books, London 2006)

Sutherland, Jon, and Canwell, Diane, *U-Boats at World Wars I and II: Rare Photographs from Wartime Archives (Images of War)* (Pen & Sword Maritime, Barnsley 2009)

Steffen, Dirk, 'The Holtzendorff Memorandum of 22 December 1916 and Germany's Declaration of Unrestricted U-boat Warfare', *The Journal of Military History*, Vol. 68, No. 1, 1/2004, pp. 215-224

Stock, M B, and Smythe, P M, 'Does Nutrition during Infancy Inhibit Brain Growth and Subsequent Intellectual Development?', *Archives of Disease in Childhood*, No. 38, 1964

Stoker, Donald J, *Girding for Battle, The Arms Trade in a Global Perspective, 1815-1940* (edited with Grant, Jonathan A, Praeger, Westport, Connecticut 2003), Chapter 6, Forsén, Björn, and Forsén, Annette, 'German Submarine Exports, 1919-35', pp. 113-33.

Swetman, Deryck, 'The Flanders U-Boat Flotilla, A Nest of Vipers Spawned by Allied Intelligence?', MA Maritime Studies, *University of Portsmouth*, 2003/2004

Tarrant, V E, *The U-boat Offensive 1914-1945* (Cassell, London 1989)

Ten Cate, J H, 'Das U-Boot als geistige Exportware: Das Ingeniuerskantoor voor Scheepvaart N.V., 1919-1957' in Melville R, et all, ed., *Deutschland und Europa in der Neuzeit, Festschrift für Karl Otmar, Freiherr von Aretin, zum 65* (Stuttgart, 1988)

Tennent, A J, *British Merchant Ships Sunk by U boats in World Wars l and ll* (Pen & Sword Maritime, Barnsley 2009)

Termote, Tomas
  *Krieg Unter Wasser: Unterseebootflottille Flandern 1915-1918* (E S Mittler, Hamburg 2015)
  *War Beneath the Waves: U-boat Flotilla Flandern 1915-1918* (Uniform, London 2017)

Terraine, John
  Mons, The Retreat to Victory (Batsford, London 1960)
  *Business in Great Waters, The U-Boat Wars, 1916-1945* (Leo Cooper, London 1989)
  *The Smoke and the Fire* (Leo Cooper, London 1992)

Terry, C Sanford, ed., *Ostend and Zeebrugge, April 23: May 10, 1918, The Dispatches of Vice-Admiral Sir Roger Keyes and other Narratives of the Operations* (Oxford University Press, 1919)

Thomas, Lowell, *Raiders of the Deep* (Garden City Publishing, New York 1932)

Thomazi, A, 'La Guerre Navale dans la Zone des Armées du Nord' (1924; Payot, Paris 1928)

Tooley, Hunt, *The Western Front, Battle Front and Home Front in the First World War* (Macmillan, Basingstoke 2003)

Trentmann, Frank, and Just, Flemming, editors, *Food and Conflict in Europe in the Age of the Two World Wars* (Macmillan, Basingstoke 2006)

Tuchman, Barbara W, *The Guns of August – August 1914* (Four Square, 1964)

Tucker, Spencer C, editor, *The European Powers in the First World War, An Encyclopedia* (Garland Publishing, New York 1999)

Turner, L C F, *Origins of the First World War* (Edward Arnold, London 1970)

Ullrich, Volker, trans. Beech, Timothy, *Bismarck* (1998; Haus Publishing, London 2015)

Vagts, Alfred, *A History of Militarism: Civilian and Military* (Revised edition; Free Press, New York 1967)

Vigness, Paul G, *The Neutrality of Norway in the World War* (Stanford University 1932; Kessinger Reprint, USA, 2016)

Vincent, C Paul, *Politics of Hunger: The Allied Blockade of Germany, 1915-19* (Ohio University Press, 1985)

Ward-Jackson, C H, *Stephens of Fowey, A Portrait of a Cornish Merchant Fleet 1867-1939* (National Maritime Museum, London, Maritime Monographs and Reports, No 43, 1980)

Warner, Philip, *The Zeebrugge Raid* (William Kimber, London 1978)

Wegener, Vice Admiral Wolfgang, trans. Herwig, Holger H, *The Naval Strategy of the World War* (1929; Naval Institute Press, Annapolis, Maryland 1989)

Weinreb, Alice, *Modern Hungers, Food and Power in Twentieth-Century Germany* (Oxford University Press 2017)

Weir, Gary E, *Building the Kaiser's Navy, The Imperial Naval Office and German Industry in the von Tirpitz Era, 1890-1919* (United States Naval Institute, Annapolis, Maryland 1992)

Williamson, Gordon, *U-boats of the Kaiser's Navy* (Osprey, Oxford 2002)

Willis, Edward F, 'Herbert Hoover and the Blockade of Germany, 1918-1919' in Cox et al, eds., *Studies in Modern European History in Honor of Franklin Charles Palm* (Bookman, New York, USA, 1956), pp. 81-104

Willmott, H P, *World War I* (Dorling Kindersley, London 2012)

Wilson, Keith, edited, *Forging the Collective Memory, Government and International Historians through Two World Wars* (Bergahn Books, Oxford 1996)

Wilson, Michael, *Baltic Assignment, British Submariners in Russia: 1914-1919* (Leo Cooper, London 1985)

Winick, Myron, and Noble, Adele, 'Cellular Response in Rats during Malnutrition at Various Ages', *Journal of Nutrition*, No. 89, 1966, pp. 300-6

Winter, Jay, ed, *The Cambridge History of First World War*, Vols. I-III (Cambridge University Press, 2014)

Winter, Jay, and Prost, Antoine, *The Great War in History: Debates and Controversies, 1914 to the Present* (Cambridge University Press 2005)

Winton, John, *Convoy: The Defence of Sea Trade 1890-1990* (Michael Joseph, London 1983)

Wislicenus, Georg, *Deutschlands Seemacht, sonst und jetzt* (1895; Grunow, Leipzig 1901)

Wodiczko, Krzysztof, *The Abolition of War* (Black Dog, London 2012)

Woodward, E L, *Great Britain and the German Navy* (Clarendon Press, Oxford 1935)

Yarnall, John, *Barbed Wire Disease, British and German Prisoners of War, 1914-1919* (History Press, Stroud 2011)

Zweig, Stefan, trans. Bell, Anthea, *The World of Yesterday* (1942; Pushkin, London 2009)

Zweiniger-Bargielowska, Ina, Duffett, Rachel, and Drouard, Alain, editors, *Food and War in Twentieth Century Europe* (Ashgate, Farnham 2011)

Chris Heal's books are available through selected Hampshire retailers and major internet booksellers. Find details at www.candspublishing.org.uk.

### The War of the Raven (2023) (*sister history to Saints & Sinners*)

Georg Gerth volunteered for a u-boat command to counter England's attempt to blockade and starve Germany. His patrols in 1917 took him into the English Channel where his faulty equipment led to terrifying experiences. He engaged his enemy with torpedoes, canon, machine guns, bombs and even a revolver.

Gerth became infamous when his u-boat stranded south of Calais. It was falsely claimed it had been captured by the Belgian cavalry. The intelligence gain from the wreck and crew was substantial and, to this day, kept very quiet. Confined on a French Atlantic island, Gerth attempted a daring escape. He was kept in prison till long after the war ended as part of the bargaining around the Versailles Treaty.

The War of The Raven is the true story of Gerth's career, backed by extensive research and supported by private interviews with his descendants, finally discovered in Bavaria.

### Bad Moon Rising (2023)

Three novellas about despair: 'The Voice of Rage and Ruin, The End of Alton'; 'Bad Times Today, The Sad Life of Mary May'; 'Don't Go Round Tonight, Earth's Last Second'.
*The line between cosy normality and disaster is thin. All it takes is a malign or uncaring person. Then your world collapses. And there's usually nothing you can do about it.*

### The Winchester Tales (2022) (*concluding part of the Ridge Trilogy*)

An Anglo-Norman love story set during the invasion of England after 1066.
*Gilbert of Bayeux, orphan, linguist and administrator, is brought to Winchester by Bishop Odo in 1067 to mastermind the appropriation of the land of the Saxon thegns fallen at Hastings. For the next forty years in Hampshire, he treads a precarious path through the Norman occupation. His great love, Ailgifu, is an outspoken mead seller from Medstead. His servant, Lēofric, provides challenging and dangerous company.*

### Ropley's Legacy (2021) (*second part of the Ridge Trilogy*)

The Ridge Enclosures, 1709 to 1850: Chawton, Farringdon, Medstead, Newton Valence and Ropley and the birth of Four Marks.
*The very first private parliamentary enclosure in England was in 1709 in Ropley. Driven by the less than saintly bishop of Winchester, it was a highly contested land grab seeking to make money by taking control of the common fields. Over 150 years, the government sanctioned theft spread to all the neighbouring ridge villages.*

*The Four Marks Murders* (2020) (*updated second edition; first part of the Ridge Trilogy*)
*In this true-life thriller, Chris Heal investigates deliberate and untimely deaths in what was thought to be one of the quiet backwaters of Hampshire. The twenty murders begin in Roman times with over half since 1900 and three within the last few years. They beg the question, 'Is Four Marks the murder capital of Southern England?*

*Reappearing* (2020)
*The semi-autobiographical sequel to* Disappearing*. If an elderly couple save you from a bad death in the Sahara, there's an honest debt to be paid. But this couple have conflicting plans. The only escape is down the River Niger where some unpleasant people await. The hunt is on for an elusive father who fought for the French across the globe in the dog days of empire.*

*Disappearing* (2019)
*A nomad with a violent past, infuriated by petty bureaucracy and the surveillance society, determines to live happily ever after, throwing off identity and leaving no trace. Things go awry: fighting for Biafran successionists, gun running in Morocco, murder in Brussels, terrorists in Nairobi and a deathly Saharan escape. Semi-autobiographical.*

*Sound of Hunger* (2018)
The depth and breadth of this book is staggering. You would have to read a dozen others to get anywhere close to what's given you. The author wants you to know that WW1 was not won by the titanic slaughters, but by the slow starvation of the civilian populations of Germany and Austria. This is mature erudition from a man of three score and five who has produced a magnum opus to which I say, 'Bravo, Sir'. This is the kind of book I love because as soon as you finish it you start reading it again to see what you missed and enjoy it all over again.

**Jack V Sturiano**
This handsomely produced volume will be recognised as a distinctive and valuable contribution to the history of the First World War. Its author has been very careful in his research and shows both commendable levels of objectivity combined with real imaginative sympathy for his subjects. This is gripping stuff and should not disappoint its audiences. Four years into the publishing jamboree that is the War's centenary, here is a title that stands out and deserves its place on (and one hopes frequently off) the shelf.
**Dr Richard Sheldon**
A major contribution to WWI military history … excellent work … the author writes extremely well and his style is both lucid and engaging … such a scholarly source book is a welcome addition to my bookshelf … an objective, dispassionate foreigner's view of German history.
**Col John Hughes-Wilson (retd.)**